Savoring Provence

WILLIAMS-SONOMA

Savoring Provence

Recipes and Reflections on Provençal Cooking

Recipes and Text
DIANE HOLUIGUE

General Editor
CHUCK WILLIAMS

Recipe Photography
NOEL BARNHURST

Travel Photography
JASON LOWE

Illustrations
MARLENE McLOUGHLIN

BORDERS.

FRANCE

ARDÈCHE

DRÔME

GARD

HAUTES-A

SISTERON

AL
HAUTE-

ORANGE

CARPENTRAS

VAUCLUSE

LA DURANCE

AVIGNON

APT

MANOSQUE

LE VERDON

CAVAILLON

MONTAGNE DU LUBÉRON

PROV

LES BAUX-DE-PROVENCE

ARLES

GRAND

BOUCHES-
DU-RHÔNE

AIX-EN-PROVENCE

RHÔNE

MARTIGUES

PASTIS
51

MARSEILLE

72
HUILE

TOULON

GOLFE
DU
LION

MER MÉDITERR

ITALIE

ALPES DE PROVENCE

ALPES-MARITIMES

MENTON

NICE

GORGES DU VERDON

GRASSE

CANNES.

CÔTE D'AZUR

ENCE

VAR

SAINT-TROPEZ

HYÈRES

ÎLES D'HYÈRES

NÉE

0   20   40 KM

0   20   40   MI

Contents

L'INTRODUCTION

The Provençal Table

THE EXCITEMENT IS PALPABLE as I drive my car southward from Paris. I have only to pass Montélimar and suddenly Provence is before me. This vast, imaginary triangle runs left to the Alps and down to the Riviera and the Italian border, its right arm straddling the Rhône River to join the Mediterranean Sea at Aigues-Mortes, myth-making town of the Crusaders from which Saint Louis set off to conquer Jerusalem. Under the Romans, and in its apogee under Good King Réne (1409–80), Provence extended much farther west. No longer a political entity, it is now generally defined through the five administrative *départements* bequeathed by Napoléon to modern France—Vaucluse, Var, Bouches-du-Rhône, Alpes-Maritimes, and Alpes-de-Haute-Provence—and parts of the Drôme and the Ardèche around Nîmes in the Gard.

On the roadside, a huge pink stone monument to the sun, La Porte du Soleil, tells me that I have arrived. "You are now entering the Land of the Midi," it proclaims—the land of the midday sun. Could one ask for a more beguiling declaration than this?

As tourists, we are often afraid of clichés. We try to show our savoir faire by steering clear of the so-called tourist traps and the well-trodden byways. In truth, the most familiar paths always pass by the sights that best define the beauty of a region, and Provence abounds with them.

Left: The seaside city of Nice on the Côte d'Azur conveys an air of easy elegance. **Top:** A wall of rock looms behind tiny Moustiers-Sainte-Marie in the Alpes-de-Haute-Provence. Where the crags give way to a ravine, the waters of the Riou cascade down to the village. An iron chain suspended across the cleft dangles a golden star placed by the residents of Moustiers, a tradition dating from the thirteenth century. **Above:** Sturdy turnips and other vegetables are essential components in the Provençal pantry.

Imagine going to Provence and bypassing the perched, cobblestoned village of Èze, or not joining the bustling throng in their rowdy evening walk along the plane tree–lined Cours Mirabeau in Aix-en-Provence. Imagine driving the winding Riviera highway known as the Grande Corniche and ignoring the view of a thousand houses clinging to the hillside above the coastline far below, or avoiding the crush that awaits the opening of the Picasso Museum at Valauris.

Imagine coming to Provence and not eating a daube or leaving without having tasted an *anchoïade* or a *soupe de poissons,* a *socca* from a vendor in Old Nice, a bouillabaisse in Marseilles, a crab soup in Toulon. Imagine not going to the markets to experience the displays of lavender, honey, terra-cotta *toupins* of olives, and plaited bundles of fresh garlic, and the plethora of fresh herbs, seasonal fruits, and regional cheeses. Why ask for an apple when figs are falling from the trees, a Camembert when goats treading these craggy hillsides yield some of the world's best goat cheeses?

Whenever I am in Provence, I return to paths I have traveled for years. I love the Nice flower market, with its Monday bric-a-brac stalls and its nighttime carnival of bustling restaurants. I am awed by the bright red town of Roussillon, gouged from iron-rich earth that gave the color ocher to the artist's palette. I revel in a visit to the nearby white village of Gordes, built stone by stone from the rocks of the Lubéron. I drive through the tree-shaded streets of Saint-Rémy or watch the men, blue berets on their heads, playing *pétanque* in Saint-Paul-de-Vence. I marvel yet again at the stony scrubland, the burning yellow rays of the summer sun, even the icy visit of the mistral that funnels down the Rhône and brings rain that restores to clarity the translucent aquamarine that Colette called the "ferocious blue" of the Mediterranean Sea.

I never tire of the climb to the stony heights of Les Baux-de-Provence, its white cliffs gouged out in the perfectly square blocks that gave the world its first bauxite. Rising from a bare rock promontory, the town claims some

Left: The northern Camargue supports the cultivation of rice in specialty varieties, among them the red rice known as *le riz Flamade.* **Top:** Outside a restaurant in Cucuron, an old cart laden with pumpkins and onions welcomes visitors to the weekly Tuesday market. Most villages in Provence have market day at least once a week—the bigger the town, the more numerous the market days. Hub cities such as Aix-en-Provence boast a lively daily *marché.* **Above:** Fresh, locally made goat cheeses, or *chèvres,* are temptingly offered for tasting at the farmers' market in Velleron.

of the best views in the Bouches-du-Rhône, sweeping right across to the sleepy city of Arles, where Van Gogh painted sunflowers and cafés in vibrant yellows and vivid blues.

The geography, too, is alive with myth. The Alps possess a natural beauty that rivals the alpine regions of bordering Switzerland and Italy. The Riviera, that jewel of the glitterati, is home to place names—Antibes, Saint-Tropez, Cannes, Juan-les-Pins—as famous as the stars who frequent them. The sparsely populated, rocky scrubland belongs to stubborn, hard-working farmers who eke out a living against the odds. This is the unyielding countryside of novelist Marcel Pagnol, whose hero, Jean de Florette, toiled in vain to breathe life without water into his stony soil.

The marshy flatlands of the Rhône delta are host to little black bulls and great white horses that run unherded through the brackish waters that lap the shore. The richer soils of the valley of the Rhône River, the only bene-volent countryside in Provence on which to grow food crops, yield a bounteous fruit and vegetable harvest and most of the region's better wines. Count among them the fabled reds of Châteauneuf-du-Pape, the sweet white Muscat de Beaumes-de-Venise, the reds of Gigondas, and Tavel, signature rosé of France.

Man's imprint in the area dates from the Neolithic Age, as evidenced by pottery and agricultural remains found near Châteauneuf-les-Martigues. Ligurians, Celts, and Phocaeans in turn occupied the region, enriching it with the disparate cultures of a succession of invaders, marauders, and traders.

No one left a greater imprint than the Romans. Vestiges of their magnificent engineer-ing feats remain today in the two great forums of Arles and Nîmes, and in numerous amphi-theaters. Orange has the foremost example, its tiered stone seating and formidable stage wall—called "the finest wall in my Kingdom" by Louis XIV—continuing to serve as a theater for summer festivals. Large sections of the aque-ducts that disseminated water in Roman days still exist; the three-tiered Pont du Gard not far from Nîmes is definitely the most impressive.

History has also laid the table of the region. The Provençaux are lovers of olives, garlic, herbs, seafood, goat cheeses, lamb, salad greens, figs, red peppers (capsicums), and eggplants (aubergines). To modify Brillat-Savarin, here it is "tell me what you eat and I'll tell you *where* you are." A regional cuisine is also, by definition, a cliché: local products birthing local dishes over time. It is the very opposite of fashion and demands that expectations are always met. What comes to the table in Provence today is essentially the same as it has been for centuries.

The marvelous writings of Jean Giono, born in Manosque in 1885, when it was largely isolated from the valleys below, carry an over-whelming impression of the permanence of Provençal life, of its deep-rooted solidarity with the land. Giono's heroes exist only as part of their landscape, and of the past, grow-ing the same limited produce, catching the same fish, and hunting the same game as their forebears did. It is a way of life that has the rituals of eating at its heart.

Top: Two men assess the day's business at the fish market in the ancient port city of Marseilles. **Above:** When small and tender, the artichokes of early spring are often enjoyed raw. For larger globes, slow braising is favored, especially in the Alpes-Maritimes. **Right:** Perhaps the single most evocative aroma of Provence is that of lavender, which thrives in high, dry, and sunny regions such as the Valensole Plain in the Alpes-de-Haute-Provence. Harvest takes place at the height of summer's heat, when the essence rises into the spiky flowers.

Giono pictures a peasant returning from the fields. Covered with sweat and dust, and parched with thirst, he consumes a glass of the wine he has made himself, reveling in its familiar, earthy character. As he drinks, he tastes the rows of grapes he planted, nurtured, and plucked from the vine. Two men cement their friendship hunting wild boar; two others enhance the family weekend with freshly caught fish. Elsewhere, head down, shaping the loaves and razoring their silhouette with the asymmetrical slits of the local *fougasse,* a mother works quietly, her labor synonymous with peace, maternity, and seduction.

The people of Provence have bent their backs for food, have known hunger, have lived through the good harvests and the bad. Nothing about the family meal is offhand. Food is a constant topic of conversation, and those who can return home for the pleasure of sharing their midday meal at the family table always do.

In the company of others, one savors not only the meal but also time, fraternity, a respect for history, an appreciation for the role of nurturing, and a shared cultural heritage.

LES ENTRÉES

*Simple combinations~
olives, charcuterie,
cheeses~are traditional
openers to a meal.*

Preceding pages: Poppies carpet the Vaucluse. **Top:** To meet the demands at Apt's busy market, the olive merchant's offerings must be plentiful. A wealth of varieties, picked at varying stages of ripeness, lend themselves to dozens of traditional and innovative preparations. **Above:** High above the village of Castellane, the chapel of Notre-Dame-du-Roc crowns the massive outcrop. **Right:** Selective pruning, carried out atop the three-legged ladder called a *chevalet*, revitalizes olive trees for the coming *olivades,* or olive-gathering days, from autumn until year's end.

IT'S A PARTICULAR BELIEF OF MINE, and a belief that has not yet failed me, that one gets more insight into a cuisine from looking at its appetizers than from the dishes of any other part of the meal.

The cooking of Provence is one of the most recognizable regional styles in France, and when asked to come up with a list of Provençal ingredients, few would get them wrong. The landscape's innumerable olive trees yield an abundance of green and black fruits for the table and golden oil for embellishing salads and for cooking. Sun-ripened fruits and vegetables from backyard gardens or from the lush commercial holdings of the Rhône Valley; fish and shellfish from the sea; sausages and mountain hams; cheeses from the milk of goats and sheep; and thyme, rosemary, fennel, and other wild herbs from the hillsides—all contribute to the Provençal menu. Nature's bounty seems to know no bounds, and it translates into the most marvelous first courses for which one could possibly wish.

First and foremost among these gifts is certainly the olive. By mid–October, the green

olive is already on the tree, but a taste would find it bitter to the point of inedible. Before green olives are acceptable for the table, they must be given an alkaline bath in lye or wood ash, and then a soaking in several changes of water for ten days. After that, they are placed in brine along with such typical flavorings of the region as coriander seed, bay leaves, and orange peel, and then set aside for a couple of months until palatable.

Olives that mature on the tree until black are fully ripe and will fall from the branches of their own accord. In Provence, this occurs from around mid-December to late January, depending on the microclimate. Locals insist that the best specimens come after the first frost and have only to be layered with salt, but for the most part, ripe olives are harvested by shaking the tree around the turn of the year. Many are brined for long conservation, and it is these that are used for cooking. But, for

a more interesting flavor, afterward they may be drained and marinated with herbs and olive oil or combined with other flavorings that make them all the more appealing for the aperitif table or for use in the salad appetizer.

For the most part, the precious golden oil gleaned from the olive between December and February, taken only from the first pressing and sold simply as "pure" olive oil, is the oil the Provençaux use for cooking. The oils pressed as extra virgin (those with less than 1 percent acidity), and particularly those from the four areas that have gained an *appellation d'origine contrôlée* (A.O.C.)—Nyons, in the Drôme Provençal where it borders the Vaucluse, was the first to gain the status in 1994—are the most aromatic and those to use in salads, to drizzle over best-of-the-season tomatoes with shredded basil, or to add to other preparations where the taste of uncooked oil is paramount to the dish.

As starters to a meal, simple combinations are among the most loved: an appetizer plate of slices of air-cured sausage, a variety of olives, hard-boiled eggs, roasted red peppers (capsicums), and artichokes, for example, or a slice of rabbit or hare pâté with vinegary *cornichons* and crusty bread. Equally popular is a plate of grated or sliced raw vegetables (crudités) with either a vinaigrette or, more commonly, a bowl, placed in the center of the plate, containing sun-colored aioli, the pungent, garlic-rich olive oil–based mayonnaise that is one of the treasures of the region.

It always amazes me how much the Provençaux love their vegetables raw, and I don't mean carrots, cucumbers, tomatoes, and other things that everyone eats raw. The first of the season's tiny, pointed, purple artichokes are preferred crunched raw between the teeth. It is thought better to boil them in vinegared water and maintain their youth under oil, so that one might bring them out preserved for the rest of the year, rather than eat them when they are larger and begin to form their hairy choke in the center. The case is much the same for the tiny *fèvettes,* the first of the fava (broad) beans that appear in spring. My friend Huguette's mother, Niçoise to the core, adores them peeled, dipped in salt, and slipped into the mouth raw, but never sets them on the table again once they mature.

Summer is an extended season in Provence, to the extent that northerners call this part of France the Midi—the place where the sun shines overhead at midday—so light appetizers prevail. Composed salads are popular, with the colorful *salade niçoise* of romaine lettuce, slender green beans, artichokes, favas, tomatoes, and tuna probably the best known. But so are small *mesclun* salads constructed of a nest of field greens and on top anything the market or the pantry can offer, from mushrooms or slivers of smoked or roasted chicken or duck to a scattering of mixed vegetables and slices of hard-boiled egg or a slice or two of goat cheese laid over an oil-fried crouton.

The soups of Provence have personality and come in all forms. There are puréed soups made from almost any vegetable, either singly or combined: carrots, tomatoes, leeks, red

Left: Golden *pommes de terre nouvelles,* or new potatoes, from Velleron's farmers' market, might make their way into *salade niçoise,* a favorite salad of the Provençaux. **Below:** Cèpes, the highly prized quarry of mushroom hunters in the autumn woodlands, are dried for year-round use. **Bottom:** Throughout the Mediterranean, the pressing of the olive yields oil ranging from amber to jewel green. Flavored oils take on the subtle character of their herbal infusions, such as *basilic* and *romarin,* basil and rosemary.

Above: Outdoor bistros do brisk business in the convivial city of Aix-en-Provence. **Right:** In the Vaucluse, the citizens of Châteauneuf-du-Pape call their home the village of *vignerons,* or "vintners," and rightfully so, for there life centers on the making of its world-renowned wines. The vineyards are lined with stones called *galets* that soak up the sun's heat, which helps boost the sugar content of the thirteen grape varieties planted there. Vines were first established in 1317 by Pope John XXII on the gentle slopes surrounding his summer residence. Since the sixteenth century, the papal château has lain in picturesque ruins, but from its one still-standing tower the superb views include another fantasy castle, now converted to a luxury hotel.

peppers, white beans, radish leaves, nettles, even garlic. The last is viewed as part calmant, part medicine, the cure for all ills. A broth might contain a garden of vegetables (*soupe au pistou* being the most renowned) or something as simple as leeks and potatoes. There is rabbit soup and chicken soup, and, near the coast, all manner of seafood soups.

When something hot other than soup is required, Provence brings on a bevy of vegetable starters. Sometimes they come in the form of a tart, such as the pizzalike, onion-and-anchovy-garnished *pissaladière* of Nice or tartlets filled with shallots braised in red wine or with cherry tomatoes and goat cheese embellished with shredded fresh basil. Stuffed zucchini (courgettes) and stuffed eggplants (aubergines) are common starters as well. Usually they are halved lengthwise and filled with a stuffing of rice and mixed vegetables, with black olives dotted here and there. Sometimes a small amount of ground meat or ham is added to the stuffing, and each diner is served a half vegetable, hardy enough for even a good-sized appetite.

The stuffed vegetables par excellence are *les petits farcis,* served mostly in the Alpes-Maritimes, the Var, and the Bouches-du-Rhône. The Toulonnais have made them an art form. The little hollowed-out rounds of eggplant, zucchini, and tomato are sized perfectly to match, their mounded stuffings containing only the neatest diced vegetables and meat. The presentation—usually at least four arranged symmetrically on the plate, doused with a little olive oil, and sprinkled with parsley—leaves nothing to be desired. More surprisingly, I have come across cucumber as a cooked vegetable, halved and braised in tomato sauce, either as a starter or as a vegetable dish.

Numerous dips are also part of the Provençal appetizer menu, including the mouth-watering purée of roasted eggplant called *caviar d'aubergines* and the Niçoise version of the anchovy-laced *bagna cauda.* The avocado is well acclimatized to the sunny Midi, where it is served with a vinaigrette or with seafood, and the region's bountiful figs are sometimes wrapped with *jambon de montagne* (air-dried ham from the mountains). A few of the lighter

Below: Comfort, utility, and a certain panache characterize the clothing of the Provençaux. **Bottom:** The color of asparagus depends on the amount of light it receives as it grows. White spears have been completely shielded, whereas shoots exposed to sunlight are gradually tinged purple and then turn to green, the color preferred in the Midi. **Right:** In eastern Provence, the rolling landscape begins its ascent to the Alps.

pasta dishes from around Nice, in small portions, may also be used as appetizers. Finally, there is seafood, especially such local specialties as oysters from Bouzigues, mussels from Carteau, salted mullet roe *(poutargue)* from Martigues, sea urchins from Marseilles, and *tellines* (tiny clams) from the Camargue. The locals prefer their oysters, mussels, and sea urchins served raw as appetizers, plated on ice and eaten directly from the shells, at most with a squeeze of lemon or a drop of vinegar. Mussels sometimes come steamed open with a little wine, sometimes baked, or perhaps tossed with a *persillade.* It is common to bring scallops and *bouquets roses* (large shrimp/prawns) to the table this way as an appetizer. In fact, if there is no fish course between the starter and the main meal, small seafood dishes are commonly served at the beginning of the meal.

All that remains is to set the table, lay out the pastis or a refreshing rosé, and pull up a chair for the aperitif. The Provençaux love color, so chances are that the table is laid with a cloth printed in bright blue or red, with wheat sheaves or olives in contrasting greens and dazzling yellows. The plates and bowls are likely of terra-cotta or another pottery in mustard yellow or bright blue or green. In Provence, primary colors rule the day, and honest, primary flavors rule the table. The appetizer's role is to whet the palate, relax the diner, and set the tone for the meal to come. Like the chatter at the table of a successful meal, it should rise slowly to a high pitch as the pleasures of the unfolding menu, and of the company, progress. A meal with family and friends takes time, but time is never of the essence in Provence.

Alpes-de-Haute-Provence

Galette au Chèvre et aux Tomates

goat cheese and tomato tart

To give the dish a lightness—and the cook the possibility of using purchased pastry dough—I have made this little galette with puff pastry rather than the olive oil–based shortcrust pastry that is traditionally used. The rustic nature of the original still shines through in the combination of potatoes, tomatoes, and the ubiquitous cheese made from the milk of myriad goats that roam the hillsides of Haute Provence—all products that the farmers of the area have readily at hand.

The basil oil can be stored in a cool, dark place for up to 2 months. It is also excellent in green salads, tomato salads, and ratatouille, and drizzled over lamb or poached seafood.

BASIL OIL

1 bunch fresh basil

about 1½ cups (12 fl oz/375 ml) peanut oil or grapeseed oil

1 cup (8 fl oz/250 ml) olive oil

1 lb (500 g) puff pastry, homemade (page 249) or purchased

4 round yellow-fleshed potatoes, about 2 inches (5 cm) in diameter

5 very round, very red tomatoes, about 2 inches (5 cm) in diameter

sugar for sprinkling (optional)

10 oz (315 g) fresh goat cheese

4 fresh basil leaves, torn into small pieces

olive oil for brushing

To make the basil oil, pluck the basil leaves from their stems. Place the stems and about ½ cup (½ oz/15 g) of the leaves in a small saucepan. Add enough peanut oil or grapeseed oil to cover. Heat the oil and basil slowly over low heat, then remove and let stand for 10 minutes.

Transfer the contents of the pan to a blender and purée until smooth. Pour the purée through a fine-mesh sieve placed over a pitcher, then transfer to a clean bottle. Let cool completely and then add the olive oil. You should have about 2½ cups (20 fl oz/625 ml) basil oil.

Preheat an oven to 400°F (200°C).

On a floured work surface, roll out the puff pastry ⅛ inch (3 mm) thick. Using a sharp knife and a small plate as a template, cut out six 5-inch (13-cm) rounds and place the rounds on a lightly oiled large baking sheet. Prick them with a fork to prevent them from rising, cover with a second baking sheet, and place an ovenproof weight on top. Bake until brown and crisp, 18–20 minutes, pressing down twice on the top sheet to expel any air from the rounds. Remove from the oven, lift off the weight and top baking sheet, and set the pastry rounds aside to cool.

In a saucepan, combine the potatoes with salted water to cover. Bring to a boil over high heat, reduce the heat to medium-high, and boil until tender, about 10 minutes. Drain and let cool completely, then peel and slice ¼ inch (6 mm) thick. Set aside at room temperature. Slice the tomatoes to the same thickness as the potatoes. If you like a slightly caramelized flavor, cut them thicker (⅓ inch/9 mm), sprinkle lightly with sugar on one side, and panfry on the sugared side for a moment to brown, then remove quickly. Carefully transfer to parchment (baking) paper to cool. Thinly slice the cheese.

Preheat the broiler (griller).

Alternating the tomato, potato, and cheese slices, arrange them in a spiral pattern to cover each pastry round. Distribute the basil evenly among the pastries, placing the pieces in the gaps between the vegetables and cheese. Brush the surface of each tart lightly with olive oil.

Slip the baking sheet under the broiler 5 inches (13 cm) from the heat source and broil (grill) until glazed and warmed through, 2–3 minutes.

Carefully transfer each tart to the center of a warmed plate. Drizzle a line of basil oil around the tart and serve immediately.

serves 6

Fresh goat cheeses are best around April, when milk is most plentiful.

Alpes-Maritimes

Pan Bagnat

niçoise sandwiches

Here, all the ingredients of a salade niçoise come together in a baguette. Literally "moist bread," the pan bagnat, *a specialty of the Côte d'Azur, owes its unique flavor to the custom of making this picnic favorite well in advance and topping it with a weight to compress the ingredients in their own moisture and the region's superb olive oil.*

1 baguette, halved crosswise, or 2 long, crusty bread rolls

1 clove garlic, halved lengthwise

about 6 tablespoons (3 fl oz/90 ml) olive oil

8 soft lettuce leaves such as butter (Boston) lettuce

1 tomato, sliced

1 hard-boiled egg, peeled and sliced

10 small black olives, pitted

10 English (hothouse) cucumber slices

4–6 green or red bell pepper (capsicum) strips

½ cup (4 oz/125 g) olive oil–packed canned tuna, flaked

4 olive oil–packed anchovy fillets, cut into pieces

salt and freshly ground pepper to taste

❧ Split the baguette halves or the bread rolls in half horizontally, without cutting all the way through. Remove a little of the soft crumb from the center of each portion to create a slight hollow. Rub the cut surfaces of the bread with the cut sides of the garlic clove. Drizzle 2 tablespoons of the olive oil over the cut surface of the bottom of each baguette half or roll and then drizzle 1 tablespoon of the oil over the cut surface of the top half.

❧ Place 2 of the lettuce leaves on each bottom half. Top with the tomato and egg slices, olives, cucumber slices, and bell pepper strips, dividing them evenly. Scatter the tuna and anchovy pieces in among the layers. Season with salt and pepper and finish each sandwich with 2 lettuce leaves.

❧ Close each sandwich and wrap in aluminum foil or plastic wrap, pressing together well. Weight the sandwiches lightly with a cutting board. Let stand in a cool place for up to 4 hours.

❧ Unwrap the sandwiches and serve.

serves 2

Bouches-du-Rhône

Champignons à la Grecque

marinated mushrooms

Despite its name, this recipe is as at home in Mediterranean France as it is in Greece, and it is one of the most popular dishes on the Provençal buffet or outdoor luncheon table. Choose very small, very white, tightly closed mushrooms so that they can be left whole. If you cannot find any, use larger mushrooms and halve or quarter them with their stems attached. The marinated mushrooms store well in the refrigerator for up to a week.

¼ cup (2 fl oz/60 ml) olive oil

2 shallots, finely chopped

¾ cup (6 fl oz/180 ml) beef stock (page 251)

½ cup (4 fl oz/125 ml) dry white wine

juice of 1 lemon

3 cloves garlic, finely chopped

2 teaspoons tomato paste

½ beef bouillon cube

bouquet garni (page 246), with the addition of 1 small celery stalk

½ teaspoon fresh thyme leaves

salt and freshly ground pepper to taste

1 lb (500 g) fresh white button mushrooms, brushed clean

3 tablespoons chopped fresh flat-leaf (Italian) parsley

❧ In a frying pan large enough to accommodate all the mushrooms, warm the olive oil over medium heat. Add the shallots and sauté until softened, about 45 seconds. Add the beef stock, wine, lemon juice, garlic, tomato paste, bouillon cube, bouquet garni, and thyme and season lightly with salt and pepper. Bring to a boil, reduce the heat to low, and simmer gently for 10 minutes to blend the flavors.

❧ Add the mushrooms and cook until softened, about 3 minutes. Using a slotted spoon, transfer to a serving dish. Raise the heat to high and reduce the liquid by about two-thirds, about 2 minutes. If the liquid is too salty, do not reduce as much.

❧ Discard the bouquet garni and adjust the seasoning. Add the chopped parsley, then spoon the reduced liquid over the mushrooms. Let cool and serve.

serves 6–8

Alpes-Maritimes

Palmiers au Basilic

basil-scented savory cookies

These small, very Provençal cookies, ideally partnered with an aperitif, can also be spread with tapenade *(page 59) or topped with shredded Gruyère cheese.*

20 fresh basil leaves

4 cloves garlic, roughly chopped

¼ cup (2 fl oz/60 ml) olive oil, plus oil for brushing

½ lb (250 g) puff pastry, homemade (page 249) or purchased

sea salt

❧ Preheat an oven to 400°F (200°C).

❧ In a small food processor, combine the basil and garlic cloves and process until a paste begins to form. With the motor running, add the ¼ cup (2 fl oz/ 60 ml) olive oil in a slow, steady stream, processing until a smooth paste forms.

❧ On a floured work surface, roll out the puff pastry into a rectangle about 15 by 12 inches (38 by 30 cm). Spread the basil paste thinly over the pastry surface. Make a small imprint on the long side at the top of the rectangle, positioning it at the midpoint. Make a second imprint in the same position at the bottom of the rectangle, indicating an imaginary line down the center. Roll the 2 narrow ends of the pastry sheet inward, not too tightly, brushing with a little olive oil to help it hold together. When the rolls meet at the center, press together very lightly, then place in the freezer for 20 minutes.

❧ Lightly oil a baking sheet. Remove the pastry roll from the freezer, place on a work surface, and cut crosswise into pieces about ⅜ inch (1 cm) thick. Transfer each piece to the prepared baking sheet, laying it on a cut side. When the baking sheet is full, sprinkle the pastries with the sea salt, then pass a rolling pin very lightly over each piece to spread the salt a little and to help it adhere.

❧ Bake until golden, about 15 minutes. Using a spatula, transfer the pastries to a rack and let cool completely before serving.

makes 20–22 pastries

Alpes-de-Haute-Provence

Oeufs à la Tripe

egg, onion, and tomato gratin

Before modern transportation made a variety of foods readily available the year around, the rural people of Alpes-de-Haute-Provence fed themselves as much as possible from what they could grow. The cows provided milk, and the vegetable plot at the back of the house yielded Swiss chard, cardoons, fennel, and other produce. In turn, the local ingredients were combined with a white sauce, dusted with cheese, and baked into gratins such as this one.

6 tablespoons (3 fl oz/90 ml) olive oil

6 large yellow onions, thinly sliced

TOMATO SAUCE

¼ cup (2 fl oz/60 ml) olive oil

8 large tomatoes, peeled, seeded, and coarsely chopped

3 fresh oregano sprigs or 12 fresh basil leaves, shredded

salt and freshly ground pepper to taste

1 heaping tablespoon tomato paste, or to taste

3 tablespoons chopped fresh flat-leaf (Italian) parsley

6 hard-boiled eggs, peeled and halved lengthwise

BÉCHAMEL SAUCE

3 cups (24 fl oz/750 ml) milk

5 tablespoons (2½ oz/75 g) unsalted butter

3 tablespoons all-purpose (plain) flour

salt and freshly ground pepper to taste

freshly grated nutmeg

1 tablespoon shredded Gruyère cheese

¼ cup (1 oz/30 g) shredded Gruyère cheese

4 teaspoons unsalted butter

❧ Oil an oval or rectangular baking dish measuring about 9 by 14 inches (23 by 35 cm).

❧ In a large frying pan over medium heat, warm the olive oil. Add the onions and fry, stirring continuously, until softened, about 2 minutes. Cover with parchment (baking) paper cut to the diameter of the pan, reduce the heat to low, and simmer, stirring occasionally, until tender, about 20 minutes longer. Transfer to the prepared dish. Set aside.

❧ To make the tomato sauce, in a frying pan over medium heat, warm the olive oil. Add the tomatoes and sauté until they start to soften, about 2 minutes. Add the oregano or basil and season with salt and pepper. Reduce the heat to low and cook, uncovered, until a thick, pasty sauce forms, about 15 minutes. If there is too much liquid, raise the heat to high and cook briskly to evaporate it, stirring to prevent scorching. Stir in the tomato paste and parsley and spoon the tomato sauce evenly over the onions.

❧ Arrange the egg halves, cut sides down, over the tomato sauce, placing them so that they are evenly spaced over the surface.

❧ Preheat an oven to 450°F (230°C).

❧ To make the béchamel sauce, pour the milk into a small saucepan and place over medium heat just until it starts to boil. In a deep saucepan over medium heat, melt the butter. Whisk in the flour and cook, stirring, for about 2 minutes. Stir in the hot milk and bring to a boil, stirring continuously, until thickened and smooth. Remove from the heat and season with salt, pepper, and nutmeg. Stir in the 1 tablespoon Gruyère cheese. Pour the sauce evenly over the eggs.

❧ Sprinkle the surface of the gratin with the Gruyère cheese and dot with the butter. Bake until the cheese is melted and the top is golden brown, 5–8 minutes. Bring to the table and serve.

serves 8

Les Fromages de Chèvre

The craggy hillsides and rocky, infertile soil of the *garrigues* and the lower Alps, with their sparse vegetation and small fragrant bushes, are ideal goat country, and, not surprisingly, Provence's best-known cheeses are made of goat's milk. Manufacture is centered around Banon in the Alpes-de-Haute-Provence, although individual farmers making cheeses from the milk of small herds elsewhere in the Alps and in the Var and the Vaucluse are championed locally.

Le Banon de Banon, sometimes called *le vrai Banon* (true Banon), is the most famous Provençal goat cheese. It is sold bound in chestnut leaves tied with raffia, and the production is large enough for export out of the region. Banon is sold in various stages of maturation, as are most goat cheeses. As it ages from soft and fresh to a firmer, drier product, the flavor grows stronger.

Notable also from Banon is lou Papé, its rind washed during maturation to give the cheese a stronger flavor; la tomme fraîche and la tomme ancienne, both drier, smoother cheeses with a firm exterior; le Mescaré, a cheese of mixed ewe's milk and goat's milk; and the extraordinary cacheil, made by mashing offcuts (leftovers from the primary cheeses produced) with eau-de-vie. The result is a runny, exceptionally strong cheese that is for converts only!

Provence delivers most of its goat cheeses in small, round shapes called *crottins* or in log-shaped *bûches*, some of which are flavored with chopped olives or rolled in walnuts. Other goat cheeses, like the famous faiselle de chèvre and brousse, are little more than very fresh drained curds, which are typically doused with cream, sprinkled with sugar, and eaten with a spoon. Fresh goat cheeses are best around April; by summer, milk is scarce and matured cheeses reign.

Goat cheeses, like most cheeses in France, are served primarily as a course before dessert, but the semimatured products come into their own in cooking, melting delightfully under heat. I have eaten them mixed with olives in puff pastries, sandwiched between vegetables, or sitting on a crouton atop a bed of greens as a first course.

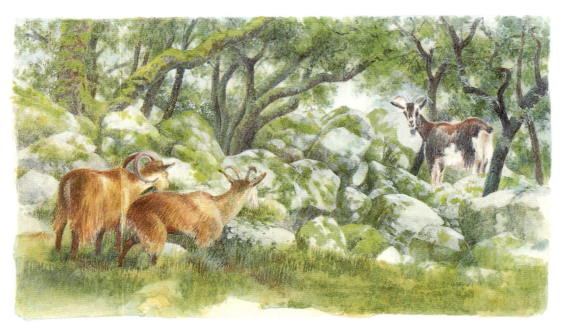

Vaucluse

Crottin de Chèvre et Sa Petite Salade

warm goat cheese with curly endive salad

Crottins *(small, round goat cheeses) can be bought at any stage of maturity. Only the fresh to semimature types work for this presentation.*

6 croutons, made from baguette slices and fried (page 247)

6 small, round fresh or semimature goat cheeses, each about 1 oz (30 g)

6 handfuls (about 6 oz / 185 g) chicory (curly endive) leaves, dandelion leaves, arugula (rocket), or mesclun

24 walnut halves

¾ cup (6 fl oz / 180 ml) extra-virgin olive oil

3–4 tablespoons sherry vinegar or red wine vinegar

1 teaspoon honey

salt and freshly ground pepper to taste

2 tablespoons chopped fresh chives

❦ Preheat a broiler (griller).

❦ Lay the croutons on a baking sheet and place a small goat cheese on each crouton.

❦ Make a nest of the greens on each individual plate, leaving the center free for the cheese-topped crouton. Break up the walnuts. In a small bowl, whisk together the olive oil, vinegar, honey, salt, and pepper.

❦ Slip the baking sheet under the broiler about 6 inches (15 cm) from the heat source and broil (grill) until the cheese just begins to melt at the edges, about 2 minutes. Using a spatula, carefully transfer a cheese-topped crouton to the center of each plate. Scatter the walnuts over the salads, dividing them evenly. Spoon a couple of tablespoons of vinaigrette over both the croutons and the greens. Garnish with a sprinkling of the chives and serve at once.

serves 6

Alpes-Maritimes

Crudités

raw vegetables with dips

A large platter of attractively arranged raw vegetables is found on dining tables throughout France, but the vegetables are often treated only to a bath of oil and vinegar or a bland mayonnaise. In Provence, the lively dips of the area, most notably aioli—garlic mayonnaise—and anchoïade—anchovy sauce— elevate this simple array to something extraordinary.

The ideal way to eat this classic dish? Seated at a rustic wooden table under the shade of an olive tree in an herb-edged garden, with a pitcher of locally produced wine close by and the white-hot sun and vivid blue sky of the Mediterranean overhead.

AIOLI

3–6 cloves garlic

3 egg yolks

2 teaspoons Dijon mustard

1¼–1¾ cups (10–14 fl oz/310–430 ml) olive oil

salt and white pepper to taste

white wine vinegar or fresh lemon juice to taste

ANCHOÏADE

1 cup (8 fl oz/250 ml) olive oil

6 salt-packed anchovies, about 4 oz (125 g) total weight, filleted and rinsed (page 246)

3 cloves garlic, crushed

1 tablespoon Dijon mustard

2 tablespoons red wine vinegar

12 baby artichokes, no more than 1½ inches (4 cm) in diameter, trimmed (page 246) and halved lengthwise

16 baby carrots, peeled

3 heads Belgian endive (chicory/witloof), leaves separated

3 celery stalks, halved lengthwise, then cut crosswise into 2-inch (5-cm) batons

1 small head cauliflower, divided into florets

1 bunch baby radishes, trimmed

2 red and/or green bell peppers (capsicums), seeded and cut lengthwise into strips ½ inch (12 mm) wide

18–20 fresh white button mushrooms, brushed clean and stem ends trimmed

❧ To make the aioli with a handheld electric mixer or a wire whisk, finely mince the garlic, using the smaller amount for a lighter flavor and cutting away any green sprout visible at the center of each clove. Place the garlic in a small bowl and add the egg yolks and mustard. Beat for a few moments until blended. Begin adding the oil drop by drop, beating continuously. Once an emulsion forms, add the oil in a very fine, steady stream, continuing to beat until the aioli has thickened to the desired consistency. It should be thick enough to cling to the vegetables. The more oil used, the thicker the result. Season with salt, white pepper, and vinegar or lemon juice, then cover and refrigerate until serving. You should have 1½–2 cups (12–16 fl oz/375–500 ml).

❧ To make the aioli in a food processor, coarsely chop the garlic, place in the food processor, and pulse to chop as finely as possible. Add the egg yolks and mustard and pulse again briefly. With the motor running, add the oil in a very fine, steady stream, then proceed as directed for mixer method.

❧ To make the *anchoïade,* in a small saucepan over low heat, combine ½ cup (4 fl oz/125 ml) of the olive oil and the anchovies and cook slowly for 15 minutes to blend the flavors. Remove from the heat, let cool, and, using a whisk, beat the mixture until a paste forms. Add the garlic, mustard, and vinegar and whisk to combine. Add the remaining ½ cup (4 fl oz/125 ml) olive oil slowly at first, then in a fine, steady stream, whisking continuously. Cover and refrigerate until needed. You should have about 1½ cups (12 fl oz/375 ml). Alternatively, transfer the cooled anchovy-oil mixture to a food processor and process to a paste, then proceed as directed for the hand method, adding the oil with the processor running.

❧ Arrange the vegetables on 1 or more large platters. Place the bowls of aioli and *anchoïade* in the center of the platter(s) or alongside. Serve at once.

serves 6–8

Pungent, sun-colored aioli is a culinary treasure of Provence.

Alpes-Maritimes

La Socca

chickpea flour crepes

In Provence in the past, chickpea flour was more common than it is today, and this pancakelike snack was once a greater part of the family diet. Today, socca lives on in street stalls and marketplaces as a favorite early-morning food of the fishermen, laborers, and shoppers who regularly purchase a hearty piece of it, wrapped in a paper napkin. The chickpea flour gives the socca its unique flavor and texture, while the sizzling-hot surface on which the crepes are cooked delivers the appetizing bubbles and charred spots.

2 cups (16 fl oz/500 ml) water

1⅔ cups (8 oz/250 g) chickpea (garbanzo bean) flour

3 tablespoons olive oil

1 teaspoon salt

freshly ground pepper to taste

☙ Put the water in a bowl, then whisk in the chickpea flour, olive oil, and salt, continuing to whisk until no lumps remain. Let stand for 30 minutes.

☙ Place a 12-by-16-inch (30-by-40-cm) heavy-duty baking sheet in an oven. Preheat the oven to 500°F (260°C).

☙ Remove the baking sheet from the oven, brush with oil, then quickly pour the batter onto the sheet. It should be about ⅛ inch (3 mm) thick.

☙ Burst any bubbles in the batter with the tip of a knife. Turn the oven setting to broil (grill) and slip the baking sheet under the broiler (griller) about 5 inches (13 cm) from the heat source.

☙ Cook until the entire surface of the crepe is golden and is lightly charred in places, 2–3 minutes. Quickly transfer to a cutting board and cut into squares or rectangles. Dust generously with pepper and serve immediately.

serves 4

Alpes-Maritimes

Soupe au Pistou

vegetable broth with pesto

It is the last-minute addition of the wonderfully pungent basil paste known as pistou *that both gives this dish its name and moves an otherwise simple vegetable soup into the realm of the sublime. Named for the pestle with which it is traditionally ground into a paste,* pistou *is a specialty of Nice, with obvious links to the Italian pesto that originated in nearby Genoa. The closer one is to the Italian frontier, notably in the area of Nice, the more the local* pistou *resembles its Italian counterpart, while in more distant reaches—in the Alps, for example—the recipe is lightened by adding a bit of tomato to the mix.*

1 cup (7 oz/220 g) dried beans, preferably half cannellini and half red kidney or black-eyed peas

4 qt (4 l) water

1 large yellow onion, chopped

2 celery stalks, sliced

½ lb (250 g) green beans, trimmed, left whole if thin or cut into 1-inch (2.5-cm) lengths if large

2 large zucchini (courgettes), trimmed, halved lengthwise, and then sliced crosswise

3 large, very red tomatoes, peeled, seeded, and coarsely chopped

salt and freshly ground pepper to taste

PISTOU

3 cloves garlic, sliced

40 fresh basil leaves

1 small tomato, peeled, seeded, and chopped (optional)

3 tablespoons olive oil

½ cup (2 oz/60 g) grated Parmesan cheese

salt and freshly ground pepper to taste

3½ oz (105 g) vermicelli, broken into 3-inch (7.5-cm) lengths, or small macaroni

2 tablespoons tomato paste, or to taste

❧ Pick over the dried beans, discarding any grit or misshapen beans. Rinse well, place in a large bowl, and add water to cover generously. Let the beans stand overnight.

❧ Drain the beans and place in a large soup pot. Add the 4 qt (4 l) water and bring to a boil over high heat. Reduce the heat to low and cook, uncovered,

for 30 minutes. Add the onion, celery, green beans, zucchini, and tomatoes and season lightly with salt and pepper. Continue to cook, uncovered, until the beans are nearly tender, about 30 minutes longer.

❧ Meanwhile, make the *pistou:* Combine the garlic and basil in a mortar and grind with a pestle until a paste begins to form. Add the tomato, if using, and fully incorporate into the mixture. Add the oil, a little at a time, working it into the basil mixture until a smooth paste forms. Mix in the Parmesan and season with salt and pepper. Alternatively, combine the garlic and basil in a food processor and process until finely chopped. Add the tomato, if using, and process until fully incorporated. With the motor running, slowly add the oil, processing until a smooth mixture forms. Add the Parmesan and process to mix, then season with salt and pepper. Set aside.

❧ Add the pasta to the soup pot and cook until the pasta and the beans are tender, 12–15 minutes longer. Taste and adjust the seasoning with salt and pepper, then stir in the tomato paste.

❧ Stir 2 tablespoons of the *pistou* into the soup until well blended. Ladle the soup into warmed wide soup bowls or into a tureen. Swirl 1 heaping tablespoon of the *pistou* into the soup in each bowl, or swirl 3 or 4 heaping tablespoons into the soup in the tureen. Pass the remaining *pistou* at the table.

serves 10

Alpes-Maritimes

Olives Sautées

warm black olives

Only occasionally are olives served warm, but this quick method of heating them to transform their flavor results in an ideal appetizer.

1 lb (500 g) large, fleshy black olives

3 tablespoons olive oil

3 slices air-cured ham (page 247), torn into bite-sized pieces

8 fresh sage leaves

3 bay leaves, broken up if large

2 red bird's-eye chiles, sliced

1 tablespoon sea salt

❧ Drain the olives, rinse, and pat dry. Warm the oil in a frying pan over medium heat. Add the olives and fry, stirring constantly, until heated through, about 2 minutes. Add the ham, the sage and bay leaves, and lastly the chiles. Mix briefly, add the salt, and stir to mix evenly without dissolving the salt.

❧ Transfer to a serving bowl and serve at once.

serves 8–10

Alpes-Maritimes

Olives en Marinade

marinated olives

For serving with aperitifs or as part of an array of hors d'oeuvres, locals like to marinate cured olives with oil, garlic, and herbs.

10 oz (315 g) brine-cured black olives

6 oz (185 g) brine-cured green olives

2 cloves garlic

3 or 4 peppercorns

3 or 4 fresh thyme sprigs

leaves from 1 long fresh rosemary or fennel sprig

1 bay leaf

1 red bird's-eye chile (optional)

olive oil to cover

❧ Drain the olives. Place in a preserving jar with a glass lid attached with a wire and bales; select a jar at least one-third larger than the volume of the olives. Intersperse among the olives the garlic, peppercorns, thyme, rosemary or fennel, and bay leaf, and the chile, if using.

❧ Add olive oil just to cover the olives, then cap the jar. Store in a cool, dark place, allowing the olives to marinate for at least 3 weeks before serving. If stored submerged in olive oil and tightly capped, the olives will keep indefinitely.

serves 8–10

Bouches-du-Rhône

Calmars Marinés

marinated squid

One of the simplest appetizers to make, this squid can be passed in bowls to accompany drinks or served on a platter as part of a mixed hors d'oeuvre spread.

2 lb (1 kg) small squid

6 tablespoons (3 fl oz/90 ml) olive oil

3 tablespoons fresh lemon juice, or to taste

2 cloves garlic, crushed

1 red bird's-eye chile, sliced (optional)

¼ cup (⅓ oz/10 g) chopped fresh flat-leaf (Italian) parsley

freshly ground pepper to taste

❧ Clean the squid as directed on page 250. Cut the smaller section of each body crosswise into narrow rings. Cut the wider sections lengthwise into long, narrow strips. Cut the tentacles into pieces of varied length, leaving some of the shorter, thinner ones in twos or threes for an interesting variation in shapes.

❧ Bring a saucepan three-fourths full of water to a boil. Add the squid. As soon as the water returns to the boil, usually 20–30 seconds, remove from the heat, drain well, and let the squid cool.

❧ Place the cooled squid in a serving bowl. Add the olive oil, lemon juice, and garlic, and the chile, if using. Toss well. Just before serving, add the parsley and pepper and toss again.

serves 8

Vaucluse

Fougasse

stuffed flat bread

I have fond memories of driving through Carpentras and noticing that nearly every bakery window was filled with fougasse. Soon I discovered that the town is home to a group of proud bakers devoted to upholding the tradition of making this regional flat bread. Before long, my husband, Gérard, and I were sitting on an old bridge in the sun with a bottle of wine and a loaf of fougasse from one of the local bakeries. As we pulled it apart, it revealed a stuffing of anchovies and grattons (bits of crispy fried duck skin). It made a splendid summer meal. If desired, use a combination of anchovies, olives, and ham for the filling.

SPONGE

⅔ cup (3½ oz / 105 g) bread (hard-wheat) flour

½ cup (4 fl oz / 125 ml) lukewarm water

1 cake (1 oz / 30 g) fresh yeast, or 2½ teaspoons (1 envelope) active dry yeast

DOUGH

2¾ cups (14 oz / 400 g) bread (hard-wheat) flour

1 teaspoon salt

1 cup (8 fl oz / 250 ml) lukewarm water

2 tablespoons olive oil

20 olive oil–packed anchovy fillets; or ½ lb (250 g) large, fleshy black olives, pitted and coarsely chopped; or 2 cups (12 oz / 375 g) coarsely chopped cooked ham

salt and freshly ground pepper to taste

olive oil for brushing

To make the sponge, place the flour in a small bowl. Place the lukewarm water in a cup, crumble in the yeast, and stir to dissolve. Pour the dissolved yeast into the flour and stir until blended. Cover the bowl with oil-coated plastic wrap and let rise in a warm place until doubled in bulk, 30–40 minutes.

To make the dough by hand, place the flour on a lightly oiled work surface and make a large well in the center. Sprinkle in the salt and add the sponge, water, and olive oil. Using a fork, blend the liquid with the sponge, gradually breaking down the wall of flour until the flour is incorporated. Then knead the dough until it is light and elastic, 8–10 minutes. The dough is fairly wet, but do not add more flour; instead, dust your hands with flour and continue kneading. Form the dough into a ball, place in a lightly oiled bowl, turn to coat with oil, cover the bowl with a damp kitchen towel, and let the dough rise until doubled in bulk, 45–60 minutes.

❧ To make the dough in a food processor, use a plastic blade and, if possible, reduce the speed of the processor as necessary to prevent the dough and the machine from overheating. Combine the flour and salt in the processor. Add the sponge, water, and oil. Process until the mixture comes together and begins to form a ball at the top of the blade. Turn out the dough onto a lightly floured work surface and knead until it is light and smooth, 2–4 minutes. Form the dough into a ball, place in a lightly oiled bowl, turn to coat with oil, cover the bowl with a damp kitchen towel, and let the dough rise until doubled in bulk, 45–60 minutes.

❧ Preheat an oven to 450°F (230°C). Have ready a fine-nozzled mister filled with water.

❧ Turn out the dough onto a floured work surface. Punch it down and roll out into a 20-by-8-inch (50-by-20-cm) rectangle. Spread the anchovies, olives, or ham over half of the rectangle, leaving a ¾-inch (2-cm) border uncovered. If not using anchovies, season with salt and pepper. Fold the rectangle in half to form a loaf 10 inches (25 cm) long and 8 inches (20 cm) wide, then transfer to a baking sheet. Using a sharp knife, make 7 or 8 slits, spacing them about 2 inches (5 cm) apart and extending them through to the work surface. Pull the slits open well, so that they do not close during baking. Here and there, lightly press the exposed edges of the dough to the bottom layer, so some stay closed during baking. Brush with olive oil, cover with a damp kitchen towel or oiled plastic wrap, and let rest for 30 minutes.

❧ Remove the towel or plastic, place the flat bread in the oven, and quickly spray 3 gusts of water into the top and bottom of the oven. Bake until the bread is golden brown, about 25 minutes, misting the oven again 5 minutes before removing the bread from it. (The misting ensures a crisper result.)

❧ Remove the bread from the oven, transfer to a rack to cool, and immediately brush with olive oil. Serve warm or at room temperature.

makes 1 loaf

Les Fougasses

In central-south Provence, especially in the Lubéron and south to the Camargue, bakers' windows feature a unique style of flat bread, *la fougasse,* immediately recognizable from the irregularly spaced slits that mark its surface. Normally radiating out from an imaginary center like veins from the spine of an oak leaf—or sometimes trellislike in their patterning—these slits contribute to the crustiness of the breads by cutting across their doughy centers, effectively clamping the top and bottom together at intersections along the surface.

Fougasses are made in many forms, from fan-shaped loaves to small rolls that look like hands, fingers extended. The sixth-generation Fassy family bakery in Maillane, near Saint-Rémy, makes such a specialty of *fougasses* that they offer twenty-five varieties, all of them sourdough leavened.

But my favorites are the rectangular loaves into which the baker folds a stuffing, such as chopped pungent black olives, crispy fried duck or goose skin bits called *grattons,* ham, anchovies, or even Roquefort cheese from Aveyron. Copiously garnished within, these loaves make an ideal picnic lunch with little more than a bottle of wine. In Nice, a sweetened version of the bread, *fougassette,* is a Christmas tradition.

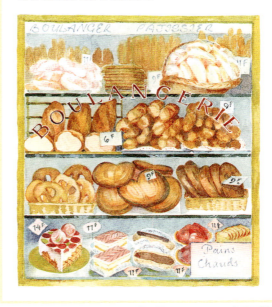

Vaucluse

Soupe à la Tomate aux Fines Herbes

tomato soup with fines herbes

Tomato soup is only as good as the tomatoes that are used to make it, so it is no wonder that this soup is synonymous with the summer months, when the reddest, juiciest, most flavorful specimens are in the market. Also best in this season are the pungent, leafy green herbs that the French call fines herbes: *parsley, chervil, chives, basil, and tarragon.*

3 tablespoons olive oil

1 large yellow onion, finely chopped

2 lb (1 kg) ripe tomatoes, peeled, seeded, and coarsely chopped

1 tablespoon sugar

½ celery stalk, finely chopped

6 cups (48 fl oz / 1.5 l) water

1 tablespoon tomato paste, or to taste

salt and freshly ground pepper to taste

5 green (spring) onions, including tender green tops, thinly sliced

⅓ cup (½ oz / 15 g) chopped fresh flat-leaf (Italian) parsley

⅓ cup (½ oz / 15 g) chopped fresh chervil

12 fresh basil leaves, chopped

☙ In a large soup pot over medium heat, warm the oil. Add the onion and sauté until softened, about 1 minute. Add the tomatoes and stir until they release their liquid, about 2 minutes. Add the sugar and continue stirring until all the liquid evaporates and the tomatoes begin to stick—or even caramelize—a little on the bottom of the pan, 2–3 minutes. Add half of the celery, the water, and the tomato paste and mix well. Season lightly with salt and pepper, then bring to a boil, reduce the heat to low, and simmer, uncovered, for about 30 minutes.

☙ Using a handheld blender or a potato masher, partially purée the soup, leaving the tomato fairly chunky. Add the remaining celery and simmer for 5 minutes longer to blend the flavors.

☙ Just before serving, add the green onions, parsley, chervil, and basil and stir to blend. Taste and adjust the seasoning. Ladle into bowls and serve.

serves 6

Alpes-Maritimes

Salade Niçoise

niçoise salad

Arguably one of the best-known salads in the world, the salade niçoise appears in a host of variations. It can certainly be eaten without tuna, but the fish is a typical addition. There are those who swear that the salad should never see a potato or any cooked vegetable, and many cooks from Nice insist that it's not worth making the salad at all if the market has no fava beans or artichokes small enough to be eaten raw. The staples of the salade niçoise, however, are lettuce, tomatoes, green beans, eggs, anchovies, and Niçoise olives. Call it one without these and any properly reared Niçoise housewife will quickly challenge you.

6 small, waxy potatoes, unpeeled (optional)

20–24 baby green beans, trimmed

½ lb (250 g) fresh tuna, or 1 can (7 oz/220 g) tuna packed in olive oil

3 tablespoons olive oil, if using fresh tuna

1 head butter (Boston) or romaine (cos) lettuce, leaves separated

9 small firm tomatoes, cut into wedges

5 small white onions, each 2 inches (5 cm) in diameter, sliced

1 green bell pepper (capsicum), seeded and cut lengthwise into narrow strips

1 celery stalk, sliced

1 small, slender English (hothouse) cucumber, peeled or unpeeled, sliced

12 olive oil–packed anchovy fillets, halved lengthwise

6 baby artichokes, trimmed (page 246) and halved lengthwise (optional)

15–18 young, tender fava (broad) beans, peeled (page 247) (optional)

⅔ cup (3 oz/90 g) Niçoise olives

12 fresh basil leaves, roughly torn into pieces

6 hard-boiled eggs, peeled and quartered lengthwise

VINAIGRETTE

¾ cup (6 fl oz/180 ml) extra-virgin olive oil

3–4 tablespoons fresh lemon juice or red wine vinegar

2 cloves garlic, crushed

salt and freshly ground pepper to taste

❧ If using potatoes, bring a saucepan three-fourths full of salted water to a boil. Add the potatoes and cook until tender, about 10 minutes. Drain, place under running cold water until cool, and drain again. Cut into slices ¼ inch (6 mm) thick. Set aside.

❧ Refill the saucepan three-fourths full of salted water and bring to a boil. Add the green beans to the pan and blanch until tender, 2–3 minutes. Drain, place under running cold water until cool, and drain again. Set aside.

❧ If using fresh tuna, cut into slices 1 inch (2.5 cm) wide. In a large frying pan over high heat, warm the olive oil. Add the tuna slices and sear lightly on both sides, about 2 minutes total. Remove from the heat, let cool, and cut into pieces 2 inches (5 cm) long. If using canned tuna, drain and separate into large flakes.

❧ Line a large, wide salad bowl with the lettuce leaves. Add the green beans, tomatoes, onions, bell pepper, celery, cucumber, anchovies, and tuna, and the potatoes, artichokes, and fava beans, if using. Scatter the olives and the basil over the top.

❧ To make the vinaigrette, in a bowl, whisk together the olive oil, lemon juice or vinegar to taste, garlic, salt, and pepper. Pour over the salad and toss. Top the salad with the eggs and serve.

serves 6

Alpes-Maritimes

Beignets de Fleurs de Courgettes

zucchini flower fritters

Fritters made with zucchini flowers are associated with Provence. A visit in spring would be incomplete without sampling them.

1 cup (5 oz / 155 g) all-purpose (plain) flour

2 eggs, separated

1 tablespoon olive oil

1 cup (8 fl oz / 250 ml) milk

30 zucchini (courgette) flowers

peanut oil or grapeseed oil for deep-frying

salt to taste

3 cups (24 fl oz / 750 ml) Tomato Sauce (page 67), heated (optional)

❧ Place the flour in a bowl. Make a well in the center and add the egg yolks, olive oil, and 3 tablespoons of the milk. Whisk the ingredients in the well until blended. Stirring constantly, incorporate the flour a little at a time. Add the remaining milk, a little at a time, continuing to stir until the batter is smooth. Let stand for 1 hour.

❧ Remove the pistils from the zucchini flowers. Rinse the flowers only if necessary, then pat dry.

❧ In a bowl, whisk the egg whites until firm peaks form. Carefully fold the egg whites into the batter.

❧ Pour peanut oil or grapeseed oil to a depth of 3 inches (7.5 cm) into a deep saucepan and heat to 325°F (165°C) on a deep-frying thermometer. Dip the flowers, two at a time, into the batter and lower gently into the hot oil. Fry in batches, 4–6 at a time, until golden, 1½–2 minutes. Using a wire skimmer or slotted spoon, transfer to paper towels to drain. Keep warm in a low oven.

❧ Arrange the fritters on a platter, sprinkle with salt, and serve immediately. If desired, spread a small pool of the tomato sauce on each warmed individual plate. Arrange the fritters on top of the sauce, sprinkle with salt, and serve.

serves 6

Alpes-Maritimes

Raviolis Tout Nus

naked ravioli

The County of Nice is linked to the history of Naples through the House of Savoy, and the Italian border is close by, so it is no wonder that the locals love their pizza and pasta. This recipe, however, is not really ravioli but meatballs with a humorous name. They are traditionally served with a chunky tomato sauce and topped with Gruyère or Parmesan cheese.

SAUCE

1 large yellow onion, chopped

1 carrot, peeled and chopped

1 celery stalk, chopped

3 tablespoons chopped fresh flat-leaf (Italian) parsley

leaves from 2 fresh thyme sprigs, chopped

leaves from 2 fresh tarragon sprigs, chopped

2 cloves garlic, minced

3 shallots, minced

¼ lb (125 g) ground (minced) pork

¼ lb (125 g) ground (minced) veal

2 tablespoons olive oil

4 tomatoes, peeled, seeded, and chopped

3 tablespoons tomato paste, or as needed

¼ cup dried cèpe mushrooms, soaked in water to cover for 1 hour, drained, and finely chopped

4 cups (32 fl oz / 1 l) water

salt and freshly ground pepper to taste

RAVIOLI

1 large bunch Swiss chard, large stems removed and leaves coarsely chopped

¾ lb (375 g) ground (minced) pork

¾ lb (375 g) ground (minced) veal

1 scant cup (3½ oz / 105 g) shredded Gruyère cheese

1 clove garlic, finely chopped

1 cup (¾ oz / 20 g) chopped fresh flat-leaf (Italian) parsley

3 eggs, lightly beaten

salt and freshly ground pepper to taste

pinch of freshly grated nutmeg

about 1 cup (5 oz / 155 g) all-purpose (plain) flour

To make the sauce, combine the chopped onion, carrot, and celery on a cutting board and mince together as finely as possible. (This will ensure that they are fully integrated into the texture and flavor of the sauce.) Transfer to a small bowl, add the herbs, garlic, and shallots, and mix well. Combine the pork and veal in a separate bowl and mix well.

In a saucepan over medium heat, warm the olive oil. Add the chopped vegetable mixture and stir for 2–3 minutes. Add the meat mixture and mix thoroughly. Add the tomatoes, the 3 tablespoons tomato paste, and the mushrooms and pour in the 4 cups (32 fl oz/1 l) water. Bring to a boil over high heat, reduce the heat to low, and simmer, uncovered, stirring from time to time, until reduced by half, about 1 hour. Season with salt and pepper and adjust the flavor with tomato paste if a deeper tomato flavor is needed. Remove from the heat and set aside.

To make the ravioli, bring a large saucepan three-fourths full of salted water to a boil. Add the Swiss chard and cook until tender, about 5 minutes. Drain well and squeeze as dry as possible, then chop again and press out any excess liquid.

In a bowl, combine the chard, pork, and veal and mix well. Add ⅓ cup (1½ oz/45 g) of the Gruyère cheese, the garlic, and the parsley and mix well. Mix in the eggs. Season with salt, pepper, and nutmeg. Form the mixture into balls about 1 inch (2.5 cm) in diameter. Spread the flour on a plate and roll the balls in the flour, tapping off the excess.

Bring a large saucepan three-fourths full of salted water to a boil over high heat. Plunge the meatballs into the boiling water, reduce the heat to medium, and boil until cooked through, 8–10 minutes. Meanwhile, reheat the tomato sauce.

When the meatballs are ready, using a slotted spoon, transfer them to warmed individual plates, dividing them evenly. Spoon the tomato sauce over the top, then sprinkle evenly with the remaining ⅔ cup (2 oz/60 oz) cheese. If flameproof plates are used, they can be placed under a preheated broiler (griller) briefly to melt the cheese. Serve at once.

serves 6

Var

Petits Pâtés aux Olives

little olive pastries

I spotted this dressy puff pastry appetizer in the sophisticated beach resort of Saint-Tropez, with its clutch of great restaurants.

1⅓ cups (6½ oz/200 g) large, brine-cured black olives, plus chopped olives for garnish (optional)

3 tablespoons olive oil

1 small, round mature goat cheese, about 3½ oz (105 g), grated

1 tablespoon finely chopped fresh rosemary, plus 6 small sprigs

½–¾ cup (2½–4 oz/75–125 g) all-purpose (plain) flour, for rolling out pastry

1 lb (500 g) puff pastry, homemade (page 249) or purchased

1 egg, lightly beaten

❀ Pit the olives, then finely mince the flesh. Place in a bowl and stir in the olive oil with a fork. Add the goat cheese and stir to mash the mixture lightly. Add the chopped rosemary and mix well. Preheat an oven to 375°F (190°C). Lightly oil a baking sheet.

❀ On a floured work surface, roll out the pastry about ¼ inch (6 mm) thick. Using a sharp knife and small plates as templates, cut out six 5-inch (13-cm) rounds, then cut out six 4¼-inch (10.5-cm) rounds. Transfer the smaller rounds to the prepared baking sheet.

❀ Divide the olive mixture among the pastry rounds on the baking sheet, spooning it into the center of each round. Brush the edges of the rounds with the beaten egg, and then cover each with a large pastry round, pressing the edges together firmly with your fingers. Brush the tops with the remaining egg.

❀ Bake the pastries until golden brown, about 20 minutes. Transfer to a rack and let cool slightly. Serve warm. Garnish with the chopped olives, if desired, and a small rosemary sprig.

serves 6

Les Olives

With its gnarled, twisted trunk and its narrow silver leaves blowing in the wind, the olive tree is a prevailing image of the Provençal landscape. It lives in backyards, in the wild, in hillside pastures, and in commercial groves, particularly in the Var, the Vaucluse, and the Bouches-du-Rhône.

Its fruit, bitter at birth, yields first the green olive, then the black. The unripe green olives, harvested around November, must be taken from the tree, then bathed in lye and cured in salt to render them palatable. Ripe, black olives eventually fall from the tree, but in December and January, farmers can be seen manning small tractors fitted with large rubber "arms" that grasp and shake the trunks, releasing the fruits onto large cloths spread beneath the branches. Black olives need no alkaline treatment. They can be simply sun-dried or salt-cured for the table.

One day, in the Marché de Fourvilles in Cannes, I counted the olive merchant's wares and found no less than thirty-six different offerings. Green, fleshy *picholines* sat alongside green, pointed *lugnes*. There were black Kalamatas, large *violettes* from Tunisia, green Sévillanes, and the aptly named huge *mamouths*. Some, like the *tanche,* are better known by their place of origin (Nyons), as are the Niçoise, their tiny shape and succulent flesh perfect for topping salads and tarts.

On display were pitted, smashed, bruised, and cracked olives suitable for eating and for cooking in classic daubes and ragouts. Then came those with flavorings, strictly destined for the aperitif or buffet table. These were marinated in oil; peppered or mixed with chopped chile or minced herbs; tossed with garlic and capers, garlic and orange peel, or thyme, red peppers (capsicums), onion, and capers; or even "smeared with anchovy." Also offered to tempt the palate were large bowls of much-loved local specialties: *à la façon grecque* (braised with stock and lemon juice), *à la camarguaise* (with *crème d'anchois* and garlic), and *à la sicilienne* (mixed with lemon).

Vaucluse

Terrine de Veau aux Fruits Confits

veal pâté with dried apricots and hazelnuts

The charcuteries of France tend to make similar pâtés no matter where the shop, whereas restaurant chefs like to tamper with the classics to make their own creative variations. My brother-in-law Bernard, his wife, Danièle, and I first tasted this style of pâté de campagne in a tiny restaurant near Apt, the glacéed fruit capital of the world. Returning to his home in Évreux, Bernard did most of the work to create his own version of this very moist, apricot-studded pork-and-veal terrine.

1 large or 2 small pork tenderloins, about ½ lb (250 g) total weight

1½ lb (750 g) pork fatback

3 shallots, sliced

2 or 3 cloves garlic, sliced

½ cup (4 fl oz / 125 ml) Madeira, equal parts Madeira and port, or equal parts Madeira and brandy

1½ lb (750 g) ground (minced) pork

1½ lb (750 g) ground (minced) veal

1 lb (500 g) pork or veal liver, cut into cubes

leaves from 3 large fresh thyme sprigs or ½ teaspoon dried thyme

1 egg

2 tablespoons salt

freshly ground pepper to taste

4 bay leaves

handful of hazelnuts (filberts) or pistachio nuts

about 15 dried apricots

boiling water, as needed

cornichons

coarse country bread, sliced

❧ Cut the pork tenderloins into long, thin batons about ¼ inch (6 mm) wide and the length of the tenderloin. Cut about 3 oz (90 g) of the pork fatback in the same manner. Place all the batons in a dish, scatter the shallots and garlic over the top, and add the wine or wine and brandy. Cover and marinate for 2 hours at room temperature or as long as overnight in the refrigerator.

❧ Drain the meat, reserving the liquid. Retrieve the shallots and garlic from the sieve. Set the meat and the liquid aside separately. Pass the garlic, shallots, remaining pork fatback, ground pork and veal, and liver through a meat grinder fitted with the medium disk, capturing them in a large bowl. Add the thyme, egg, salt, and pepper and pour in the reserved liquid. Mix well with your hands.

❧ Position a rack in the middle or in the lower third of an oven and preheat to 375°F (190°C).

❧ Select a lidded earthenware or porcelain terrine with a capacity of about 2 quarts (2 l). Place 2 bay leaves on the center of the bottom of the terrine. Working your way up the height of the terrine, assemble the pâté by beginning with a ¾-inch (2-cm) layer of the ground meat mixture. Continue adding the ground meat mixture, interspersing it with the batons of meat and pork fatback and scattering the nuts and apricots here and there as you proceed. End with a ¾-inch (2-cm) layer of ground meat, mounding it attractively.

❧ Press 2 bay leaves onto the top of the ground meat, placing them at a diagonal. Cover the terrine with aluminum foil, prick the foil all over with the tip of a knife, and place the lid on the terrine.

❧ Place the terrine into a large, deep baking dish. It should fit snugly. Fill the baking dish three-fourths full with boiling water. Carefully transfer to the oven rack, then pour in additional boiling water to fill the dish as full as possible. Bake for 1½–1¾ hours. Turn off the oven, leave the oven door ajar, and let the terrine cool in the oven until the water is no longer too hot to handle. If you prefer the top of your pâté caramelized, remove the lid and foil for the last 20 minutes of cooking, replacing it before leaving the terrine in the oven to cool.

❧ When the pâté has cooled, remove the lid and foil and sponge the side and bottom of the vessel to remove any grease. Rinse the lid and then re-cover the terrine. Refrigerate for 2–3 days before serving.

❧ Remove the pâté from the refrigerator. Set out the *cornichons* in a small bowl. Cut the pâté into slices about ½ inch (12 mm) thick and serve with the bread slices.

makes 1 terrine; yields 15–18 slices

Bouches-du-Rhône

Tapenade

anchovy and black olive spread

Tapenade has multiple uses. It can be spread on toasted bread to accompany an aperitif, as it is here, or it can be used as a dip for crudités (page 41). It also appears as an accompaniment to grilled or poached fish; as a filling for rolled meats, especially veal, beef, lamb, and rabbit; and as a complement to squid preparations. If making the tapenade in advance of serving, place in an airtight container and store in the refrigerator for up to 10 days. For longer storage, pour a thin film of olive oil over the top and place in the refrigerator for up to 2 months.

½ lb (250 g) large, brine-cured black olives, pitted

2 cloves garlic, crushed

6 salt-packed anchovies, about 4 oz (125 g) total weight, filleted and rinsed (page 246)

3 tablespoons salt-packed capers, rinsed

7–8 tablespoons (3½–4 fl oz/100–125 ml) olive oil

TOASTED BAGUETTES

8 tablespoons (4 fl oz/125 ml) olive oil, plus oil for brushing

2 baguettes, cut into slices ½ inch (12 mm) thick

❧ In a food processor or blender, combine the olives, garlic, anchovies, and capers and process to a paste. With the motor running, slowly add the olive oil in a fine, steady stream, adding only as much as needed to form a spreadable consistency. Transfer to a bowl. You should have about 2 cups (16 fl oz/ 500 ml) *tapenade.*

❧ To toast the baguette slices, warm 1 tablespoon of the oil in a ridged stove-top grill pan over medium-high heat, quickly distributing the oil over the surface of the pan with a paper towel.

❧ Working in batches, brush both sides of the baguette slices with oil, arrange in the pan, and toast until golden on one side, about 2 minutes. Using a spatula, turn and toast on the second side until golden, about 1 minute. Repeat to toast the remaining slices, adding more oil to the pan as needed. Arrange the toasts on a platter.

❧ Serve the *tapenade* accompanied with the toasts.

serves 6

Alpes-de-Haute-Provence

Aïgo Boulido

garlic soup

A variation of this soup runs through most of the alpine regions of France, including the Provençal Alps and the Pyrenees. In these areas, the high concentration of vitamin C present in garlic is looked upon by shepherds—and doting mothers—as a means of warding off winter's ills. Most rustic recipes simply call for stirring egg yolks into the finished soup. This version, with its whole poached eggs, comes from the departmental capital of Digne, long a stopping-off point for alpine tourists and well known for its thermal baths. The city lies on the famous road built by the Romans through Italy to northern France, a byway that later became la Route Napoléon.

8 cups (64 fl oz/2 l) water

20 cloves garlic, coarsely chopped

10 fresh sage leaves

salt and freshly ground pepper to taste

6 eggs

12 croutons, made from dense sourdough loaf and grilled (page 247)

2 tablespoons chopped fresh flat-leaf (Italian) parsley

6 tablespoons (3 fl oz/90 ml) olive oil

❧ In a soup pot over high heat, combine the water, garlic, and sage, bring to a boil, and boil until the garlic is soft, about 15 minutes. Remove the pot from the heat and, using a slotted spoon, scoop out the sage and garlic. Discard the sage and mash the garlic with a fork. Return the garlic to the pot of water and season with salt and pepper.

❧ Return the water to a boil, then reduce the heat so the liquid gently simmers. One at a time, break the eggs into a small bowl and slip into the simmering liquid. Cook until the whites are opaque and the yolks are soft and still liquid, about 2 minutes.

❧ Place 2 croutons in the bottom of each of 6 wide soup bowls. Using a slotted spoon, quickly and care-fully remove 1 egg at a time from the simmering soup and transfer to the bowls, placing 1 egg on the bread in each bowl. Top each egg with 2 ladlefuls of the soup, then sprinkle on the parsley, dividing evenly. Drizzle 1 tablespoon of the oil into each bowl and serve at once, before the eggs cook any further.

serves 6

Alpes-Maritimes

"Sandwiches" d'Aubergine et Fromage de Chèvre

eggplant and goat cheese sandwiches

I encountered this modern variation on the traditional vegetable dish known as aubergines en éventail *(page 193) in an upmarket restaurant in the Cap d'Antibes, where it was served as an eye-appealing starter. It combines the Provençal love for two local products, eggplant and goat cheese. Look for a semi-mature goat cheese that will slice easily. In Provence, this would be a pyramid-shaped cheese or a cylinder about 1½ inches (4 cm) in diameter.*

3 globe eggplants (aubergines), each 2–3 inches (5–7.5 cm) in diameter

salt

about ¾ cup (4 oz/125 g) all-purpose (plain) flour

olive oil for frying and brushing eggplant

6 very firm, very round tomatoes

20–24 fresh basil leaves, shredded, plus 6 sprigs for garnish

10 oz (315 g) semimature goat cheese (see note), cut into slices ⅓ inch (9 mm) thick

extra-virgin olive oil for serving

❦ Cut the unpeeled eggplants lengthwise into slices about ⅓ inch (9 mm) thick. You will need 18 slices in all. Place the slices in a colander, sprinkle with salt, and let stand for 30 minutes to drain off the bitter juices. Pat the slices dry with paper towels. Spread the flour on a plate and coat the eggplant slices on both sides with the flour, tapping off the excess.

❦ Pour olive oil to a depth of about 1 inch (2.5 cm) into a wide frying pan and heat to 325°F (165°C) on a deep-frying thermometer. Add 2 or 3 eggplant slices and fry, turning once, until golden, about 4 minutes total. Transfer to paper towels to drain. Repeat with the remaining slices.

❦ Preheat an oven to 300°F (150°C). Oil a large baking sheet.

❦ Set aside 6 eggplant slices with the peels intact on one side. Arrange 6 of the remaining slices on the baking sheet. Slice the tomatoes into thin, uniform slices. Place 3 or 4 tomato slices on top of each eggplant slice, overlapping the tomato slices slightly. Scatter some shredded basil and some slices of goat cheese over the tomatoes. Top with a second layer of eggplant slices and more tomato slices, basil, and cheese. Finish with the reserved eggplant slices, so each stack resembles a whole eggplant. Brush the tops lightly with olive oil.

❦ Bake the sandwiches until slightly softened and warmed through, 5–8 minutes. Transfer to warmed individual plates. Garnish with the basil sprigs and drizzle with extra-virgin olive oil. Serve at once.

serves 6

The craggy hillsides, rocky soil, and small, wiry bushes of Haute Provence are ideal goat country.

Alpes-Maritimes

Tarte Renversée aux Tomates Séchées

upside-down tart with oven-dried tomatoes

This tart, a variation on the Norman specialty tarte Tatin, *exploits the marvelously intense tomatoes that have been dried in the oven.*

10 oz (315 g) puff pastry, homemade (page 249) or purchased

3 tablespoons unsalted butter

1 tablespoon olive oil

1 tablespoon sugar

15 shallots

½ cup (4 fl oz / 125 ml) water

leaves from 1 fresh thyme sprig

salt and freshly ground pepper to taste

10–12 oven-dried tomatoes halves (page 68)

☙ On a lightly floured work surface, roll out the puff pastry into a round about ⅛ inch (3 mm) thick. Cut into a round about 10½ inches (26.5 cm) in diameter. Place in the freezer for 15–20 minutes.

☙ Preheat an oven to 400°F (200°C). Select an ovenproof frying pan 10 inches (25 cm) in diameter. Place over high heat and melt the butter with the oil. Add the sugar and stir for 40–50 seconds. Add the shallots and toss for 30 seconds. Add the water, cover, reduce the heat to low, and simmer until evaporated, about 5 minutes. Let cool completely.

☙ Distribute the shallots in the pan. Sprinkle with the thyme, salt, and pepper. Place the tomatoes, skin side down, among the shallots. Remove the pastry from the freezer and lay over the pan. Quickly trim the edges to the size of the pan. Make 4 knife slits in the pastry and bake until browned, 20–25 minutes.

☙ Remove from the oven, cover with a round serving plate slightly larger than the diameter of the pan, and invert the plate and pan together, releasing the tart onto the plate. Carefully lift the pan off the tart. Cut into wedges to serve.

serves 6

Le Pissalat

A glance at the *pissaladière,* the traditional onion flat bread of Provence, often gives rise to comparison with the Italian pizza, which is not surprising in light of the similar-sounding names and the history of Nice as an Italian city-state. What few people realize is that the *pissaladière* takes its name from the fermented fish paste that originally served as the pungent base beneath the onion, a role now played by a few anchovies arranged on top. Called *le pissalat,* the fish paste was a direct descendant of the Roman fish paste *garum,* and was designed, as was *garum,* as a means of conserving the fishermen's harvest of anchovies and sardines.

The already strongly flavored fish were combined in roughly equal amounts, treated to a spicy blend of salt, ginger, peppercorns, chiles, cinnamon, and cloves, and then placed in an earthenware crock, or *toupin.* The mixture was turned daily but otherwise left to bubble and ferment like a witches' brew for a week or longer, at which point the partially decomposed mass was mashed and then sieved to produce the highly flavored paste. Finally, it was bottled and topped with oil to prevent oxidation. Some older folks still make *pissalat* at home and use it for picnics, at which it is relished spread thickly on bread or croutons.

Alpes-Maritimes

Pissaladière

onion and anchovy tart

The pissaladière *is one of the most recognizable dishes of Nice, where squares of the warm, just-baked tart are often sold by street vendors.*

1 cup (8 fl oz/250 ml) lukewarm water

1½ oz (45 g) fresh yeast, or 1 tablespoon active dry yeast

2¾ cups (13 oz/410 g) all-purpose (plain) flour

2 tablespoons olive oil, plus ⅓ cup (3 fl oz/ 80 ml)

pinch of salt

3 lb (1.5 kg) yellow onions, sliced

leaves from 3 or 4 fresh thyme sprigs

salt to taste

20 olive oil–packed anchovy fillets

18–20 small black olives

❦ Place the water in a cup, crumble in the yeast, and stir to dissolve. In a food processor, combine the flour and dissolved yeast and process for 15 seconds. Add the 2 tablespoons oil and pinch of salt. Process until the mixture forms a ball. If it is too dry, dribble in a little water; if it is too wet, add a little flour. Transfer to a floured work surface, knead briefly, and shape into a ball. Place in an oiled bowl, turn to coat with oil, cover with a damp kitchen towel, and let rise until doubled in bulk, about 1 hour.

❦ Meanwhile, in a deep frying pan over medium heat, warm the ⅓ cup (3 fl oz/80 ml) olive oil. Add the onions and sauté for about 2 minutes. Add the thyme, reduce the heat to low, and cook, stirring occasionally, until the onions are soft, about 40 minutes.

❦ Preheat an oven to 475°F (245°C). Have ready a 12-by-16-inch (30-by-40-cm) baking sheet. Turn the dough out onto a floured work surface and roll into a rectangle about 10 inches (25 cm) by 14 inches (35 cm). Transfer to the baking sheet. Salt the onions lightly and spread evenly over the dough. Arrange the anchovies in a grid pattern on top. Dot with the olives. Let stand in a warm place until the dough rises around the topping, about 15 minutes.

❦ Bake until crisp and browned, 18–20 minutes. Remove from the oven and serve hot, warm, or at room temperature, cut into squares.

serves 8

Bouches-du-Rhône

Escargots à la Ventrèche

snails braised with sausage

La ventrèche is a type of fresh sausage made from the belly (ventre) of the pig. It is served in the Bouches-du-Rhône, and this somewhat unusual combination of sausage and snails is found throughout the area.

1 can (7 oz/220 g) snails, drained, rinsed, and drained again

2 tablespoons red wine vinegar

3 fresh thyme sprigs

3 bay leaves

¼ cup (2 fl oz/60 ml) olive oil

6 thin, well-seasoned fresh pork sausages, about 1 lb (500 g) total weight, cut into 1-inch (2.5-cm) lengths

2 yellow onions, chopped

2 small red bell peppers (capsicums), seeded, cut lengthwise into their natural lobes, and then cut crosswise into slices ⅜ inch (1 cm) wide

2 lb (1 kg) ripe tomatoes, peeled, seeded, and roughly chopped

salt and freshly ground pepper to taste

Place the snails in a bowl. Drizzle with the vinegar, stir, and set aside for 30 minutes. Fill a large saucepan three-fourths full of water. Add 1 of the thyme sprigs and 1 of the bay leaves and bring to a boil. Plunge the snails into the boiling water, return the water to a boil, and then immediately drain.

In a heavy frying pan over medium heat, warm the olive oil. Add the sausages and fry for about 5 minutes. Add the onions and fry, stirring, for about 5 minutes longer. Add the bell peppers, stir once or twice, then add the tomatoes. Reduce the heat to low, add the remaining 2 thyme sprigs and 2 bay leaves, and season with salt and pepper. Simmer gently uncovered, stirring occasionally, until the tomatoes soften into a light sauce, about 20 minutes. Add the snails, stir through the sauce, cover, and cook over low heat for about 15 minutes. Remove and discard the herbs. Spoon into warmed individual bowls and serve.

serves 6

Alpes-Maritimes

Bagna Cauda

vegetables with hot anchovy sauce

Given its history under the Houses of Savoy and Sardinia—the County of Nice was finally ceded to France in 1860—Nice has many connections with the cooking just across the Italian border. The Niçois, with their plentiful supply of anchovies, consider this dish as much their own as do the Piedmontese or the Ligurians. Bagna cauda, meaning "hot bath," is surrounded with vegetables and served in much the way that an aioli is served. Since the sauce needs to be kept warm, it is best made in a fondue pot or similar saucepan with a burner placed under it.

15–18 small boiling potatoes, each about 1½ inches (4 cm) in diameter, peeled

12 baby beets, each about 1 inch (2.5 cm) in diameter

12 whole baby leeks, or 2 large leeks, including tender green tops, sliced

3 or 4 celery stalks, halved lengthwise, then cut crosswise into 4-inch (10-cm) batons

12 baby carrots, peeled, or 3 large carrots, peeled and quartered lengthwise

1 small cauliflower, cut into florets

6 baby artichokes, trimmed (page 246) and quartered lengthwise

12 green (spring) onions, including 2–2½ inches (5–6 cm) of the green tops, trimmed

1 large bunch radishes, trimmed

2 large red bell peppers (capsicums), seeded and cut lengthwise into strips about ½ inch (12 mm) wide

30–35 cherry tomatoes

3 heads Belgian endive (chicory/witloof), leaves separated

SAUCE

15 salt-packed anchovies, about 7 oz (220 g), filleted and rinsed (page 246)

6 cloves garlic, sliced

scant 1 cup (7 fl oz/220 ml) olive oil

freshly ground pepper to taste

In a saucepan, combine the potatoes with water to cover. Bring to a gentle boil over medium-high heat and cook, uncovered, until tender, 12–15 minutes. Drain and set aside to cool completely.

If the beet greens are attached, cut them off, leaving about ½ inch (12 mm) of the stem intact. Do not peel. In a saucepan, combine the beets with water to cover. Bring to a gentle boil over medium-high heat and cook, uncovered, until tender, 10–12 minutes. Drain and, when cool enough to handle, trim off the stems and root ends and slip off the peels. Set aside.

Bring a saucepan three-fourths full of water to a boil. Add the leeks and blanch for 1 minute if whole baby leeks, or for 2 minutes if sliced large leeks. Drain, immerse under running cold water to stop the cooking, and drain again. Cut whole leeks on the diagonal into 2-inch (5-cm) lengths. Set aside.

Arrange all the vegetables on large platters. About 20 minutes before serving, begin making the sauce. In a fondue pot or similar saucepan, combine the anchovies, garlic, and olive oil. Place over low heat and stir continuously with a wooden spatula, mashing the anchovies until they are reduced to a purée, for 15–20 minutes. Be careful not to let the mixture boil. The garlic should become translucent but never brown, and the anchovies must not be allowed to become crisp. Season with pepper.

Transfer the pan holding the sauce to a tabletop burner. Bring the platters of vegetables to the table. Let diners help themselves to vegetables and drizzle them with the warm sauce.

serves 8

Alpes-Maritimes

Les Petits Farcis

stuffed vegetables

This recipe for "little parcels" comes from Kathie Alex, who teaches the cuisine of the region at her mas (homestead), la Pitchoune, near Grasse.

TOMATO SAUCE

2½ tablespoons olive oil

2 yellow onions, chopped

2 lb (1 kg) tomatoes, peeled, seeded, and chopped

2 cloves garlic, finely chopped

bouquet garni (page 246), with the addition of 1 each fresh summer savory and basil sprig

1 orange zest strip, preferably dried, about 1 inch (2.5 cm) wide

salt and freshly ground black pepper to taste

pinch of cayenne pepper (optional)

2 tablespoons chopped fresh basil or flat-leaf (Italian) parsley (optional)

12 small tomatoes, each about 2 inches (5 cm) in diameter

salt to taste

3 zucchini (courgettes), each about 7 inches (18 cm) long and 1¾ inches (4.5 cm) in diameter

⅔ cup (5 fl oz/160 ml) olive oil

1 large yellow onion, finely chopped

¾ lb (375 g) spicy bulk pork sausage meat

1 teaspoon dried herbes de Provence

3 tablespoons chopped flat-leaf (Italian) parsley

2 cloves garlic, finely chopped

1½ cups (3 oz/90 g) fresh bread crumbs

¼ cup (1 oz/30 g) grated Parmesan cheese

1 or 2 eggs, lightly beaten

2 tablespoons fine dried bread crumbs

1 cup (8 fl oz/250 ml) hot water

❧ To make the tomato sauce, in a large, heavy frying pan over medium heat, warm the olive oil. Add the onions and sauté for about 10 minutes. Do not allow to color. Add the tomatoes and cook uncovered, stirring occasionally, until they have rendered their juice, about 15 minutes. Add the garlic, bouquet garni, and orange zest and season with salt. Stir once, reduce the heat to low, and simmer uncovered, stirring occasionally, until the liquid is reduced

by about one-third, 20–30 minutes. Discard the bouquet garni and zest and season with salt and black pepper. If desired, add the cayenne and stir in the basil or parsley, if using.

❧ Meanwhile, cut a thin slice off the stem end of each tomato. Using a teaspoon, scoop out the center, discarding the seeds and juice and reserving the flesh. Salt the inside of each tomato, then place upside down on a wire rack to drain. Trim the ends of the zucchini. Slice each zucchini crosswise into 4 equal lengths. One at a time, stand the pieces upright on an end. Using a melon baller, scoop out their centers, leaving the bottom intact and forming walls about ⅜ inch (1 cm) thick. Be careful not to cut through the walls. Reserve the flesh.

❧ Fill a large saucepan three-fourths full with salted water and bring to a boil. Slip the zucchini pieces into the boiling water, bring the water back to a boil, reduce the heat to low, and simmer, uncovered, until just softened, about 4 minutes. Using a slotted spoon, lift out the zucchini pieces and plunge into a bowl of ice water. When the pieces are cool, place them, hollowed side down, on a kitchen towel to drain.

❧ Preheat an oven to 350°F (180°C). Oil a baking dish large enough to hold the vegetables in a single layer without touching.

❧ Chop the reserved zucchini and tomato flesh. In a small frying pan over low heat, warm 3 tablespoons of the olive oil. Add the onion and sauté for about 10 minutes. Do not allow to color. Add the chopped zucchini and tomato, season with salt, and continue to cook, stirring and tossing, until softened, about 15 minutes. Transfer the zucchini-tomato mixture to a bowl. Add the sausage meat, *herbes de Provence*, parsley, garlic, fresh bread crumbs, and Parmesan cheese and stir to mix well. Add 1 egg and drizzle in about 2 tablespoons of the remaining olive oil. Using your hands, mix together thoroughly. If the stuffing seems too dry, mix in another egg.

❧ Arrange the tomato and zucchini shells in the prepared baking dish. Sprinkle the cavity of each with a little salt and drizzle with some of the remaining olive oil. Using a teaspoon, distribute the stuffing evenly among the vegetables, pressing gently with the back of the spoon. Sprinkle with the dried bread crumbs, then drizzle with the remaining olive oil. Pour the hot water into the bottom of the dish.

❧ Bake the stuffed vegetables until the stuffing is golden brown, about 30 minutes. Warm the sauce over low heat. Spoon some of the sauce on each plate. Arrange the vegetables on top and serve.

serves 6

Alpes-Maritimes

La Trouchia

swiss chard omelet

La trouchia is a style of vegetable omelet unique to the Nice area, where it is made exclusively with Swiss chard. One is tempted to draw comparisons with the Italian frittata, and a keen eye will also spot that it bears a distinct resemblance to the tians *(layered vegetable dishes) found in Provence.*

6 tablespoons (3 fl oz/90 ml) olive oil

1 yellow onion, finely chopped

1 lb (500 g) Swiss chard, stems removed and leaves coarsely shredded

7 eggs

1 scant cup (3½ oz/105 g) grated Parmesan cheese

1 clove garlic, finely chopped

2 tablespoons chopped fresh flat-leaf (Italian) parsley

salt and freshly ground pepper to taste

8–10 small black olives

☙ In a nonstick frying pan over medium heat, warm 3 tablespoons of the olive oil. Add the onion and sauté until softened, about 1 minute. Add the Swiss chard and cook, stirring, just until the chard has wilted. Reduce the heat to low and cook, stirring often, until tender, 5–6 minutes total. Set aside to cool.

☙ In a bowl, using a fork, beat the eggs until blended. Stir in half of the Parmesan cheese and all of the garlic and parsley. Season with salt and pepper, then add the cooled chard mixture and stir briefly to mix.

☙ Wipe out the frying pan with a paper towel and return to low heat. Add the remaining 3 tablespoons olive oil. When the oil is hot, add the egg mixture and stir gently with the fork. Stop stirring as soon as the eggs start to set, then allow the pan to rest on the heat until the eggs start to become firm, 3–4 minutes. Place a plate over the pan and, holding the plate and pan together, invert them and lift off the pan. Slip the omelet back into the pan and return to low heat. Sprinkle the remaining Parmesan evenly over the top and cook, without disturbing, for 2–3 minutes.

☙ Slide the omelet from the pan onto a serving plate and dot the top with the olives. Cut into wedges and serve at once.

serves 4–6

Alpes-Maritimes

Salade de Tomates Séchées au Four

salad of oven-dried tomatoes

The Provençal housewife traditionally dried small plum tomatoes on racks in the sun. Strung on fine thread, these decorative mainstays of the kitchen cupboard would tide her over to the next harvest. Modern cooks prefer a softer, moister product. Here, the result becomes a warm, flavorsome salad. To store the tomatoes, let cool, place in a covered container, and refrigerate for up to 1 week.

OVEN-DRIED TOMATOES

12–15 plum (Roma) tomatoes

2 teaspoons sugar

salt and freshly ground pepper to taste

¼ cup (2 fl oz/60 ml) olive oil

3 shallots, finely chopped

2 cloves garlic, finely chopped

3–4 tablespoons olive oil

about 2 teaspoons red wine vinegar or sherry vinegar

8–10 fresh basil leaves, torn or coarsely sliced

salt, if needed

freshly ground coarse pepper to taste

☙ To dry the tomatoes, oil a large baking sheet. Halve the tomatoes lengthwise. If they are large, make the first cut off center, then cut the larger piece in two. Trim away the cores. Place the pieces, cut side up, on the prepared baking sheet.

☙ Sprinkle the sugar evenly over the tomatoes, then season with salt and pepper and drizzle with the olive oil. Place in an oven, turn on the oven to 150°F (65°C), and leave in the oven for 8–9 hours or as long as overnight. The tomatoes will be semidried. If you are short of time, set the oven at 225°F (110°C) and reduce the cooking time to 3–4 hours. Check occasionally to make sure that the tomatoes are not baking but drying.

☙ Time the tomatoes to come out of the oven 30 minutes before the salad is to be served. Place in a large bowl and add the shallots and garlic. Moisten with olive oil, drizzle with vinegar, add the basil, and toss gently. Add salt, if needed, and pepper and serve.

makes 24–45 tomato pieces; serves 6

Bouches-du-Rhône

Gougères du Soleil

choux puffs of the sun

The classic gougères *are small, cheese-flavored* choux *puffs from Burgundy. One day, a home cook in Arles offered me this not-so-classic variation. The puffs were rich with the strong flavors of sun-dried tomatoes, local olives, and the ubiquitous anchovy. She called them simply "my* gougères.*" They were full of the flavors of the south, and as I looked at her sunny, geranium-covered terrace and tasted the refreshing Camargue rosé in my glass, I promptly bestowed upon her creation a name befitting their character,* gougères du soleil.

The dough for choux *pastry is made by mixing flour into boiling water, then adding eggs. It is easy to prepare, but the ratio of water and flour is crucial. Be sure to measure both ingredients carefully. Sifting the flour onto parchment (baking) paper allows the flour to be poured quickly into the water just after it comes to a boil.*

CHOUX PASTRY

1 cup (5 oz / 155 g) all-purpose (plain) flour

1 cup (8 fl oz / 250 ml) water

5 tablespoons (2½ oz / 75 g) unsalted butter, cut into small dice

pinch of salt

4 eggs

3 tablespoons finely diced Gruyère cheese

4 olive oil–packed anchovy fillets, drained, patted dry, and diced

5 oil-cured black olives, pitted and chopped

3 sun-dried tomatoes, drained and patted dry if oil packed, diced

1 clove garlic, finely chopped

salt and freshly ground pepper to taste

❦ If using an electric oven, position a rack in the center. If using a gas oven, position a rack in the upper third. Preheat to 400°F (200°C). Line 2 baking sheets with parchment (baking) paper.

❦ To make the *choux* pastry, sift the flour onto a sheet of parchment paper and set aside. Pour the water into a saucepan that is deep rather than wide and add the butter and salt. Bring to a boil over high heat, stirring to ensure that the butter has melted completely by the time the water reaches a boil.

❦ Reduce the heat to medium and add the reserved flour all at once, stirring briskly with a wooden spatula rather than a spoon (the bowl shape tends to trap the flour). Continue stirring until the flour rolls off the walls of the saucepan and clings in a ball to the spatula, 30–40 seconds, evaporating as much water as possible without scorching the pastry. Remove from the heat. Transfer the pastry to a bowl and let cool for 3 minutes. Add the eggs, one at a time, stirring to blend completely before adding the next egg.

❦ Fold the Gruyère cheese, anchovies, olives, tomatoes, garlic, salt, and pepper into the pastry. Using 2 spoons, scoop up portions of the pastry and form into balls about 1¼ inches (3 cm) in diameter, spacing them about 2 inches (5 cm) apart on the prepared baking sheets. You should have about 30 puffs.

❦ Bake the puffs until golden brown, about 20 minutes. Turn off the heat, open the door, and let the puffs dry for 5–10 minutes (if not allowed to dry, the puffs will be soft rather than crispy). Remove the baking sheets from the oven and tap gently on a countertop to release the puffs.

❦ Transfer the hot puffs to a bread basket lined with a napkin and serve immediately.

serves 6

Northerners call this part of France the Midi — the place where the sun shines overhead at midday.

Les Rosés de Provence

Nothing goes better with the brash, pungent flavors of Provençal food than the local rosé wines. The Provençaux have made the production of rosés an art form, turning out young, fresh, crisp, evocative, and, for the most part, drier wines than any of their many namesakes. Arguably the best rosé in the world, Tavel, a wine of deep, rich hue and a full finish, claims the title of premier rosé of France. It comes from the town of the same name, which lies just north of Avignon. Tavel vintners have been making rosé since the tenth century, as have vintners in nearby Lirac, another rosé name of renown. Among the other top producers of red wine in Provence, only Gigondas and Domaine Tempier in Bandol make rosé.

Most other rosés are generic wines, made and served locally with neither fuss nor pretension. Drunk young, fresh, and dry as an aperitif or with an appetizer, fish, or a light white-meat course, even the unheralded ones are trustworthy enough to be ordered by carafe in most restaurants. I cannot pass up the chalky gray-pink rosé of the Camargue, *gris de gris de Listel*. One of the least expensive rosés on the market, and also one of the driest, this intriguing wine sits beautifully with the strongly flavored, garlic-infused and oil-drenched food with which it was intended to be served.

LES PRODUITS DE LA MER

Seafood dishes are guided by the motto faites simple~ "make it simple."

GIVEN A COASTLINE just over two hundred miles (350 km) long between Menton and Aigues-Mortes—much of it difficult to reach due to mountains and cliffs rising from the sea's edge, and the salt and silt-logged marshes of the Rhône delta—it is astonishing how much of the Provençal diet is associated with fish and shellfish. One finds fishing communities in small inlets everywhere along the Mediterranean shore, and the fishermen who live there are descended from men who for centuries pulled their living from the depths of the sea. Once a haven for small rockfish and for larger, oilier fish from waters farther from shore, the Mediterranean is now largely overfished. What is reeled in is as expensive as meat and, in the case of prized fish like the *rascasse* (scorpion fish), *loup de mer* (sea bass), and *rouget barbet* (red rock mullet), more expensive. Still, the Provençaux love their products of the sea, and their most renowned dishes are a celebration of this fact.

Just how scarce these prized fish are is apparent in the retail markets, where trestle tables offer only a few of each type and often small in size. Mussels, squid, imported shrimp

Preceding pages: New paint refurbishes an old boat in Marseilles. **Top:** This bounty of the sea will be transformed into a host of delectable Provençal dishes. **Above:** From these rocky waters come the *rouget barbet,* or red mullet, and the *rouget grondin,* or sea robin, superior fish of the Mediterranean. **Right:** The hardworking fishermen of Marseilles bring in a steady harvest for seafood-loving Provençaux.

(prawns), whelks, clams, and other seafood, however, are found piled high.

Trailing in the wake of Provençal chef André Perez around la Criée, the wholesale fish market of Marseilles, I learned to recognize the colorful fish of the Mediterranean. He pointed out the anemic–skinned *saumonette,* ideal for poaching, and the similarly pink, but less spotty, lingcod, the larger specimens of which grow up in the deeper, more distant waters and whose fleshy medallions are ideal for steaming or for panfrying. There is the ugly, spiny *rascasse,* rare now, but without it the cooks of Marseilles would not even contemplate making their famed bouillabaisse, and the cousin of the *rascasse,* the red *chapon.* The *baudroie* (monkfish), the giant-headed stargazer, the John Dory, and the little red mullets, sea robins *(rougets grondins),* and other rockfish that add complexity to bouillabaisse are also much loved grilled. The popular, affordable sardine is grilled, deep-fried, sautéed, boned and rolled stuffed with spinach and walnuts, or prepared *en escabèche,* that is, cooked in a spiced vinegary marinade and served cold.

Left: Le Vieux Port, the Old Port of Marseilles, is aptly named—ships have docked here for twenty-six centuries. The commercial anchorage has moved to the north of the city, but the port still welcomes pleasure craft. **Below:** Plump and fresh from the market, these *rougets barbets,* or red mullets, are ideal for preparing *en papillotes,* in paper packets that are a delight to open at the table. **Bottom:** *Pétanque* is Provence's popular version of the game of *boules.* Its name derives from the Provençal dialect for *pieds tanqués,* meaning feet planted on the ground, which describes the stance of *pétanque* players, as opposed to the long strides taken by adherents of *boules.*

Anchovies, too, are inexpensive and plentiful, particularly around Nice, where in spring they rise in hoards to spawn. Apart from being grilled or fried, they are preserved between layers of sea salt, the intense result ideal for hors d'oeuvres. Traveling away from the coast, one encounters market displays of trout caught in the freshwater torrents that flow from high in the Alps and occasionally displays of perch or the rare *omble chevalier* from mountain lakes.

If bouillabaisse is the most famous Provençal soup, it is not the only one. The beautiful *bourride,* a broth made from white-fleshed fish and served creamy and rich with an emulsion of garlicky aioli, is nearly as renowned. Every home cook uses the fish varieties available in the marketplace, simmering them with tomatoes, saffron, leeks, and other vegetables, to make the family's *soupe de poissons.* The russet-colored *sauce rouille,* named for the addition of pimiento to its base of aioli, is as much an accompaniment to these home-style soups as it is to bouillabaisse.

Bouillabaisse can trace its history back twenty-five hundred years to the arrival of the Phocaean Greeks, but its evolution—through the addition over the centuries of saffron, fennel, orange peel, and finally tomatoes—

has been right here, giving Marseilles the right to call the dish its own. The mystique of bouillabaisse is legendary. When Parisian chef Raymond Oliver, a well-known gastronomic chronologist and a highly ethical man who backs his years of study with one of the best collections of old French culinary manuscripts in the country, went on television to make a bouillabaisse, he wound up in the courts with a subpoena from the Marseillais Fishing Cooperative. No doubt he would not have ventured to make it without the *rascasse* and the requisite amount of local fish. Perhaps he was not using water from Marseilles!

Although the fish soups are models of sophistication, with fish, as with most of Provençal cookery, the motto *faites simple* (make it simple) prevails. Two common threads run through this tradition: a respect for the integrity of each ingredient and the use of local produce to dress the centerpiece of any dish. As always, olive oil is the cooking medium, and herbs and garlic the major additions. In the past, families had a fireplace in the kitchen, and fish was simply painted with oil, garlic, and herbs and thrown on the hearth to grill. Nowadays, as the whim dictates, it is pan-fried, broiled, grilled over an outdoor fire, or baked in the oven.

Also adhering to the *faites simple* premise is the tradition of poaching seafood. Water rather than stock is the medium, and the flavorings here, too, are local. Fennel or coriander seed and the ubiquitous orange peel give the liquid its flavor, and the fish or shellfish is more than likely served in a little of the reduced liquid rather than with a *velouté* (thickened stock-enriched sauce) or a buttery or cream sauce as it would be farther north.

Below: At Provençal fish markets, cooks can purchase the seagoing counterpart to the common garden snail, as well as such delicacies as sea urchins, prized for their roe, and the small oysterlike shellfish called *vioulets*. **Bottom:** Obliging fishmongers will cut steaks to order at the marketplace on the Quai des Belges in Marseilles. **Right:** From the golden sands of Fréjus-Plage, the coast curves east to Saint-Raphaël. Both of these resorts are highly valued as family vacation destinations.

From the eastern township of Nice to the township of Nîmes in the *département* of Gard in the extreme west, history has made salt cod *(morue)* a central item of the Provençal diet. Yet this dried fish does not come from local shores. A prolific nineteenth-century olive oil and salt trade with Scandinavia left Provençal traders with the problem of finding cargo to fill the holds on the return journey, and the local North Sea cod, heavily dried, was a hardy, imperishable product ideal for the trip. This "stick fish," as the Norwegians called it, became an affordable alternative to the fresh fish of the Mediterranean and has remained popular with the Provençaux, as it has in the port cities of Italy, Spain, and Portugal. In Nice, salt cod is stewed with tomatoes, anchovies, garlic, and olives in the traditional *estocaficada,* a dish that borders on the mythic. Indeed, a club of purists intent on protecting the recipe's integrity has existed since 1905. But it is *brandade,* salt cod purée, and the traditional manner of cooking it in Nîmes that are perhaps best known internationally.

Any seafood cooked *à la provençale* is likely to be prepared with garlic and parsley. Anything *à la toulonnaise* contains tomatoes and mussels. The famed *esquinade* is a Toulonnais specialty of small crabs cooked in mussel juice, the meat removed and combined in the half shell of the mussel, and then baked. *Favouilles* are small crabs found only along the shore near Toulon, while larger spider crabs (blue swimmers) are at home everywhere along the coast. The Marseillais feast upon all manner of *fruits de mer* raw. The two greatest delicacies are sea urchin roe and the unique little amorphous black-shelled creature called the *vioulet,* a fleshy yellow shellfish rich in iodine. Cooks in Martigues grate salted mullet roe *(poutargue)* into olive oil, and between Antibes and Menton, cooks make fritters and *rissoles* of tiny mixed fish called *nonats.* While octopus, squid, and cuttlefish are found all along the coast and served fried, grilled, and braised, the tiny fingernail-sized clams called *tellines* live only around Arles and the Camargue, where they are dug from the sandy beaches and sautéed in a *persillade.* All in all, a feast from heaven made from a harvest from the sea.

Var

Pot-au-Feu de Poisson

fish stew

Every area of France has its own pot-au-feu. The Provençal version of this large "pot on the fire" contains fish from the nearby Mediterranean, tomatoes, leeks, fennel, garlic, and that special-occasion spice, saffron.

SEAFOOD

4 lb (2 kg) mixed white-fleshed whole fish such as red snapper, porgy, orange roughy, lingcod, sea perch, and Atlantic salmon, cleaned

24 small mussels, scrubbed and debearded

16 sea scallops

12 large shrimp (prawns), peeled and deveined

STOCK AND VEGETABLES

2 small or large fennel bulbs, trimmed and cut lengthwise into quarters if small or sixths if large

1 leek, white part only, cut into 4-inch (10-cm) lengths

4 celery stalks, cut into 4-inch (10-cm) lengths

5 tomatoes, peeled, seeded, and quartered

¼ cup (2 fl oz/60 ml) olive oil

2 yellow onions, minced

3 cloves garlic, minced

3 tablespoons minced fresh flat-leaf (Italian) parsley

salt and freshly ground black pepper to taste

¼ teaspoon saffron threads, crushed and steeped in 2 teaspoons hot water

pinch of cayenne pepper

1¼ cups (10 fl oz/310 ml) dry white wine

SAUCE

fresh white bread crumbs, from 2 thick slices day-old sourdough bread

3 large red bell peppers (capsicums), roasted (page 246)

salt and freshly ground black pepper to taste

tiny pinch of cayenne pepper

pinch of powdered saffron (optional)

3 tablespoons chopped fresh flat-leaf (Italian) parsley

about 24 croutons, made from baguette slices and toasted (page 247)

♛ Fillet most of the fish into chunky pieces about 5 by 3 inches (13 by 7.5 cm). Reserve 1 lb (500 g) of the heads and larger bones or tails for the stock. Cut larger, thicker fish across the bone into steaks.

♛ To make the stock, cut the fennel, leek, celery, and tomatoes as indicated, saving enough trimmings to yield about 1 cup (5 oz/155 g) finely chopped vegetables. In a saucepan over medium heat, warm the olive oil. Add the onions, garlic, and parsley and sauté until fragrant. Add the finely chopped vegetables and the fish heads and bones or tails. Season with salt and black pepper and add the saffron and cayenne. Pour in the white wine and 4 cups (32 fl oz/1 l) water, bring to a boil, and cook rapidly, uncovered, for about 30 minutes. Remove from the heat and strain through a sieve lined with cheesecloth (muslin) placed over a clean saucepan.

♛ Place the mussels in a saucepan, discarding any that fail to close to the touch. Cover, place over high heat, and cook, shaking the pan from time to time, until the mussels open, 3–5 minutes. Transfer the mussels to a plate, discarding any that failed to open. Pass the juices through a fine-mesh sieve lined with cheesecloth (muslin) placed over a bowl. Set aside. Remove 8 of the mussels from their shells.

♛ Bring the strained stock to a boil over high heat. Add the fennel, leek, and celery, and cook until just tender, about 4 minutes. Add the tomatoes when the other vegetables are cooked. Reduce the heat to medium-low, lower the fish pieces into the stock, and simmer until opaque throughout, 6–8 minutes. Halfway through the cooking time, add the scallops and shrimp. Remove from the heat and add all the mussels. Season with black pepper and a little of the reserved mussel juice.

♛ Meanwhile, make the sauce: In a bowl, combine the bread crumbs with about ½ cup (4 fl oz/125 ml) water. Let stand until the water is absorbed. Squeeze out the excess water, then place the moistened crumbs in a blender or food processor. Add the bell peppers and process until puréed. Season with salt, black pepper, cayenne, and, if lacking color, a little saffron. Add a small ladleful of the stock from the stew and process again. Transfer to a small saucepan and place over medium heat, stirring until heated through.

♛ Transfer the fish, shellfish, and vegetables to a platter. Ladle in the stock. Drizzle with some of the sauce and sprinkle with the parsley. Serve the remaining sauce in a bowl alongside the croutons.

serves 8

La Criée

For centuries in Marseilles, everyone, merchants and consumers alike, went to la Criée, a great cavernous structure in le Vieux Port (Old Port), to buy their fish. The wonderfully expressive name—literally, "The Shout"—evokes the scene perfectly: the bustle, the jostling, the noise.

Brawny men with fish-filled boxes piled high on carts would trundle them through the crowds, rolling them one by one into place on the podium to have their contents called by species, by merchant, by the origin of the catch. The auctioneer, eyes alert, pointing, negotiating, would gauge the cries of the crowd as prices were shouted from the floor. He would push the bids upward, raising the prospective buyers' voices to a fever pitch, then bang! the hammer would slam down as the deal was sealed, and the auctioneer would swiftly move on.

The fish are gone now from la Criée. Although the name is etched into the facade of the building, the structure has become the Théâtre National de la Criée. Walking through it, one can see the original vaulted glass-paned ceiling and remnants of the old concrete floors. The nostalgic visitor can imagine the atmosphere of the onetime market, where wholesale vendors labored through the night, to be replaced by a retail trade of small market stalls during the day.

La Criée itself has moved to a much larger, highly modern complex in l'Estaque, a western coastal suburb of Marseilles, which it shares with the city's wholesale meat market. The market is now known as la Nouvelle Criée du Chalutage (the New Criée of the Fishing Fleet), but only the name retains the romance. Limited to professional buyers, and with high security, its large waterfront sheds are the portrait of efficiency, ensuring smooth dispersal of seafood from the coast of Provence to the rest of France.

One or two fishing boats continue to anchor daily among the pleasure cruisers in the Old Port, the skippers selling their catch directly to the public. The householder who fancies a greater variety will find plenty of choice from the decks of boats docked a little farther along the coast in the bays of Martigues, Carro, Sausset-les-Pins, or Carry-le-Rouet.

Alpes-Maritimes

Gratin de Coquilles Saint-Jacques à la Mediterranéenne

scallops gratin, mediterranean style

Try to find a fishmonger that sells scallops still in their shells for this eye-appealing dish. Ask him or her to open the shells and remove the scallop meats, since a large tough area must be discarded and only the central eye and coral (orange section) are retained. Once you have the shells, they may be scrubbed and reused. If you can locate only already-shelled scallops, look for small ovenproof porcelain shells made by such French companies as Apilco and Pillivuyt.

16 sea scallops (see note)

4 green (spring) onions, including tender green tops, sliced

2 firm tomatoes, peeled, seeded, and cut into ⅓-inch (9-mm) dice

½ cup (2½ oz/75 g) diced mixed red and green bell pepper (capsicum)

2 tablespoons salt-packed capers, rinsed and drained

salt and freshly ground coarse pepper to taste

1 cup (8 fl oz/250 ml) olive oil

2–3 tablespoons chopped fresh flat-leaf (Italian) parsley

☙ Preheat an oven to 475°F (245°C).

☙ Lay each scallop in the center of its bottom shell. Arrange 4 filled shells per person on ovenproof plates. Place the plates on baking sheets.

☙ Scatter an equal amount of the green onions, tomatoes, bell pepper, and capers around each scallop. Sprinkle with salt and pepper. Drizzle evenly with the olive oil.

☙ Bake until the scallops are opaque throughout, about 3 minutes. Remove from the oven, sprinkle with the parsley, and serve immediately.

serves 4

Calmars aux Petits Pois

squid braised with peas

I discovered this recipe in Toulon, the great French naval military harbor, where cooks slowly braise squid and cuttlefish with excellent results.

2 lb (1 kg) medium to large squid

5 tablespoons (2½ fl oz/75 ml) olive oil

1 small yellow onion, chopped or thinly sliced

1 lb (500 g) tomatoes, peeled, seeded, and coarsely chopped

1 clove garlic, finely chopped

about 1 cup (8 fl oz/250 ml) water

2 fresh thyme sprigs

2 small bay leaves

salt and freshly ground coarse pepper

2⅓ cups (12 oz/375 g) fresh or frozen shelled English peas (about 2½ lb/1.25 kg unshelled)

tomato paste to taste (optional)

☙ Clean the squid as directed on page 250. Cut the small tubular parts of the body into rings. Cut the larger parts lengthwise into strips the width of fettuccine and 4–5 inches (10–13 cm) long. Include the tentacles, cut into similar lengths.

☙ In a saucepan over medium heat, warm the olive oil. Add the onion and sauté for about 1 minute. Add the tomatoes and garlic, cover, and simmer for about 5 minutes. Add the squid and the water just to cover. Stir in the thyme sprigs and bay leaves. Season with salt and pepper. Bring to a boil, reduce the heat to low, cover, and simmer until the squid is tender, about 50 minutes.

☙ Add the peas and simmer until tender, 15–20 minutes if using fresh peas and 5 minutes if using frozen peas. Taste and adjust the seasoning, adding a generous grinding of pepper. Add a little tomato paste to taste, if desired. Remove the thyme sprigs and bay leaves and discard. Ladle into warmed shallow bowls and serve at once.

serves 6

Bouches-du-Rhône

Loup Farci sur Son Lit de Légumes

sea bass on a bed of vegetables

This dish is a baked variation of loup grillé au fenouil, *arguably the most famous whole-fish preparation in Provence. The grilled version is a simple dish, with the unscaled sea bass enveloped in dried fennel stalks and a little fresh fennel and placed in a special fish-shaped wire grill basket that allows it to stand over the hot coals. After the fish is turned and cooked on the second side, a little pastis or Pernod is tossed over the fish, causing the fennel to emit a marvelously fragrant anise-scented smoke that rises up and infuses the bass. The baked whole fish presented here is in the same vein but simpler to manage, and because the recipe includes vegetables, it is a complete meal.*

Even in Provence, large sea bass is becoming increasingly hard to find—and expensive—but the dish may also be made with snapper or porgy.

1 sea bass, 4½ lb (2.25 kg), cleaned but unscaled

2 bay leaves

4 large fresh thyme sprigs

5 fennel stalks with ferns attached

salt and freshly ground pepper to taste

olive oil for brushing fish, plus ½ cup (4 fl oz/ 125 ml)

2 large lemons, each cut into 6 wedges

4 tomatoes, each cut into 4 wedges or, if large, into 6 wedges

2 zucchini (courgettes), trimmed and sliced

3 thin carrots, peeled and each cut crosswise into thirds

3 yellow onions, cut into small wedges

6 cloves garlic, sliced

¾ cup (6 fl oz/180 ml) dry white wine

2 tablespoons Pernod or pastis (optional)

☸ Preheat an oven to 400°F (200°C).

☸ Rinse the fish, running your hands over it to remove any loose scales. Pat dry with paper towels and fill the cavity with the bay leaves, thyme sprigs, and fennel. Sprinkle the cavity with salt and pepper, then brush the exterior with olive oil and sprinkle with salt and pepper.

☸ Oil a baking dish large enough to hold the fish. Scatter the lemons, tomatoes, zucchini, carrots, and onions to cover the bottom of the dish. Drizzle the ½ cup (4 fl oz/125 ml) olive oil over the vegetables and distribute the garlic evenly throughout the vegetables. Season with salt and pepper and center the fish on top.

☸ Bake for 15 minutes, then pour the wine and the Pernod or pastis, if using, evenly over the vegetables to moisten them. Bake for 15 minutes longer. Rotate the dish 180 degrees to ensure that the fish cooks evenly, and turn the vegetables with a spatula to keep them evenly moist. Continue to bake until the vegetables are tender and the fish is cooked through, 20–30 minutes longer. To test the fish for doneness, pierce with a sharp knife. The flesh should be opaque at the bone.

☸ To serve, use 1 or 2 wide metal spatulas to lift the fish gently onto a cutting board. Using a slotted spoon, transfer the vegetables to a large warmed platter. Strain the liquid in the dish into a sauceboat to use as a sauce. With a sharp knife, sever the skin at the gills and tail, then lift it away from the fish. The scales will hold the skin together, so it should come away easily. Carefully turn the fish, skin-free side down, onto the vegetables on the platter. Remove the skin on the second side. Pour a little of the sauce over the fish and serve at once. Pass the remaining sauce at the table.

serves 6

Bouches-du-Rhône

Le Grand Aïoli

salt cod, chicken, and snails with vegetables and aioli

The name aioli is used not only for the classic garlic-flavored mayonnaise of Provence, but also for one of the great rustic springtime meals of the region. In the case of the latter, it is a true Provençal celebration of nature's bounty, a traditional one-course feast of salt cod, chicken, and snails surrounded by a variety of vegetables and served with the garlicky mayonnaise.

2 lb (1 kg) salt cod fillet

1 cup (7 oz/220 g) dried chickpeas (garbanzo beans) or 3 cups (21 oz/655 g) drained canned chickpeas

STOCK

8 cups (64 fl oz/2 l) water

1 large carrot, peeled and sliced

1 leek, including green top, split lengthwise

1 yellow onion, studded with 2 cloves

2 cloves garlic

bouquet garni (page 246), with the addition of 1 each small celery and fennel stalk

20 small boiling potatoes, preferably yellow fleshed

15 baby artichokes, trimmed (page 246)

2 bunches baby carrots, peeled

8 small onions

8 zucchini (courgettes), trimmed and quartered lengthwise

1 lb (500 g) baby green beans, trimmed

1 large cauliflower, cut into florets

16–20 baby beets, trimmed with ½-inch (12-mm) stem intact

4 dozen snails, canned in salted water

1 capon or boiling chicken, 4½–5 lb (2.25–2.5 kg), or 5 chicken breasts, about ½ lb (250 g) each

8–10 hard-boiled eggs, peeled

Aïoli (page 41), made with 8–10 cloves garlic, 3 egg yolks, 1 tablespoon Dijon mustard, and 3 cups (24 fl oz/750 ml) olive oil

❦ Begin preparing the salt cod at least 2 days in advance of serving. Place in a large bowl, add water to cover generously, cover, and refrigerate for at least 24 hours or preferably 48 hours, changing the water at least 5 times during that period.

❦ The day before serving, pick over the dried chickpeas, discarding any grit or misshapen beans. Rinse well, place in a bowl, add water to cover, and let soak overnight. Drain, place in a saucepan with water to cover by about 3 inches (7.5 cm), and bring to a boil. Reduce the heat to low, cover, and cook until tender, about 30 minutes. Drain and set aside. If using canned chickpeas, rinse well, drain, and set aside.

❦ The day of serving, make the stock: In a large saucepan, combine the water, carrot, leek, onion, garlic, and bouquet garni. Bring slowly to a boil over medium-high heat. Cover, reduce the heat to low, and simmer gently for 30 minutes. Remove from the heat, strain through a fine-mesh sieve, and return to the saucepan. Set aside to cool.

❦ The potatoes, artichokes, carrots, onions, zucchini, green beans, cauliflower, and beets must be cooked separately in boiling salted water. Place in the salted water, bring to a boil, and cook, uncovered, just until tender, according to the following timings: potatoes, 20–25 minutes; artichokes, about 20 minutes; carrots, about 12 minutes; onions, about 6 minutes; zucchini, about 5 minutes; green beans, 4–5 minutes; cauliflower, 3–4 minutes; and beets, 10–12 minutes. Drain the vegetables. Peel the skins off the beets. Put all the vegetables on 1 or more platters and set aside.

❦ Drain the snails, rinse well, and set alongside the vegetables. Place the whole capon or chicken or the chicken breasts in the cooled stock, bring to a boil over medium-high heat, reduce the heat to low, cover partially, and cook until opaque throughout, about 1 hour and 20 minutes for the whole bird and 8–10 minutes for the breasts. Transfer to a cutting board and carve into large pieces. Keep warm.

❦ Drain the salt cod, transfer to a saucepan, add cold water to cover, and place over medium heat. Bring slowly to just under a boil and simmer, uncovered, until tender, 8–10 minutes. Drain and keep warm.

❦ While you are cooking the cod, reheat all the vegetables, including the chickpeas, in the stock, heating only one type at a time. Reheat the beets last, as they color the stock. Each batch should take 3–4 minutes. Then heat the snails in the stock.

❦ Arrange the cod, chicken, snails, vegetables, and eggs in separate piles on large platters and bring to the table. Set out the aioli in 1 or more bowls. Serve immediately.

serves 8

Alpes-Maritimes

La Petite Friture

deep-fried baby fish

Small fish—baby sardines, baby anchovies, tiny red mullets, and other rockfish—are caught in nets while fishermen are harvesting larger specimens. These fish are nonetheless well appreciated and are grouped together in batches in the market, the price scrawled in pencil on the paper on which they lay. Although whitebait comes mainly from the Atlantic, many vendors add it to the mix. Often sold as "fish for the soup," they are also commonly deep-fried to a golden crisp and served as a separate fish course, a single luncheon dish or a light supper. A mesclun salad and a crisp local white or rosé are the only accompaniments.

1¼ lb (625 g) mixed tiny fish or whitebait

about ¾ cup (6 fl oz/180 ml) milk, or
as needed

1 cup (5 oz/155 g) all-purpose (plain) flour

olive oil for deep-frying

salt and freshly ground pepper to taste

1 cup (1 oz/30 g) fresh flat-leaf (Italian) parsley
sprigs, well dried (optional)

2 lemons, cut into wedges

☙ In a bowl, combine the fish with milk just to cover. Let stand for 30 minutes.

☙ Place the flour in a bowl. Drain the fish well and add them to the flour. Toss to coat well with the flour, then transfer to a sieve and shake the sieve to rid the fish of excess flour. Set aside.

☙ Pour olive oil to a depth of 1½ inches (4 cm) into a deep saucepan and heat to 325°F (165°C) on a deep-frying thermometer. When the oil is ready, carefully add about one-third of the fish. Use a wire skimmer to move the fish around the pan to keep them separate, and turn them to ensure even cooking. When they are golden brown, after 1½–2 minutes, transfer to paper towels to drain. Repeat with the remaining fish in 2 batches.

☙ Sprinkle the fish with salt and pepper. If desired, toss the parsley sprigs into the hot oil for a couple of seconds and scoop out onto paper towels to drain.

☙ Arrange the fish on a large platter and toss the crisped parsley over them, if using. Serve immediately with the lemon wedges.

serves 6

Les Nonats

A specialty—by decree—of the Alpes-Maritimes, *nonats,* or *poutines,* are transparent, almost microscopic fish pulled from local waters. When the County of Nice became part of France in 1860, the government granted the fishermen between the Cap d'Antibes and Menton the right to keep the fingerlings and undersized fish that came up with the harvest in their nets. These tiny specimens, nowadays often mixed with *sardinettes* (baby sardines), tiny anchovies, and whitebait (though originally *nonats* were white fish only), can be bought in markets along the Riviera only during a forty-five-day period that falls between February and April.

When the fish are fresh, they cling together like a transparent gel. Cooks gather them into little patties, coat them in flour, and fry them to a crisp in a deep-fry basket. Another favorite use is in *sartagnade,* which calls for panfrying them in olive oil, pressed together and turned as one, to yield a crisp-fried cake of tiny fish that can be cut into wedges. In former times, the *nonats* were a staple of the fishermen's diet and helped extend the household budget. Although I have occasionally seen them scrawled on a menu as a dish of the day in little bistros boasting local specialties, today they are prepared mainly as a curiosity.

Var

Soupe aux Moules

mussel soup

Every region of France with a coastline also has a mussel soup. Most are simple broths that aim to catch the juice as the mussels open; transform its flavor with a little garlic, onion, or parsley; and soften the salty sea brine with a little white wine, beer, or cream. This version of mussel soup is a little more complicated than many, with rich results.

4 tablespoons (2 oz/60 g) unsalted butter

2 carrots, peeled and finely diced

2 leeks, white part only, finely diced

2 celery stalks, finely diced

2 potatoes, peeled and diced

2 tomatoes, peeled, seeded, and diced

bouquet garni (page 246)

3–5 cups (24–40 fl oz/750 ml–1.25 l) water

1 cup (8 fl oz/250 ml) dry white wine

4 lb (2 kg) mussels, scrubbed and debearded

¼ lb (125 g) slab bacon, cut crosswise into pieces ½ inch (12 mm) wide

salt and freshly ground pepper to taste

⚜ In a large saucepan over low heat, melt 3 tablespoons of the butter. Add three-fourths each of the carrots, leeks, and celery and sauté until shiny and well coated with butter, about 2 minutes. Add the potatoes, tomatoes, bouquet garni, and 3 cups (24 fl oz/750 ml) of the water. Raise the heat to high and bring to a boil. Reduce the heat to low, cover, and simmer slowly until the vegetables are tender, about 30 minutes.

⚜ Meanwhile, in a large soup pot over high heat, bring the wine to a boil. Add the mussels, discarding any that fail to close to the touch, cover, and cook over high heat, stirring once, until the mussels open, 2–3 minutes. Remove from the heat and discard any mussels that failed to open.

⚜ Set aside 24 mussels in their shells for garnish. Pluck the remainder from their shells and set the meats on a plate. Strain the mussel liquor through a fine-mesh sieve lined with cheesecloth (muslin) set over a bowl. Set aside.

⚜ Rinse the soup pot, add the remaining 1 tablespoon butter, and place over medium heat. Add the bacon and sauté until the fat is rendered and the bacon begins to crisp, about 1 minute. Add the remaining carrots, leeks, and celery and stir over medium heat until shiny and half-cooked, about 2 minutes.

⚜ Remove the bouquet garni from the saucepan and discard. Add about ¼ cup (2 oz/60 g) of the shelled mussels and half of the mussel liquor and mix well. Purée with a handheld blender in the pan, or transfer to a blender or food processor and purée until smooth. Slowly add the remaining mussel liquor, tasting as you do. Stop adding it if the soup becomes too salty. You will need 3–4 cups (24–32 fl oz/ 750 ml–1 l) liquid in all. If the liquor is too salty, use water instead. Pour the puréed soup through a medium-mesh sieve onto the vegetables and bacon. Taste and season with salt, if needed, and pepper.

⚜ Add the remaining mussels, both shelled and unshelled, to the soup and reheat gently to serving temperature. Ladle into wide soup bowls, placing 3 mussels in their shells in the center of each bowl. Serve at once.

serves 8

Alpes-Maritimes

Thon à la Méridionale

grilled tuna with herbs

Tuna, with its firm red flesh and meaty texture, lends itself to grilling. Here, the flavor is highlighted with the fresh herbs of the south: rosemary, thyme, and fennel. Swordfish or marlin may be substituted.

6 tuna steaks, each 5 oz (155 g) and 1 inch (2.5 cm) thick

2–3 tablespoons olive oil, plus oil for brushing grill rack

¼ cup (¼ oz/7 g) fresh rosemary leaves, lightly chopped if desired

leaves from 3 large fresh thyme sprigs (about 1 tablespoon)

1 tablespoon fennel seed, crushed

salt and freshly ground pepper to taste

6 tablespoons (3 fl oz/90 ml) extra-virgin olive oil

☙ Brush the tuna steaks with the 2–3 tablespoons olive oil. Combine the rosemary, thyme, and fennel seed on a sheet of parchment (baking) paper or a cutting board, mixing well, then spread in a thin layer. Press the tuna onto the herbs, coating both sides. Cover and allow the herbs to infuse the tuna for at least 30 minutes or up to 2 hours.

☙ Prepare a fire in a grill.

☙ Brush the grill rack with olive oil. Place the tuna steaks on the rack. Grill until the first side is nicely colored, 2½–3 minutes, rotating the fillets 45 degrees after about 1½ minutes to create grid marks on the surface. Turn the fillets, season with salt and pepper, and grill until done as desired, about 2 minutes longer for medium-rare. This is how the tuna steaks are preferred in Provence—seared on the outside and pink on the inside. (The tuna can also be cooked on a ridged cast-iron grill pan on the stove top, using similar timing.)

☙ Transfer the tuna to warmed individual plates, drizzle each steak with 1 tablespoon of the extra-virgin olive oil, and serve immediately.

serves 6

Alpes-de-Haute-Provence

Truite à l'Oseille

baked trout with sorrel

When Provence is mentioned, most outsiders think of sun, sand, and the wide, blue Mediterranean Sea. Of course, they overlook the mountainous stretches that make up much of the region. The east and northeast, through the départements of the Alpes-Maritimes and Haute Provence and westward into the Vaucluse, boast great expanses of alpine land-scapes, with gorges, lakes, and clear mountain streams offering freshwater bounty such as trout.

6 trout, about 6 oz (185 g) each, cleaned

salt and freshly ground pepper to taste

2 tablespoons unsalted butter

about 1 cup (6 oz/185 g) multicolored mixed vegetable julienne made from carrots, turnips, snow peas (mangetouts), celery, or similar seasonal vegetables

⅓ cup (3 fl oz/80 ml) crisp, lightly acidic white wine such as a Riesling

1 cup (8 fl oz/250 ml) heavy (double) cream

12–15 sorrel leaves, coarsely chopped

❧ Preheat an oven to 400°F (200°C). Butter a baking dish large enough to accommodate the trout in a single layer. Rinse the fish, pat dry, and season inside and out with salt and pepper. Set aside.

❧ In a frying pan large enough to hold the vegetables, heat the butter over medium heat. Add the vegetables and sauté until just softened, 45–60 seconds. Season with salt and pepper. Remove from the heat. Spoon the vegetable mixture into the fish cavities, dividing it evenly. Place the fish in the prepared baking dish. Pour the wine evenly over the fish. Cover the dish loosely with a piece of aluminum foil to prevent the top of the fish from drying out. Bake the fish until opaque throughout, 10–12 minutes.

❧ Using a spatula, transfer the fish to warmed individual plates and keep warm. Pour the cooking juices into a small saucepan. Add the cream and sorrel and bring to a boil over high heat. Boil, stirring, until reduced to a sauce consistency and thick enough to coat the back of a spoon, about 2 minutes. Season with salt and pepper.

❧ Spoon the sorrel sauce over the fish and serve.

serves 6

Alpes-Maritimes

Sardines Farcies au Four

baked stuffed sardines

Sardines are a favorite catch along the Côte d'Azur, where they are deep-fried or panfried or are prepared with a spicy marinade, en escabèche, and stored in the refrigerator to have on hand for a quick meal. For a special occasion, the fish are boned and stuffed with herbs. Walnuts, a common addition to the filling, are included in this version.

16 large fresh sardines

¼ cup (⅓ oz/10 g) chopped fresh flat-leaf (Italian) parsley

leaves from 1 small fresh rosemary sprig, chopped

1 tablespoon chopped fresh thyme

4 cloves garlic, finely chopped

2 tablespoons ground walnuts

1 tablespoon grated Parmesan cheese

5 tablespoons (2½ fl oz/75 ml) olive oil

♛ One at a time, hold the sardines under running cold water, squeezing the body slightly, and use your fingers to pull off the head and then pull downward to remove the backbone. Break the bone free at the tail end and discard the spine in one piece. Using a sharp knife, scrape off the scales. Rinse the fish well and place on a platter, opening the fish flat like a book. When all of the sardines are boned, set aside.

♛ Preheat an oven to 425°F (220°C). Oil a baking dish large enough to accommodate the closed sardines in a single layer.

♛ In a small bowl, stir together the parsley, rosemary, and thyme. In another small bowl, stir together the garlic, walnuts, and Parmesan. Add 2 tablespoons of the mixed herbs to the garlic mixture along with 1 tablespoon of the olive oil and mix well. Spread over the flattened sardines, then fold them closed and place in the prepared baking dish. Sprinkle evenly with the remaining mixed herbs and 4 table-spoons (2 fl oz/60 ml) olive oil.

♛ Bake the sardines until opaque throughout, about 6 minutes. Transfer to a platter and serve.

serves 4

Alpes-Maritimes

Le Blanc de Loup Belle Mouginoise

sea bass with tomatoes, mushrooms, and cucumbers

Roger Vergé has long been one of the most esteemed chefs in Provence. For many years, his Michelin-rated three-star restaurant, Le Moulin de Mougins, in the small town of Mougins, behind Cannes, and its sister restaurant, L'Amandier, a little higher up in the town, have attracted food-loving pilgrims from all over the world. They have also inspired a generation of Vergé-taught chefs, who have taken the flavors of Provence to the restaurants of the world.

His recipe for sea bass fillets calls for baking them and is deceptively easy to prepare. Colorful and appetizing, it brings some of the legend of this great chef to the home dining table. Turbot, orange roughy, lingcod, or John Dory may be substituted for the bass.

3 tablespoons finely chopped shallot

6 sea bass fillets, each 6 oz (185 g) and about 1 inch (2.5 cm) thick

3 firm tomatoes

boiling water, as needed

6 very large fresh white mushrooms, brushed clean

2 English (hothouse) cucumbers, unpeeled, thinly sliced

salt and freshly ground pepper to taste

3 tablespoons red vermouth

5 tablespoons (2½ fl oz/75 ml) dry white wine

3 tablespoons jellied fish stock (page 251)

⅔ cup (5 fl oz/160 ml) heavy (double) cream

5 tablespoons (2½ oz/75 g) unsalted butter, cut into small pieces

2 tablespoons chopped fresh chives

⚜ Preheat an oven to 400°F (200°C). Generously butter a baking dish large enough to hold the fish fillets in a single layer.

⚜ Scatter the chopped shallot over the bottom of the prepared dish. Place the fish fillets on top.

⚜ Put the tomatoes in a large heatproof bowl and pour boiling water over them. Let stand for 1 minute, then drain and immerse in cold water to cool. Carefully peel away the skin, keeping the surface as perfect as possible. Thinly slice the tomatoes. Thinly slice the mushrooms, to form slices as close as possible to the size of the tomato slices. Arrange the tomato, mushroom, and cucumber slices in three neat rows along the length of each fillet, overlapping them. Sprinkle with salt and pepper.

⚜ Pour the vermouth and white wine into the bottom of the dish. Bake until the fish is opaque throughout, about 4 minutes. Remove from the oven and, using a wide spatula, carefully transfer the fish fillets to a warmed large plate. Keep warm.

⚜ Pour the cooking juices from the baking dish into a saucepan and add the fish stock and cream. Bring to a boil over high heat and, whisking vigorously, reduce to a sauce consistency, about 1 minute. Remove from the heat, add the butter, and whisk to incorporate fully. Add the chopped chives, stir to combine, and season with salt and pepper.

⚜ Spoon some sauce onto the center of each warmed individual plate. Brush the vegetables with the sauce to give them a sheen. Gently transfer the fish fillets to the plates, placing them in the center of each pool of sauce. Serve immediately.

serves 6

La Bouillabaisse

The best Provençal cooks will tell you that producing a respectable bouillabaisse is a costly and time-consuming undertaking. But the dish itself has humble origins. It was the creation of Marseilles fishermen, who filled pots with diluted seawater, placed them over wood fires on the beach, and then added local herbs and the discards from their day's catch. When ready, fish and broth were ladled over slices of bread, and the fishermen sat down to eat.

Today, this simplicity has given way to a more complicated formula. Purists insist that at least eight species are necessary for the correct complexity of flavor, most importantly the *rascasse* (scorpion fish), without which, locals insist, it is not a bouillabaisse at all, but merely a fish soup. Garlic-rubbed toasted or fried croutons topped with *sauce rouille* have now replaced the bread, and saffron is de rigueur. Cooks around Toulon, which hotly challenges Marseilles for the right to call the soup its own, add mussels and shellfish. Only "Parisians," say the fishermen snobbishly— and for them that includes the wealthy restaurants of the rich resorts—add crayfish and lobster. In traditional recipes, water and a little wine are the primary liquids, but classic variations include substituting fish stock.

Bouches-du-Rhône

La Bouillabaisse

fish soup of marseilles

Originated by the fishermen who sailed out of the busy port of Marseilles, bouillabaisse has become a classic of the southern French table.

ROUILLE SAUCE

3 large cloves garlic, chopped

1 red bird's-eye chile, seeded and chopped

salt to taste

3 egg yolks

1¾ cups (14 fl oz/430 ml) olive oil

freshly ground pepper to taste

¼ teaspoon saffron threads, crushed and steeped in 2 teaspoons hot water (optional)

SOUP BASE

olive oil for sautéing

2 large yellow onions, sliced

2 large tomatoes, peeled, seeded, and coarsely chopped

1 leek, white part only, halved lengthwise

3 cloves garlic, chopped

½ fennel bulb, cut into 3 wedges

zest from ½ orange, cut into wide strips

1 small lemon, cut into wedges

2½–3 qt (2.5–3 l) water or fish stock (page 251) and dry white wine, in a ratio of 3 parts water or stock to 5 parts wine

2 fresh thyme sprigs

1 bay leaf

½ teaspoon saffron threads, crushed and steeped in 2 teaspoons hot water

2 teaspoons tomato paste, or to taste

salt and freshly ground pepper to taste

FISH AND SHELLFISH

6–7 lb (3–3.5 kg) whole fish such as scorpion fish, monkfish, snapper, conger eel, whiting, sea robin, ocean perch, and John Dory

2 lb (1 kg) crayfish, cut into medallions if large, halved lengthwise if small (optional)

4 small crabs, cleaned and quartered (optional)

16 mussels, scrubbed and debearded (optional)

24 small potatoes, boiled until tender, peeled, halved crosswise, and kept warm (optional)

3 tablespoons chopped flat-leaf (Italian) parsley

20 croutons, made from baguette slices and fried (page 247)

❧ To make the *rouille* sauce, in a mortar, crush the garlic and chile with a pestle, sprinkling in a pinch of salt to help the pestle grip the mixture. Add the egg yolks and whisk to combine. Add the olive oil, drop by drop, whisking constantly. When an emulsion has formed, add the oil in a slow, steady stream, whisking continuously. Season with salt and pepper. If desired, whisk in the saffron for color. Cover and refrigerate.

❧ To make the soup base, pour olive oil to a depth of ⅓ inch (9 mm) in a large, wide soup pot over medium heat. Add the onions and sauté for about 1 minute. Add the tomatoes, leek, garlic, fennel, orange zest, and lemon wedges. Add 3 ladlefuls of the water or stock and wine along with the thyme, bay leaf, saffron, 2 teaspoons tomato paste, salt, and pepper. Raise the heat to high, bring the soup to a rapid boil, and cook for 10 minutes.

❧ Leave the fish whole except for the scorpion fish and the conger eel, which should be in chunks. Start adding the firmer-fleshed fish to the pot. Ladle in enough water or stock and wine to keep the seafood almost covered with liquid. Add the crayfish and crabs, if using. Boil rapidly for 10 minutes, then add the more delicate-fleshed fish. Reduce the heat to medium-low and simmer for 10 minutes, adding the mussels, if using, during the last 4–5 minutes of cooking (discard any mussels that fail to close to the touch). Taste and adjust the seasoning with tomato paste, salt, and pepper.

❧ Using a large spatula, carefully transfer the seafood to a warmed serving platter, arranging the pieces attractively and discarding any mussels that failed to open. If serving the potatoes, place them around the edge of the platter. Sprinkle the fish and potatoes with the parsley.

❧ Pass the soup through a fine-meshed sieve into a large tureen. Put a dollop of the sauce on each of 8–10 croutons and float the croutons on the soup. Place the remaining sauce in a bowl and the remaining croutons on a plate.

❧ Bring the tureen, the platter of seafood, and the sauce and croutons to the table and serve immediately in shallow bowls.

serves 8–10

Bouches-du-Rhône

Moules au Basilic

mussels in basil butter

The mussels in this sophisticated preparation are embellished with diced tomatoes and butter flavored with the summer basil crop.

6 dozen small mussels (about 4 lb/2 kg), scrubbed and debearded

3 small, very red tomatoes, peeled and seeded

BASIL BUTTER

1 cup (8 oz/250 g) unsalted butter, at room temperature

¼ cup (⅓ oz/10 g) shredded fresh basil leaves

2 tablespoons chopped shallots

salt and freshly ground pepper to taste

fresh lemon juice to taste

❧ Place the mussels in a large saucepan, discarding any that fail to close to the touch. Cover, place over high heat, and cook, shaking the pan from time to time, until the mussels open, 3–5 minutes. Remove from the heat and, using a slotted spoon, transfer the mussels to a bowl, discarding any that failed to open. Strain the liquor through a fine-mesh sieve lined with cheesecloth (muslin) set over a bowl.

❧ Remove and discard the top shell from each mussel. Lay the mussels on a large flameproof or ovenproof serving dish or individual plates. If you lack a flameproof dish or dishes, arrange the mussels on a baking sheet and later transfer to plates for serving.

❧ Cut the tomatoes into a uniform ¼-inch (6-mm) dice. Distribute the diced tomatoes evenly on top of the mussels, using 3 or 4 pieces per mussel.

❧ Preheat a broiler (griller), or preheat an oven to 400°F (200°C).

❧ To make the basil butter, in a bowl, whisk the butter until creamy. Stir in the basil, shallots, and a small amount of the mussel liquor to taste. Season with salt, pepper, and lemon juice. Using a small spatula, evenly spread the basil butter over the mussels and tomatoes. Slip the mussels under the broiler 5 inches (13 cm) from the heat source and broil (grill) until the butter is sizzling and the mussels are heated through, 2–3 minutes. Or place in the oven and bake for about 5 minutes. Serve immediately.

serves 6

Bouches-du-Rhône

Brandade de Morue

salt cod purée

A beloved feature of the Provençal diet, brandade de morue can be simple to prepare once you learn its secrets. I received an initiation in the kitchen of a friend, Provençal chef André Perez, who lives west of Marseilles. He taught me how to achieve the necessary creamy consistency of brandade: the milk and olive oil must be warmed separately and are never added to the salt cod too quickly, or they will pool in the bottom of the pan rather than form a rich emulsion.

1 lb (500 g) salt cod fillet, preferably a thick, central cut

1 cup (8 fl oz/250 ml) olive oil

¾ cup (6 fl oz/180 ml) milk

2 cloves garlic, crushed

white pepper to taste

12 triangular croutons, made from dense sourdough bread and fried (page 247)

❧ Begin preparing the salt cod at least 2 days in advance of serving. Place in a large bowl, add water to cover generously, cover, and refrigerate for at least 24 hours or preferably 48 hours, changing the water at least 5 times during that period.

❧ The day of serving, drain the salt cod and place in a saucepan. Add water to cover, place over medium heat, and bring slowly to just under a boil. Simmer until the cod has softened and cooked through, 15–18 minutes. Drain well and, when cool enough to handle, remove any skin. Using a fork in each hand, flake the cod, removing any errant bones.

❧ In separate small saucepans over medium heat, warm ½ cup (4 fl oz/125 ml) of the olive oil and the milk. Remove from the heat. In a large saucepan over low heat, warm the remaining ½ cup (4 fl oz/125 ml) olive oil. Add the flaked salt cod and work well with a wooden spatula, mashing the cod as you stir. Add the garlic and mix well. Stirring constantly, alternately add the warmed olive oil and milk, a few tablespoons at a time, allowing each addition to be fully absorbed before adding more. When all the oil and milk is incorporated, season with white pepper.

❧ Spoon the *brandade* on the croutons and serve immediately.

serves 6

Bouches-du-Rhône

Encornets Farcis à la Tapenade

cuttlefish stuffed with tapenade

This recipe is from Saintes-Maries-de-la-Mer in the Camargue, at the base of the Rhône delta. The small seaside township is a lazy haven for tourists driving through the area, until the Gypsies come to town. The main church is the burial place of the Virgin Mary's two half-sisters and their black maid, Sarah, the patron saint of Gypsies. Year-round, a few Gypsies stay near the church to change the clothes of Sarah's statue, light candles to her image, and engage the passing tourists.

In May, Gypsies from all over Europe make a pilgrimage to the church, and the ensuing celebration swells the population of the town.

You will need only the cuttlefish bodies for this recipe, not the tentacles, so buy them already cleaned if you prefer. Squid also works well for this recipe. Accompany the stuffed cephalopods with rice.

SAUCE

2 tablespoons olive oil

1 yellow onion, finely chopped

1 clove garlic, finely chopped

12 fresh basil leaves

2 fresh thyme sprigs

1 bay leaf

salt and freshly ground pepper to taste

1 lb (500 g) tomatoes, peeled, seeded, and coarsely chopped

pinch of sugar

8 medium-large cuttlefish or squid, each 6–7 inches (15–18 cm) long

½ lb (250 g) ground (minced) veal

½ lb (250 g) ground (minced) pork

3 cloves garlic, finely chopped

1 red (Spanish) onion, finely chopped

¼ cup (2 oz/60 g) Tapenade (page 59)

4 tablespoons (2 fl oz/60 ml) olive oil

⅔ cup (5 fl oz/160 ml) dry white wine

about 1 cup (8 fl oz/250 ml) water, if needed

♛ To make the sauce, in a wide, heavy saucepan over medium heat, warm the olive oil. Add the onion and sauté until it gains an oily sheen, about 30 seconds. Add the garlic, basil, thyme, bay leaf, salt, and pepper. Stir well, reduce the heat to low, and cook slowly until the mixture softens and the flavors blend, about 10 minutes.

♛ Add the tomatoes and sugar, stir well, and continue to cook, mashing from time to time with a wooden spoon, until a chunky sauce forms, about 30 minutes longer. Remove the sauce from the heat and keep warm.

♛ Preheat an oven to 325°F (165°C).

♛ Clean the cuttlefish or squid as directed on page 250. Leave the bodies whole, and do not peel away the mottled membrane that covers each body, as it helps to color the sauce. Reserve the tentacles for another use or discard.

♛ In a bowl, combine the ground veal and pork and mix well. Mix in the garlic, onion, and *tapenade*, blending thoroughly. Add 2 tablespoons of the olive oil and 1 tablespoon of the white wine and mix again.

♛ Spoon the stuffing into the cuttlefish or squid bodies, dividing it evenly and not packing it too tightly. Secure each with a toothpick.

♛ Lay the stuffed cuttlefish or squid in a single layer in a baking dish. Spoon the sauce evenly over the top, and then drizzle with the remaining 2 tablespoons olive oil. Cover the dish with aluminum foil.

♛ Bake until a skewer inserted into the stuffed cuttlefish or squid comes out clean, 50–60 minutes. Halfway through the cooking, remove from the oven, lift the foil carefully, and add the remaining white wine to the dish. If the sauce still looks dry, add the water, distributing it evenly around the dish.

♛ Remove the dish from the oven and, using a slotted spatula, carefully lift out the stuffed cuttlefish or squid. Discard the toothpicks. Reheat the sauce, stirring, then taste and adjust the seasoning.

♛ Serve the stuffed cuttlefish or squid whole, topped with the sauce. Alternatively, cut the bodies on the diagonal into ⅜-inch (1-cm) slices, fan them out on warmed individual plates, and spoon the sauce over the top.

serves 8

Vaucluse

Cabillaud Demoiselle d'Avignon

steamed cod with vegetables

This recipe was served to me in Avignon by a hostess more concerned with her figure than most French home cooks I have met. Turbot, mahi-mahi, or even swordfish may be used in place of the cod. The fish is steamed, and the vegetables are only lightly cooked, with a minimum of extra calories.

6 cod fillets, each 6 oz (185 g) and about 4 by 3 by 1 inch (10 by 7.5 by 2.5 cm)

5 tablespoons (2½ fl oz/75 ml) olive oil

1 small eggplant (aubergine), unpeeled, cut into neat ⅜-inch (1-cm) dice

1 small zucchini (courgette), trimmed and cut into neat ⅜-inch (1-cm) dice

4 large, firm tomatoes, peeled, seeded, and cut into neat ⅜-inch (1-cm) dice

salt and freshly ground pepper to taste

6 tablespoons (3 fl oz/90 ml) extra-virgin olive oil

3 tablespoons fresh chive lengths (1 inch/2.5 cm)

♛ Place the fish on a steamer rack and set aside. Pour water into the steamer pan and bring to a boil.

♛ Meanwhile, in a small frying pan over medium heat, warm the olive oil. Add the eggplant and sauté quickly, adding the zucchini as the eggplant begins to soften. Finally, add the tomatoes just to heat through. Do not overcook or they will lose their texture. The total cooking time should be about 4 minutes. The vegetables should be crisp-tender when served. Season with salt and pepper and keep warm.

♛ Place the steamer rack over the boiling water, cover, and steam until the fish is opaque throughout, 4–6 minutes.

♛ Using a slotted spoon, transfer the vegetables to warmed individual plates, arranging them in a ring. Place a steamed fillet in the center of each ring. Drizzle 1 tablespoon extra-virgin olive oil over each fillet, garnish with the chives, and serve.

serves 6

Le Repas de Midi

In small communities and large cities alike, the arrival of midday is announced with the sound of shopkeepers and school principals simultaneously shuttering their windows and locking their doors and of townspeople flocking into the streets to return home to share the midday meal with their families. Breakfast has been simple—bread, café au lait, hot chocolate for the children—and *le repas de midi* is the main meal of the day.

The meal always begins with an appetizer, even if only sliced sausage, hard-boiled egg on a vegetable *macédoine,* or a slice of pâté. The main dish is meat or fish with an accompanying vegetable, but rarely more than one. Salad and cheese commonly follow, then fresh fruit or, for the children, maybe a fresh cheese drizzled with honey is brought to the table.

On Sunday, lunch becomes a more elaborate affair, with the table expanded to include members of the extended family. The ritual aperitif is pastis or the local Suze, Vennoise, or Figuoun, accompanied with little biscuits, a bowl of nuts, and an assortment of olives. The meal itself may open with crudités and aioli or *tapenade,* shrimp or sardines fried or rolled over spinach or walnuts, or perhaps deep-fried zucchini flowers.

The week's largest piece of meat is served on this day, and the vegetable accompaniment is carefully chosen according to tradition and season, such as leg of lamb with flageolets, steak or lamb with ratatouille, fish with sliced leeks, or a roast with a decorative *tian*. Salad comes after the main dish, then is followed by one or two good-sized cheeses purchased especially for the occasion, served with a crusty loaf (never biscuits) and lingered over for a while before dessert is set in place. Wine is poured with every course, but after cheese the red is removed and the glasses changed for a sweet muscat, maybe one of the household *ratafias* (a rum-based liqueur), or a feisty local marc with the coffee.

Sunday lunch requires dessert. An accomplished cook might make a *bavarois* or a *tarte maison* of the season's fruit. More likely, a family member will pass by the local *pâtisserie,* believing that a professional will make something suitably special.

Var

Civet de Thon

tuna braised in red wine

Civet is the name given to the traditional red wine–simmered hare in French cuisine. Tuna's dark red meat makes it a fish suitable for braising. Here, the comparison with meat is drawn further, as the fish is simmered in a rich ragout of powerful flavors. The dish also works well with monkfish or swordfish, both of which can stand up to braising. Rice is the usual accompaniment.

¼ cup (2 oz/60 g) unsalted butter

12 whole shallots, plus 1 shallot, finely chopped

3 oz (90 g) slab bacon, cut into bite-sized pieces

1 carrot, peeled and chopped

1 yellow onion, chopped

2 lb (1 kg) tuna fillet, cut into 1¼-inch (3-cm) cubes

1 tablespoon all-purpose (plain) flour

1 clove garlic, finely chopped

1 cup (8 fl oz/250 ml) dry red wine

2 tablespoons olive oil

¼ lb (125 g) fresh white mushrooms, brushed clean and left whole if small, quartered lengthwise if large

12 small oil-cured black olives

2 lemon slices, cut into tiny triangles

salt and freshly ground pepper to taste

chopped fresh flat-leaf (Italian) parsley

12 triangular croutons, made from dense sourdough bread and fried (page 247)

❧ In a small cast-iron Dutch oven or sauté pan over high heat, melt the butter. Add the whole shallots and sauté for about 1 minute. Add the bacon, fry for a few seconds, and then add the carrot and onion and stir until coated with the rendered bacon fat and butter, about 1 minute. Add the tuna cubes, sear briefly on all sides, and then sprinkle the flour over all, stirring it to the bottom of the pan and allowing it to cook for about 30 seconds.

❧ Add the chopped shallot and garlic, stir again, and then pour in the wine. Bring to a boil, reduce the heat to low, cover, and simmer gently until the fish cubes are opaque throughout, about 20 minutes.

❧ Meanwhile, in a small frying pan over high heat, warm the olive oil. Add the mushrooms and sauté until well coated with oil, about 1 minute. About 5 minutes before the tuna is finished cooking, add the mushrooms, olives, and lemon.

❧ Using a slotted spoon, transfer the tuna and vegetables to a serving dish. Raise the heat to high and boil the juices remaining in the pan until they are thickened to a sauce consistency. Season with salt and pepper. Spoon the sauce over the tuna and scatter the parsley over the tuna and vegetables. Serve the croutons on the side.

serves 4–6

Summer resorts share the Var coastline with pointus ~ old fishing boats.

Var

Cuisses de Grenouilles Provençales

frogs' legs, provence style

The lashings of garlic and parsley in this dish identify it as unmistakably Provençal. The small French frogs, once a succulent delicacy, are no longer readily available, so this recipe has been adjusted to use the more readily available, larger Asian frogs.

9 pairs frogs' legs, split

about 1 cup (5 oz/155 g) all-purpose (plain) flour

1 cup (8 oz/245 g) unsalted butter

2 tablespoons olive oil

6 cloves garlic, finely chopped

salt and freshly ground coarse pepper

2 tablespoons fresh lemon juice, or to taste

3 tablespoons chopped fresh flat-leaf (Italian) parsley

☙ Rinse the frogs' legs and pat thoroughly dry with paper towels.

☙ Spread the flour on a plate, then, one at a time, roll the frogs' legs in the flour, tapping off the excess.

☙ In a frying pan over medium heat, melt ⅓ cup (3 oz/90 g) of the butter with the olive oil. Add the frogs' legs and sauté, turning occasionally, until browned and tender, 8–10 minutes, adding the garlic during the last 3–4 minutes of cooking. Be careful not to allow the garlic to scorch.

☙ Just before the frogs' legs are tender, cut the remaining ⅔ cup (5 oz/155 g) butter into small pieces. When the legs are cooked, reduce the heat to low and add the butter pieces, stirring to melt gently. Season with salt and pepper and then add the lemon juice and then the parsley.

☙ Transfer to a warmed platter or individual plates and serve immediately.

serves 6

Bouches-du-Rhône

La Bourride

creamy fish soup

In southeastern Provençal ports, fishing villages, and coastal resort towns—from Saint-Raphaël to Saint-Tropez to Nice—this fish soup is served in nearly every restaurant and, for grand occasions, at home as well. Bourride is made unique by the addition of aioli, which is whisked into the soup in large quantity to give it an essentially creamy yellow look that is very different from the region's other great fish soup, bouillabaisse. In Provence, monkfish is the most common addition, but sea bass is also often used, as are whiting and John Dory.

STOCK

2 tablespoons olive oil

1 yellow onion, sliced

4 carrots, peeled and sliced

2 leeks, white part only, sliced

2 Swiss chard leaves, stalks removed and leaves coarsely sliced (optional)

1 fresh thyme sprig

2 orange zest strips, 2½ inches (6 cm) long and ½ inch (12 mm) wide

1¾ cups (14 fl oz/430 ml) dry white wine

6–8 cups (48–64 fl oz/1.5–2 l) water or light fish stock (page 251)

3 lb (1.5 kg) white-fleshed fish, in fillets or thick-cut medallions

salt and freshly ground pepper to taste

12 slices day-old baguette or dense sourdough bread

aioli (page 41), made with 3 egg yolks, 6 cloves garlic, and 1–1⅓ cups (8–11 fl oz/ 250–340 ml) olive oil

3 egg yolks

✲ To make the stock, in a large saucepan over medium heat, warm the olive oil. Add the onion, carrots, and leeks and sauté until softened and shiny with oil, about 1 minute. Add the Swiss chard (if using), thyme, and orange zest, stir briefly, and then pour in the wine and the water or stock. Raise the heat to high and bring to a boil. Reduce the heat to low and simmer slowly, uncovered, for 20 minutes to infuse the liquid with flavor.

✲ Strain the stock through a fine-mesh sieve and return it to the pan. Bring to a boil and boil, uncovered, until reduced by one-third. Remove from the heat and let cool slightly, about 15 minutes, before continuing.

✲ If using fillets, cut them into large chunks about 4 inches (10 cm) long. Place the fish in the cooled stock. Season lightly with salt and pepper and bring to just under a boil. Reduce the heat to low and simmer, uncovered, until the fish is opaque throughout, 8–10 minutes.

✲ While the fish is cooking, arrange the bread slices in the bottom of individual soup plates, placing 2 slices in each plate. When the fish is cooked, using a slotted spoon or wide metal spatula, carefully transfer the fish to a serving platter and keep warm.

✲ If the soup tastes too bland, boil it down to concentrate the flavor. Adjust the seasoning with salt and pepper. Moisten the bread with a little of the soup. Reserve about half the aioli to serve separately in a bowl. Whisk the egg yolks into the remaining aioli. Ladle about ¾ cup (6 fl oz/180 ml) of the hot soup into this mixture, whisk to blend well, and then return to the soup, again whisking well. Whisking continuously, reheat the soup until the egg yolks bind and thicken the soup, being very careful not to allow the soup to boil, to avoid curdling the egg yolks. If properly done, the soup will lightly coat the back of a spoon in the manner of a custard.

✲ Ladle the soup over the bread in the soup plates. Serve the fish and the reserved aioli separately. Diners alternately spoon fish and aioli into their bowls.

serves 6

Modern-day fishermen are descended from men who for centuries made their living from the sea.

Alpes-Maritimes

Mostelle Croutée aux Olives Noires

lingcod with a black olive crust

If you have time, top the fish with the olive mixture about 3 hours before cooking. This allows the crust to dry and adhere more fully to the fish. Porgy, sea bass, turbot, and halibut can be similarly prepared.

BLACK-OLIVE OIL

½ cup (4 fl oz / 125 ml) extra-virgin olive oil

1 tablespoon very finely minced brine-cured black olives

¾ cup (4 oz / 125 g) diced black olives

¼ cup (2 fl oz / 60 ml) olive oil

3 shallots, finely chopped

½ cup (1 oz / 30 g) fine white bread crumbs from day-old bread

2 teaspoons fresh thyme leaves

salt and freshly ground pepper to taste

4 thick lingcod fillets, each 6 oz (185 g) and about 4 by 3 by 1 inch (10 by 7.5 by 2.5 cm)

♛ To make the black-olive oil, in a bowl, combine the oil and minced olives. Let stand for 1–2 hours.

♛ Preheat an oven to 425°F (220°C). Oil a baking dish large enough to hold the fish in a single layer. Place the diced olives in a bowl. In a small frying pan over medium heat, warm the olive oil. Add the shallots and sauté for about 45 seconds. Raise the heat to high and add the bread crumbs, stirring until the crumbs crisp a little, 45–60 seconds. Add the crumbs to the olives in the bowl, mix well, and then stir in the thyme. Season with salt and pepper.

♛ Place the fish in the prepared baking dish. Coat the top of each fillet with the olive mixture, dividing evenly. Bake until the fish is opaque throughout, 8–10 minutes. Transfer to warmed individual plates. Drizzle a circle of the black-olive oil around each piece of fish and serve.

serves 4

Var

Rougets Barbets en Papillotes à l'Estragon

red mullet in parchment

The French habit of wrapping fish fillets in little parchment parcels is a traditional one, and I have seen this treatment used for other foods as well, such as chicken fillets. Here, the favorite small rockfish of the Mediterranean, red mullet, is used, making the recipe indisputably Provençal in origin. An alternative fish in the Var would be the less expensive sea robin, also known as the gurnard. Any rockfish fillets available would be the best choice for this classic preparation, but most white-fleshed fillets, such as whiting or garfish, would lend themselves to the method.

The packages tend to swell in the oven and look very appetizing if served immediately. They are always brought to the table, so each diner can appreciate the entrapped aroma as the paper is slit open.

VEGETABLES

6 shallots

6 baby turnips

1 bunch baby carrots, peeled

5 tablespoons (2½ oz/75 g) unsalted butter

1 teaspoon sugar

salt and freshly ground pepper to taste

6 baby zucchini (courgettes), trimmed

12 sugar snap peas or snow peas (mangetouts), trimmed

12 red mullet fillets, each about 6 inches (15 cm) long and ⅜ inch (1 cm) thick

6 tablespoons (3 fl oz/90 ml) olive oil, plus extra for brushing on parcels

salt and freshly ground pepper to taste

6 fresh tarragon sprigs

2 small lemons, unpeeled, thinly sliced to yield 18 slices

¼ cup (2 fl oz/60 ml) lemon juice

☙ First, prepare the vegetables: In a small saucepan, combine the shallots, turnips, carrots, butter, and sugar, and season with salt and pepper. Add water just to cover (about 2 cups/16 fl oz/500 ml), bring to a boil over high heat, cover partially, and boil until the water evaporates, 6–8 minutes, adding the zucchini halfway through the cooking time. Do not allow the vegetables to scorch. Remove from the heat and set aside.

☙ Preheat an oven to 350°F (180°C).

☙ Cut out six 14-inch (35-cm) squares of parchment (baking) paper. Fold each one in half and then tear off the top and bottom corners of the folded edge to round these corners slightly. To form each parcel, lay a piece of paper on a work surface and open like a book. Put 2 fish fillets on the right half of the square. Drizzle 1 tablespoon olive oil over the fish. Season with salt and pepper. Top the fish with a tarragon sprig and 3 lemon slices, and drizzle 2 teaspoons lemon juice over all. Fold the left half of the paper over the fish to cover. Then, starting from the bottom edge near the fold, fold the edge of the paper over itself every 2 inches (5 cm), working your way around the package, to enclose the fish. Repeat to make 5 more airtight parcels.

☙ Slide all the parcels onto a baking sheet and brush the tops with olive oil. Bake for 6 minutes.

☙ Meanwhile, reheat the vegetables over medium heat, stirring them to prevent scorching and adding the sugar snap peas or snow peas, which require only 1 minute or so to cook.

☙ Transfer the fish parcels to individual plates. Spoon the vegetables alongside the parcels, dividing them evenly. Serve immediately.

serves 6

Les Plateaux de Fruits de Mer

The people of Marseilles are serious seafood eaters, and a *plateau de fruits de mer*—a "seafood platter"—is regarded as a special treat in restaurants and, on festive occasions, in the home. For decades, the Toinou family has been among the best-known seafood purveyors in the city, selling their exquisitely fresh inventory from refrigerated pavement kiosks and now at their five-hundred-table, five-story restaurant in the Cours Saint-Louis.

One day, from table 252, I watched as diners partook of everything from just six sea urchins and a glass of wine to giant *plateaux*, typically two-story, round, ice-covered metal platters, one resting above the other atop a chrome tripod, both laden with a variety of the day's catch, primarily raw. What ends up on the platters depends on the season, the preferences of the diners, and the sound guidance of the waiters. That day, I tasted raw mussels from Carteau, compared Bouzigue oysters with Côtes Bleu, fished the roe from sea urchin shells, and tried the famous *vioulet*, a yellow, oysterlike shellfish unique to this area—definitely an acquired taste. Cooked shrimp, langoustines, and super *gambas* (very large prawns) completed the copious array.

Alpes-Maritimes

Crevettes au Fenouil

shrimp with fennel

Fennel and Pernod identify this dish as coming from France's sunny south. It calls for a simple method of cooking that is common to many other recipes of the region, which rely on garlic and parsley just as this one does. Leave out the fennel and Pernod and increase the garlic and you have crevettes à l'ail, *the ubiquitous garlic shrimp. Change the shrimp to scallops and you have* coquilles Saint-Jacques à la provençal, *or change to frogs' legs for* cuisses de grenouilles provençales *(page 107). This dish, as well as the others, can also be offered as a first course, in which case it will serve six.*

30–32 large shrimp (prawns), about 2 lb (1 kg) total weight, peeled and deveined

8½ tablespoons (4½ oz/140 g) unsalted butter

2 teaspoons fennel seed

1 clove garlic, finely chopped

3 tablespoons Pernod or pastis

salt and freshly ground pepper to taste

2 heaping tablespoons chopped fresh flat-leaf (Italian) parsley mixed with 1 heaping tablespoon chopped fresh dill or fennel ferns

☙ Pat the shrimp thoroughly dry with paper towels. In a frying pan over high heat, melt 2½ tablespoons of the butter until it is sizzling but has not browned. Add the shrimp, fennel seed, and garlic and sauté until the shrimp begin to change color, about 2 minutes, depending on size.

☙ Add the Pernod or pastis and carefully ignite with a long match. Let the flames extinguish naturally.

☙ Cut the remaining 6 tablespoons (3 oz/90 g) butter into small pieces and add to the pan. When it melts and forms a sauce, season with salt and pepper, then scatter the parsley and dill or fennel ferns in the pan. Mix in the herbs briefly.

☙ Spoon the shrimp onto a warmed platter and serve immediately.

serves 4

Alpes-Maritimes

Rougets Grondins Monte Carlo

sea robin monte carlo

This unusual broiled (grilled) fish dish is made with the sea robin, sometimes known as gurnard, a ubiquitous rockfish of the Mediterranean. If choosing an equivalent fish, look for another fish that rests on its belly, such as red mullet.

ANCHOVY BUTTER

½ cup (4 oz/125 g) unsalted butter, at room temperature

3 salt-packed anchovies, filleted and rinsed (page 246), or 4–6 olive oil–packed anchovy fillets

freshly ground pepper to taste

about 2 tablespoons fresh lemon juice

CROUTONS

1 day-old long white sandwich loaf, unsliced

olive oil for frying

6 small sea robins, cleaned, with heads intact, about 6 oz (185 g) each (see note)

2 tablespoons olive oil

salt and freshly ground pepper to taste

½ cup (4 oz/125 g) unsalted butter

2 shallots, finely chopped

about 1 teaspoon fresh lemon juice

3 tablespoons chopped fresh flat-leaf (Italian) parsley

♆ To make the anchovy butter, in a bowl, whisk the butter until creamy. Finely chop the anchovies and add to the butter along with the pepper and lemon juice to taste. Mix well. Set aside until serving.

♆ Preheat a broiler (griller). Oil a baking sheet.

♆ To make the croutons, cut off the crusts from the bread loaf. Then cut the loaf lengthwise into 6 equal slices. Each slice should be long enough to hold a fish. Trim each slice to resemble the shape of the fish. Pour olive oil to a depth of ½ inch (12 mm) into a frying pan and heat until a small piece of bread dropped into the oil sizzles on contact. Add the bread slices, one at a time, and fry, turning once, until golden, about 45 seconds on each side. Using tongs, transfer to paper towels to drain.

♆ Score the top of each fish, making 3 or 4 cuts on the diagonal along its length. Brush both sides of the fish lightly with the olive oil and set them, lying on their bellies, on the prepared baking sheet. Sprinkle with salt and pepper.

♆ Slip the pan under the broiler about 5 inches (13 cm) from the heat source and broil (grill) until opaque throughout, about 8 minutes.

♆ Lightly reheat the croutons in a low oven (200°F/95°C) if they have cooled completely, then spread them generously with the anchovy butter, dividing it evenly. Lay each crouton on a warmed individual plate and top with a fish.

♆ In a small saucepan over medium heat, melt the butter. Add the shallots and sauté until translucent, about 1 minute. Season to taste with a little lemon juice and pepper, add the parsley, stir quickly, and spoon evenly over the fish. Serve immediately.

serves 6

Var

Espadon des Mémés Toulonnaises

swordfish, toulon style

Dishes cooked with mussels and laden with tomato are generally given the appellation toulonnaise. Tuna may be used in place of the swordfish.

¼ cup (2 fl oz / 60 ml) olive oil

3 lb (1.5 kg) swordfish, in one piece

½ cup (4 fl oz / 125 ml) dry white wine

3 large tomatoes, peeled, seeded, and coarsely chopped

½ lb (250 g) large fresh white mushrooms, brushed clean and quartered lengthwise

12 shallots

2 fresh thyme sprigs

12 fresh tarragon leaves, chopped

salt and freshly ground pepper to taste

about 25 mussels, scrubbed and debearded

2 tablespoons chopped fresh flat-leaf (Italian) parsley

In a deep frying pan over medium heat, warm the olive oil. Add the swordfish and sauté until lightly colored on both sides, 6–8 minutes total. Raise the heat to medium-high, add the wine, and deglaze the pan, stirring to dislodge any browned bits on the pan bottom. Add the tomatoes, mushrooms, shallots, thyme, and tarragon. Season with salt and pepper. Bring to a boil, reduce the heat to low, cover, and cook until the fish is opaque, about 30 minutes.

Meanwhile, place the mussels in a saucepan, discarding any that fail to close to the touch. Cover, place over high heat, and cook, shaking the pan, for 3–5 minutes. Discard any that failed to open.

Transfer the fish to a platter. Add the mussels to the sauce. Taste and adjust the seasoning with salt and pepper. Stir the parsley into the sauce and spoon over the fish. Carve the swordfish at the table.

serves 6

LES PLATS DE RÉSISTANCE

Meats, poultry, and game are infused with the earthy seasonings native to the Midi.

Preceding pages: Nimble goats take well to Provence's varied terrain. **Top:** A quiet gate in Saint-Maximin-la-Sainte-Baume belies the town's importance as the repository of relics of Mary Magdalene. **Above:** Jacques Bon revels in the romantic life of the *gardian,* cowboy of the Camargue. **Right:** The spectacular Gorges of Verdon cut deep into the Var.

A LITTLE ELECTRIC TRAIN with just three or four carriages travels between sea-level Nice and Digne, departmental capital of the Alpes-de-Haute-Provence. First it follows the river valley of the Var, running alongside the rushing water and overlooking small farms and sheep and goats grazing on the narrow plain. Then it begins climbing, its narrow tracks working their way over bridges, through tunnels, past small villages clinging to the hillsides, and finally along a high mountain pathway to Digne. The train is one of the few ways one can still get a sense of the true interior of Provence, since nowadays a network of excellent roads cuts straight lines almost everywhere.

Today, as I drive up the new four-lane *autoroute* along the wide, forested valley of the stony-bedded Durance River—following it from Aix-en-Provence past Manosque, past the turnoff to Digne, and on to my destination, Sisteron, the lamb capital of France—I have trouble understanding the isolation expressed by the late novelist Jean Giono of Manosque, who wrote of bleak, sinuous mountain passes linking neighboring villages. I am grateful to the little train, and also to the derring-do that once

Top: In Châteauneuf-du-Pape, three festivals celebrate the tradition of wine making. On April 25, the Fête de la Saint-Marc, patron saint of vintners, begins with the blessing of the vineyards. In early August, the Fête de la Véraison heralds the first ripening of the grapes. Finally, the grand Fête des Vendanges in mid-September marks the beginning of the harvest. **Above:** Lambs thrive where wild herbs flourish in the uplands around the medieval town of Sisteron in the Alpes-de-Haute-Provence.

made me—sick with vertigo—force my car across the precipitous road through the Gorges of Verdon for a glimpse of this world. At this same time of year, hundreds of thousands of sheep once blocked this valley, part of a huge march to higher, lusher pasture led by shepherds and giving the impression, as Alphonse Daudet describes in his *Lettres de mon moulin,* that "the road itself was on the march."

The thousand tones of grayish blue below are beginning to turn into the greens of alpine scenery, punctuated with craggy white cliffs. Mount Ventoux, the highest point in the Lubéron, looks as if it is perennially snow-capped; closer, it is a white mountain of stone. This is goat and sheep country, and in the more undulating parts, I can spot sheep grazing. The pasture is not lush green grass but scores of small fragrant bushes—wild thyme, rosemary, savory, *serpolet* (known sometimes as wild thyme or *sariette*), and fennel. The few remaining sheep from the plains below come nowadays by road and train to partake of this fragrant forest, perfuming their meat with a flavor that promises a premium in the marketplace.

Although as affordable here as anywhere in France, lamb is a luxury meat, an important provider of export income, to be savored in small portions or on special occasions. There is no Easter without lamb, and the *gigot* (leg) is the preferred dish of the wedding banquet. In the home, families make a *navarin d'agneau* (lamb stew) to welcome the new spring vegetables, or braise a forequarter with a selection of root vegetables in an *estouffade,* more than they partake of prime cuts.

With the sheep carcasses sold off, Sisteron assumes its role as primary rival to Marseilles, the acknowledged place of origin, for the production of *pieds-et-paquets,* literally "feet and packages." Triangular pieces of *panse d'agneau* (the stomach lining of sheep) are used to wrap—in a particularly tricky manner without need for string—pork and *persillade* into small parcels, which are then combined with lambs' feet in an herbal broth of carrot, onion, and tomato paste and stewed for up to fifteen hours. Two Sisteron companies, Richaud et Badel and its competitor, Rizzo, vie for the market, and both are challenged

by producers in Marseilles, whose recipes differ little from those in Sisteron, except for perhaps being richer in tomato.

The small black *taureau,* a breed of Camargue cattle, is a source of more affordable meat, although production, which is mainly for the bullring, is not great and for the most part only sold locally. The *taureau* is bred in the wild—the females calving once before slaughter, and the bulls slaughtered only after their time in the bullring is finished (the European community is bent on stopping this practice)—and nourished on somewhat meager pasture. Therefore, the animals are fairly sinuous and their meat is best in long-simmered dishes. Every *gardian* (cowboy) loves a *côte de boeuf* (loin on the bone) or a porterhouse steak coated with *herbes de Provence* and grilled, but daubes and *estouffades* are the traditional dishes of the area. It is often difficult to tell one from the other, as both are marinated meats braised in wine and simmered slowly in airtight pots. The Camarguais traditionally braised their *estouffades* in heavy cast-iron pots, with lids clamped shut, over open fires outside

their low-slung, whitewashed, thatch-roofed huts. The result is the same in both cases: a syrupy-sauced ragout with the earthy flavors of root vegetables and meat that falls into soft, break-apart-with-a-spoon pieces.

Pigs are not raised on a large commercial scale in Provence. Instead, local pork is a product of a small number of animals grown on farms. Apart from being used for charcuterie—air-cured hams, sausages, terrines—pork is most often roasted or braised, with some brined for use as salt pork, and some fried in the form of small caul fat–covered *rissoles* called *caillettes*.

Poultry is the most affordable meat of Provence and graces the table more often than the others. The large, fattened capon is preferred for its succulence and mature flavor. Although more and more battery-fed poultry is sold in the markets, housewives, even in the cities, still prize, and will pay a premium for, birds raised in the barnyard by farmers who nourish their chickens, ducks, and guinea fowl with grain and allow them to run free.

Hunting is not a sport for the wealthy in Provence. Instead, it is a time-proven necessity for extending the diet and the budget of rural people. Rabbits; wild boar and its young,

Left: A faded wall shows the effects of time and the weather in Carpentras, an important market town of the Vaucluse. **Below:** Onions of all colors are mainstays of many Provençale dishes, particularly the rich, slow-simmered stews and daubes of the region. **Bottom:** The finest poultry is raised outdoors, and the birds are appropriately labeled in the marketplace as "*élevés en plein air.*"

Top: The fortitude of the Provençaux is tested every year by the mistral, the seasonal northern wind whose bone-chilling gusts are at their fiercest from winter into early spring. **Above:** A sprig or two of fragrant thyme is a key component in a bouquet garni. Wild thyme is gathered from the hills of Provence where it grows in profusion, especially on the scrublands known as the *garrigues*. **Right:** Herds of sheep are seen here and there throughout the south of France, but nowhere are they so common as in the Alpes-de-Haute-Provence, where they are brought to high mountain pastures for summer grazing and to low-lying valleys in winter.

the *marcassin;* wild ducks; partridge; and small birds were once common prey. Former treats like thrush, lark, snipe, pigeon, plover, and woodcock are now so rare that I am reminded of Marcel Pagnol's *La gloire de mon père,* where, on the odd occasion when father comes home with a small thrush, he is proclaimed a hero. *Faute de grives, on mange des merles*—"Lack of thrush, then we eat blackbird"—states an old proverb. Commercially farmed partridge, guinea fowl, quail, and pheasant, although expensive, are now more likely to be found at the table. Rabbit (prepared *en gibelotte,* braised in wine; or *chasseur,* with mushrooms) and, to a lesser extent, hare are still prevalent, and the seasonal duck migration is the highlight of the hunter's year.

Game, being wild, is rarely roasted—the long, slow braising methods required for a daube, for instance, make these muscle-bound animals more tender. Only the farmed pheasant and duck are considered good roasting birds, the latter often basted with lavender honey. The partridge comes classically as a pot-au-feu, a large "pot on the fire," with root vegetables, cabbage, and chestnuts.

Guinea fowl is an ideal barnyard animal, pecking seed around the yard. Farmers bring the birds to market alive, knowing they can return with them the following week if they do not sell. The first time I bought a guinea fowl in a local market, the lady was ready to pass it to me flapping and squawking. When I looked aghast and she realized I didn't know what on earth to do with it, she offered to kill it for me, and, city girl that I was, I had to dart along the next aisle not to see her tuck the bird's head under its wing. When I returned, I took the still-warm body in my arms and then went through further agonies, even after my husband plucked it, when I found it was up to me to empty it—a lesson for the young bride in a task that, I am happy to say, I now take in my stride. Food is of the land in Provence, and people eat better, undoubtedly, for the understanding of it.

Alpes-Maritimes

Le Tian d'Agneau Niçois

tian of lamb, nice style

Jacques Maximin, who made his name heading up the kitchen at the famed Negresco Hotel on the Boulevard des Anglais in Nice, had the classic Provençal tian in mind when he created this beautiful lamb dish stacked upon a three-layer vegetable pedestal. You will need four metal rings, each 4 inches (10 cm) in diameter and ¾ inch (2 cm) high. Alternatively, make rings of the same size from heavy cardboard, stapling the ends together and covering the rings with aluminum foil. Rather than purchase bone-in lamb, you can ask the butcher to bone the loins for you.

5 tablespoons (2½ fl oz/75 ml) olive oil

1 small yellow onion, finely chopped

4 large, ripe tomatoes, peeled, seeded, and coarsely chopped

salt and freshly ground pepper to taste

about 1 tablespoon chopped fresh basil

1 lb (500 g) spinach, stems removed

5 tablespoons (2½ oz/75 g) unsalted butter, plus 2 tablespoons cold unsalted butter, diced

pinch of freshly grated nutmeg

½ lb (250 g) fresh white mushrooms, brushed clean and finely chopped

3 boneless lamb loins, about 1½ lb (750 g) total weight (see note)

6 cloves garlic

½ cup (4 fl oz/125 ml) dry white wine

1½ cups (12 fl oz/375 ml) beef stock (page 251)

1 tablespoon truffle juice (optional)

4 black truffle slices or diced peeled tomato and chopped fresh chives (optional)

❧ In a frying pan over medium heat, warm 2 tablespoons of the olive oil. Add the onion and sauté until softened, about 2 minutes. Add the tomatoes and continue to cook, stirring occasionally, until the moisture has evaporated and the tomatoes have collapsed, 8–10 minutes longer. Season with salt and pepper, add the basil, remove from the heat, and set aside.

❧ Fill a saucepan three-fourths full of water and bring to a boil. Add the spinach and as soon as the water returns to a boil, drain and refresh the spinach under running cold water. When the spinach is cool, squeeze it between your palms to rid it of excess moisture, then chop. In a small frying pan over medium heat, melt 1 tablespoon of the butter. Add the spinach and sauté for about 45 seconds. Season with salt, pepper, and nutmeg.

❧ In a separate frying pan over high heat, warm 2 tablespoons of the olive oil. Add the mushrooms and sauté until the water they release has evaporated, about 4 minutes. Season with salt and pepper.

❧ Preheat an oven to 150°F (65°C).

❧ Trim away all traces of fat or sinews from the sirloins. In a frying pan over high heat, melt the remaining 4 tablespoons (2 oz/60 g) butter. Add the lamb and garlic and turn the lamb as needed to brown well on all sides, 4–5 minutes total. It should still be pink inside. Season the lamb with salt and pepper, then transfer to a plate, cover, and keep warm in the oven. Remove the fried garlic and set aside.

❧ Spoon off any fat from the pan, add the wine, and place the pan over high heat. Bring to a boil and deglaze the pan, stirring to scrape up any browned bits on the pan bottom. Continue to boil until reduced to 1–2 teaspoons. Add 1 cup (8 fl oz/250 ml) of the stock and the truffle juice, if using, then season with salt and pepper. Bring to a boil, stirring constantly, then strain into a bowl. Return the strained sauce to the pan and keep warm.

❧ To assemble the *tians,* rub a little of the fried garlic on the base of each dinner plate and place a metal ring in the center. Gently reheat the spinach, mushrooms, and tomatoes. Using a fork, press a layer of spinach in the bottom of each ring. Next, press a layer of mushrooms on top of the spinach. Finally, press a layer of the tomatoes on top of the mushrooms. Very thinly slice the lamb across the grain. You need 24 slices in all. (You should have enough lamb for 2 *tians* from each sirloin, but an extra sirloin has been included in case you should run short.) Using 6 slices for each *tian,* arrange them overlapping in a spiral to cover the top tomato layer.

❧ If necessary, warm the *tians* in the oven for about 30 seconds (no longer or the lamb will turn gray) before removing the rings. Lift the rings carefully from each plate to reveal the layers. Quickly stir the diced cold butter into the sauce and spoon some of the sauce around each *tian.* If desired, decorate the center of each *tian* with a truffle slice or some diced tomato and chives. Serve at once.

serves 4

Côtes de Boeuf aux Herbes

beef sirloin steaks with fresh herbs

The top sirloin or rib-eye steak is a great luxury in France and, like the leg of lamb, is often featured at wedding banquets and other festive occasions.

2 tablespoons each unsalted butter and olive oil

2 thick-cut, bone-in top sirloin steaks, each about 1½ lb (750 g)

sea salt and freshly ground pepper to taste

SAUCE

3 tablespoons unsalted butter

4 shallots, finely chopped

¾ cup (6 fl oz / 180 ml) beef stock (page 251)

2 tablespoons green mustard with herbs or Dijon mustard

3 tablespoons chopped mixed fresh flat-leaf (Italian) parsley, chervil, and tarragon

salt and freshly ground coarse pepper to taste

In a cast-iron frying pan over high heat, melt the butter with the olive oil until the mixture turns a light brown. Add the steaks and sear well, about 1 minute. Turn, sprinkle with sea salt, and brown on the second side for 1 minute longer. Turn again, reduce the heat slightly, and cook, turning once, for about 6 minutes on each side for rare, or until done to your liking. Transfer to a platter, tent with aluminum foil, and let rest for 5–8 minutes before carving.

Meanwhile, make the sauce: In a saucepan over medium heat, melt 2 tablespoons of the butter. Add the shallots and sauté until softened but not colored, about 30 seconds. Add the stock, bring to a boil, and cook until reduced by half. Remove from the heat and stir in the mustard, the remaining 1 tablespoon butter, and the herbs. Stir in any juice that has collected on the platter holding the beef. Season with salt and pepper. Pour into a warmed bowl.

Transfer the steaks to an attractive cutting board and sprinkle them with pepper, then carry the board to the table. Cut along the bone to free the meat, then carve into slices diagonally across the grain. Pass the sauce at the table.

serves 6

Bouches-du-Rhône

Nougat de Boeuf

nougat of beef

The name of this recipe comes from the layering of several different cuts of meat, giving the dish a textural look similar to that of fruit-and-nut-studded nougat candy, a Provençal specialty.

1 calf's foot, split lengthwise

1 oxtail, about 2 lb (1 kg), cut into several pieces

2 lb (1 kg) each beef brisket or rump and chuck steak

1½ lb (750 g) boneless beef shank

½ lb (250 g) salt pork

1 piece fresh pork rind, 6 by 4 inches (15 by 10 cm)

2 large tomatoes, peeled, seeded, and chopped

4 cloves garlic, finely chopped

1–2 teaspoons finely chopped orange zest

1 tablespoon tomato paste, or as needed

3 tablespoons salt-packed capers, rinsed

1 teaspoon peppercorns

salt and freshly ground pepper to taste

3 yellow onions studded with 6 whole cloves, cut into wedges

2 carrots, peeled and cut into thick slices

3 leeks, including tender green tops, cut into large chunks

large bouquet garni (page 246)

1 bottle (24 fl oz/750 ml) full-bodied dry red wine such as Cabernet Sauvignon

¼ cup (2 fl oz/60 ml) brandy

5 tablespoons (2½ fl oz/75 ml) each red wine vinegar and olive oil

2 salt-packed anchovies, filleted and rinsed (page 246), or 4 olive oil–packed anchovy fillets

☙ The day before serving, trim the excess fat and membrane from the calf's foot, oxtail, and 3 beef cuts. Cut the beef into pieces about ¼ lb (125 g) each. Cut the salt pork into thick slices about 2 inches (5 cm) long. Place the pork rind, skin side up, on the bottom of a large, preferably oval, heavy Dutch oven.

☙ In a bowl, mix together the tomatoes, the garlic, the zest, the 1 tablespoon tomato paste, 1 tablespoon of the capers, and the peppercorns. Pour one-third of the tomato mixture over the pork rind. As you layer the ingredients, sprinkle with salt and pepper. Scatter one-third of the meats over the top, along with one-third of the onions, carrots, and leeks. Top with about half of the remaining tomato mixture, the bouquet garni, and then half of the remaining meats and vegetables. Repeat using the remaining tomato mixture, meats, and vegetables. Pour in the wine, brandy, vinegar, and olive oil. Cover and refrigerate overnight.

☙ The following day, bring the pot slowly to a boil over medium heat. Reduce the heat to very low, cover tightly, and simmer for 4–4½ hours. The meat will be tender and almost melted into a syrupy sauce. About 20 minutes before the end of cooking, crush the anchovies in a mortar. Add 2 tablespoons of the cooking liquid, stir to blend, and then stir the mixture into the stew. Re-cover and continue cooking for the final 20 minutes or so.

☙ Using a slotted utensil, transfer the meat to a warmed platter. Discard the bouquet garni. Taste the cooking liquid for salt, and if it is not too salty, boil it down over high heat to a syrupy sauce consistency. Spoon off some of the fat from the surface, if desired, then adjust the seasoning with salt, pepper, and more tomato paste, if necessary

☙ Sprinkle the meat with the remaining 2 tablespoons capers and spoon some of the sauce over all. Pass the remaining sauce at the table.

serves 8–10

Vaucluse

Poulet Rôti Farci aux Courgettes

roasted chicken with zucchini stuffing

Slipping a stuffing under the skin of a chicken rather than into the cavity marvelously perfumes the breast. The most celebrated example of this method is the classic—and fittingly named—poularde demi-deuil (chicken in half-mourning), in which black truffle slices are placed under the skin, where they impart their earthy aroma.

Here, the use of a stuffing of grated zucchini and herbs has a dual purpose, to impart flavor to the meat and to keep the breast area succulent while the remainder of the chicken cooks.

2 large or 3 small zucchini (courgettes), cut or grated into a fine julienne to yield 2 cups (10 oz/315 g)

2 green (spring) onions, including tender green tops, sliced

2 tablespoons white bread crumbs from day-old bread

2 tablespoons grated Parmesan cheese

1 tablespoon chopped fresh oregano

1 teaspoon chopped fresh thyme

salt and freshly ground pepper to taste

1 roasting chicken, 4 lb (2 kg)

about 3 tablespoons olive oil

JUS (OPTIONAL)

1 cup (8 fl oz/250 ml) light chicken stock (page 251) or water

½ chicken bouillon cube if using water

salt and freshly ground pepper to taste

about ½ teaspoon tomato paste (optional)

1 tablespoon sherry or Madeira (optional)

♛ Preheat an oven to 425°F (220°C). Oil a roasting pan. In a bowl, combine the zucchini, green onions, bread crumbs, Parmesan cheese, oregano, and thyme. Season with salt and pepper and mix thoroughly.

♛ Rinse the chicken and pat dry. Make sure that the flesh around the cavity end of the bird is not exposed to the breastbone. If it is, carefully sew up loosely with a needle and kitchen string. Turn the bird and carefully open the skin that protrudes from where the neck has been removed. Slip your fingers between the skin and the flesh of the bird, easing away any membrane that holds the skin to the flesh and being careful not to tear the skin. There should now be a wide passageway between the skin and the breast into which the stuffing can be spooned.

♛ Carefully fill the cavity between the skin and the breast with the stuffing, pressing it toward the cavity end of the bird and plumping it into a rounded shape as you go. The cavity should be large enough to take the full amount of stuffing.

♛ Smooth the neck skin back over the opening and close the opening by pressing the neck skin around to the underside of the bird. This may be secured with a needle and kitchen string, but if the skin is long enough and has been firmly pressed, it should hold in place.

♛ Lay the bird, breast side up, in the prepared roasting pan. Season the top of the bird with salt and pepper and smear with the olive oil.

♛ Roast the chicken, rotating the pan 180 degrees at the midway point, until the juices run clear when a knife tip is inserted into the thigh joint, about 1¼ hours. An instant-read thermometer inserted into the thickest part of the thigh away from the bone should register 180°F (82°C). If the bird begins to overbrown, reduce the temperature to 400°F (200°C).

♛ Transfer the chicken to a cutting board, tent loosely with aluminum foil, and let rest for 10–15 minutes. Use poultry shears or sturdy kitchen scissors to cut the chicken into 4 pieces. First, carefully cut alongside the breastbone, then gently force the bird open a little and cut down along either side of the backbone. Remove the backbone and discard. Then cut each bird half in half again, following the rounded line of the leg bones so that each person getting a wing section also gets a little extra breast.

♛ If making the *jus,* add the stock or water and the bouillon cube to the roasting pan and place over high heat. Bring to a boil and deglaze the pan, stirring to scrape up any browned bits from the pan bottom. Boil down to a light, syrupy consistency and season with salt and pepper. If the sauce lacks flavor, add the tomato paste or the sherry or Madeira. Strain into a warmed serving bowl.

♛ Arrange the chicken and stuffing on warmed individual plates and serve. Pass the sauce at the table.

serves 4

Les Daubes

Some culinary observers believe that the French word *daube* is from the Spanish *dabar,* meaning "to cook in a closed environment," linking the adoption to the long-time Catalan community that populated the port of Marseilles. But most Provençaux trace the name of their favorite braised dish to the *daubière,* the tight-lidded, potbellied vessel in which it has been traditionally cooked. Nowadays, the term is applied to any braised dish that is first marinated in wine and then slowly stewed in it. Daubes are most often of beef, and the wine is most often red, but versions based on lamb, pork, venison, rabbit, poultry, and other birds, and even on fleshy monkfish, tuna, or other fish that will not disintegrate with long cooking, can be found as well.

Daubes call for long cooking in a minimum of liquid to soften the fibers of lesser cuts of meats fully, so a heavy, tight-fitting lid is essential to ensure a minimum of evaporation. Characteristically, these hearty dishes are perfumed with herbs and orange peel and simmered over very low heat until the meat can be cut with a spoon and the rendered juices have combined with the wine to become thick and syrupy. Leftover daube, refrigerated, turns into a potted meat, the reduced juices setting into a natural jelly.

Daube de Boeuf

beef daube

There are probably as many versions of the daube as there are Provençal cooks, but the common thread is the use of a marinade of red wine and spices and the long, slow cooking time, resulting in meat that is so soft and tender that it can be cut with a spoon. A finished daube is often garnished with a persillade, a mixture of finely chopped garlic and parsley.

3 lb (1.5 kg) boneless beef cheek, beef shank, or beef chuck

3 yellow onions, cut into large wedges

3 carrots, peeled and sliced into 1½-inch (4-cm) lengths or batons

5 cloves garlic, chopped

2 or 3 fresh flat-leaf (Italian) parsley sprigs

1 celery stalk, halved crosswise

5 peppercorns, lightly crushed

4 juniper berries, lightly crushed

4 whole cloves

pinch of freshly grated nutmeg

2 bay leaves

1 large fresh thyme sprig

1 bottle (24 fl oz/750 ml) Bandol red wine or other tannic red such as Cabernet Sauvignon

2 tablespoons red wine vinegar

2 orange zest strips, about ½ inch (12 mm) wide

½ lb (250 g) salt pork

2 oz (60 g) lard

2 tablespoons olive oil

2 tomatoes, peeled, seeded, and roughly chopped

1 piece fresh pork rind, 6 by 3 inches (15 by 7.5 cm)

salt to taste

3 tablespoons all-purpose (plain) flour (optional)

freshly ground pepper to taste

❧ Cut the beef into 3 roughly equal pieces. Place the beef in a large dish and add 1 of the onions and the carrots, garlic, parsley, celery, peppercorns, juniper berries, cloves, nutmeg, bay leaves, and thyme. Add the wine and vinegar, cover, and marinate overnight in the refrigerator.

❧ The next day, remove the beef from the refrigerator. Pass the marinade mixture through a sieve placed over a bowl to capture the liquid. Remove the onion and carrots from the sieve. Pat the beef and vegetables dry on paper towels. Pick out the herbs, spices, and celery from the sieve and place on a small piece of cheesecloth (muslin). Add the orange zest strips, bring the corners of the cheesecloth together, and tie with kitchen string to form a small parcel.

❧ Rinse the salt pork and cut into 2-inch (5-cm) cubes. In a large, heavy Dutch oven or sauté pan, melt the lard over medium heat. Add the salt pork and brown on all sides, about 5 minutes. Add the olive oil and the onion from the marinade. Working in batches, add the beef and brown on all sides, 10–15 minutes. Return all the beef to the pan. Add the reserved liquid and carrots from the marinade, the remaining onion wedges, the tomatoes, and the parcel of herbs. Pour in enough water just to reach to the top of the meat, then cover the beef with the piece of pork rind, skin side up. Salt lightly.

❧ Bring to a boil, reduce the heat to very low, and simmer, skimming off foam once after 5 minutes.

Cover and cook slowly for 4 hours. If desired, to reduce evaporation, mix the flour with enough water to form a paste and rub the paste into the crevice between the pan rim and the lid, to seal the lid.

❧ After 4 hours, use a knife to free the flour paste, if used, then remove the lid and check that the beef is very tender by piercing it with a knife. It will probably need a further 30–60 minutes cooking. Return the lid to its place (this time without sealing paste) and simmer slowly until the beef is so soft that it can be broken up with a spoon. When the daube is ready to serve, lift out the beef and vegetables with a slotted utensil and place on a warmed platter. Discard the parcel of herbs. The pork rind can be cut into strips and served with the meat or discarded. Keep the meat and vegetables warm.

❧ Spoon off the rendered fat, then return the pot to the stove. Taste the liquid for salt, and if it is not too salty, boil it down over high heat to a fluid sauce consistency. Season with salt and pepper, then spoon the sauce over the meat and serve immediately.

serves 8

Alpes-de-Haute-Provence

Pintade au Chou

guinea fowl with cabbage

After chicken and duck, guinea fowl is the most prevalent poultry in the Provençal larder. This classic preparation combines guinea fowls with a light broth, chestnuts, and cabbage.

2 guinea fowls, 2 lb (1 kg) each, with their livers or 6 chicken livers

STUFFING

2 oz (60 g) thick-cut sliced slab bacon, cut crosswise into pieces ½ inch (12 mm) wide

about 3 tablespoons unsalted butter, if needed

3 oz (90 g) each ground (minced) pork and veal

3 tablespoons pine nuts

leaves from 2 fresh thyme sprigs

3 shallots, finely chopped

1 clove garlic, finely chopped

salt and freshly ground pepper to taste

¼ cup (2 oz/60 g) unsalted butter

1 small yellow onion, chopped

2 large carrots, peeled and cut into 2-inch (5-cm) lengths, thicker pieces halved lengthwise

1 cup (8 fl oz/250 ml) chicken stock (page 251)

½ cup (4 fl oz/125 ml) dry white wine

16–20 dried chestnuts, soaked in water to cover overnight, drained, boiled in water for 30 minutes, and drained again

2 shallots, finely chopped

1 clove garlic, finely chopped

bouquet garni (page 246)

salt and freshly ground pepper to taste

1 small green cabbage, cut into 8 wedges

1½ teaspoons brandy or 1½ tablespoons Madeira

☙ Rinse the guinea fowls, then remove the necks and tips of the wings and set aside. Fold the neck skin over the hollow down the back and attach with a skewer or stitch with kitchen string.

☙ To make the stuffing, in a small frying pan over high heat, fry the bacon for about 1 minute. Transfer to a bowl. Add the livers to the fat in the pan, along with a little butter if necessary to prevent sticking,

and sauté until browned but still pink in the center, about 1 minute. Transfer to a cutting board and chop roughly. Add to the bowl holding the bacon. Add the ground pork and veal to the pan, place over high heat, and sauté, stirring to break up the meat, until lightly browned, 4–5 minutes. Mix in the pine nuts, thyme, shallots, and garlic and season with salt and pepper. Remove from the heat, add to the bowl, and stir to combine. Spoon the stuffing into the guinea fowl cavities, plump the birds into shape, and use skewers or kitchen string to secure the cavities closed.

☙ In a large Dutch oven over medium heat, melt the butter. Add the guinea fowls and brown on all sides, about 15 minutes. Remove from the pan. Add the onion and sauté until softened, about 3 minutes. Add the carrots, stock, wine, chestnuts, shallots, garlic, and bouquet garni. Raise the heat to high and bring to a boil, then reduce the heat to low and simmer for 5 minutes. Return the guinea fowls to the pan and season with salt and pepper. Cover and cook until the guinea fowls are done, 50–60 minutes. An instant-read thermometer inserted into a thigh away from the bone should register 175°F (80°C).

☙ About 15 minutes before the birds are ready, place the cabbage wedges on a rack in a steamer over boiling water, cover, and steam until tender, about 8 minutes. Drain off any excess liquid and keep warm.

☙ Transfer the birds to a platter and keep warm in a low (225°F/110°C) oven with the door ajar. Using a slotted spoon, scoop out the carrots and chestnuts from the liquid and transfer with the cabbage wedges to the platter.

☙ Using a wooden spoon, scrape up any browned bits from the pan bottom and then strain the sauce through a sieve into a small saucepan. Place the pan over high heat, bring to a boil, and boil down to a sauce consistency. Taste and adjust the seasoning with salt and add the brandy or Madeira. Pour into a warmed small bowl and keep warm.

☙ To serve, snip the string or remove the skewers from the birds. Using poultry shears or sturdy kitchen scissors, carefully carve each bird into serving pieces and place on warmed individual plates. Divide the stuffing, carrots, chestnuts, and cabbage among the plates. Spoon 2 tablespoons of the sauce over each portion and pass the remainder at the table.

serves 8

Alpes-de-Haute-Provence

Navarin d'Agneau

springtime lamb stew

A navarin is a lamb dish that celebrates the spring harvest. It brings together young, tender lamb and the first of the new season's baby vegetables. The sauce is lighter and less complex than those in the more robust winter casseroles. This brothlike sauce is well suited to the subtle flavors of the baby carrots, baby turnips, peas, and asparagus tips. Fava (broad) beans or haricots verts are optional additions. The most typical accompaniment is boiled new potatoes tossed in butter and parsley.

¼ cup (2 oz/60 g) unsalted butter

1 boneless leg of lamb, cut into 2-inch (5-cm) cubes

1 large yellow onion, chopped

2 tablespoons all-purpose (plain) flour

2 cups (16 fl oz/500 ml) dry white wine

2½ cups (20 fl oz/625 ml) light chicken stock (page 251) or water

bouquet garni (page 246)

4 cloves garlic, finely chopped

2 teaspoons sugar

salt and freshly ground pepper to taste

1 lb (500 g) baby carrots, peeled

16 baby turnips, peeled

1 bunch small radishes, trimmed

½ lb (250 g) shallots

1 lb (500 g) English peas, shelled

24 asparagus tips, each 3 inches (7.5 cm) long

2 tablespoons chopped fresh flat-leaf (Italian) parsley

♨ In a large Dutch oven, melt the butter over medium heat. Working in batches, add the meat and brown well on all sides, about 15 minutes for each batch. When all the meat is browned, return it to the pan, add the onion, and sauté until translucent, about 1 minute. Scatter the flour over all and cook, stirring, until some of the flour browns, about 30 seconds.

♨ Add the wine, the stock or water, and the bouquet garni and bring to a boil. Reduce the heat to low and simmer, uncovered, for 15 minutes. Stir the meat, add the garlic and sugar, and season lightly with salt and pepper. Cover and continue to simmer over low heat for about 30 minutes.

♨ Add the carrots, turnips, radishes, shallots, and peas, cover, and cook at a gentle simmer until the meat is tender, about 40 minutes. Add the asparagus 6–8 minutes before the end of the cooking time.

♨ Using a slotted spoon, transfer the meat and vegetables to a warmed serving dish and keep warm. Raise the heat to high, bring the liquid in the pot to a boil, and boil rapidly, stirring, until reduced to a light sauce consistency. Taste and adjust the seasoning with salt and pepper.

♨ Spoon the sauce over the meat and vegetables. Garnish with the parsley and serve.

serves 6

L'Agneau

Almost everywhere in Provence where flat land gives way to undulating hillside and mountain foothills is the domain of the lamb. The craggy scrubland and meager grasses in the region are compensated by fragrant herbal bushes that give the lamb a distinctive taste, which translates into a premium price in the marketplace, second only to the lamb of the salt marshes of Normandy.

Historically, the merino of the Bouches-du-Rhône was proudly grown for wool around Arles and across the open spaces of the Crau Plains. But wool prices have declined, and now almost all sheep in Provence are raised for meat. The capital of the lamb-producing regions is Sisteron, an imposing town on the Durance River. Its perched eleventh-century citadel overlooks the gaping, vertically incised gorges that make one side of the river inaccessible, while the town nestles on the other. Formerly a distribution center for both wool and meat, Sisteron now boasts the second largest abattoir in Europe in the nearby Jabron Valley, making it a large export center for Provençal lamb to the European market.

In the past, sheep from as far away as Arles and the Crau Plains were herded from their sun-dried pastures into the Durance Valley and the lower Alps to partake of the rich highland herbal pasture for the summer months. At that time, around June 15, shepherds would begin to herd over half a million sheep from the plains, leading them across villages, down roadways, along the river's banks, and up into the higher pastures. Lack of shepherds has transformed this once-romantic procession known as the *transhumance* to one of trucks and trains.

Lamb has always been the luxury meat of France and sells well throughout the country as well as locally. But meat is a smaller part of the diet than many outsiders realize. Leg of lamb and large joints are traditionally reserved for wedding banquets and special occasions. The smaller, less expensive cuts are cooked in classic dishes like *navarin* along with an assortment of vegetables or are simmered in daubes. Prime cuts, although more affordable now, are still eaten in small quantities as part of a larger meal.

Vaucluse

Râble de Lapin
en Paupiettes

little parcels of saddle of rabbit

You have only to drive through the Var to see that this
is rabbit country, with its stony outcrops, low-slung
brush, and barren gray hills. Any hunter will tell you
that you cannot do better than to obtain rabbit from
this area. He will earnestly explain that since the
rabbits feed on wild thyme, lavender, and various
herbal grasses, they are already flavored from within.

*The saddle, that is, the loin and fillets that sit between
the front and back legs of the rabbit, is the animal's
most tender meat. The animal, however, is quite lean,
particularly if it is wild and has run the fields, and
thus the meat can dry out easily. For this reason, it
is typically braised rather than roasted. Here, the moist
pork stuffing and air-cured ham deliver additional
succulence to the finished dish.*

*Few vendors sell only the saddles, but the remainder
of the rabbit can be set aside, or frozen, for use in
any ragout recipe, such as Rabbit with Wild Herbs
(page 151), or in place of the veal in Veal Chop
Ragout on page 143.*

2 large rabbits, about 3½ lb (1.75 kg) each

STUFFING
¼ lb (125 g) ground (minced) pork
¼ lb (125 g) ground (minced) veal
1 shallot, finely chopped
1 clove garlic, finely chopped
grated zest of 1 small lemon
2 fresh sage leaves, finely chopped
3 tablespoons chopped black olives
1 egg, lightly beaten
salt and freshly ground pepper to taste

8 spinach leaves, stems removed (optional)
8 thin slices air-cured ham (page 247)
or prosciutto
3 tablespoons olive oil
1 cup (8 fl oz/250 ml) dry white wine
2 fresh sage leaves
1 fresh thyme sprig
salt and freshly ground pepper to taste
2 tablespoons water

☙ Place each rabbit, belly side down, on a cutting
board. Run a sharp knife around the outline of each
leg, slice away from the tail area of the carcass, then
remove the legs. Using a cleaver or heavy knife, sever
the front legs from the saddle (loin) section. Reserve
the 4 legs for another recipe (see note).

☙ Turn the saddles belly side up and remove the kidneys and their fat. Discard the fat. Chop the kidneys
and reserve for the stuffing. Working with 1 saddle at
a time, and using a sharp, pointed knife, release the
meaty section along the stomach side of the carcass
and, without cutting it off, turn the carcass and continue around onto the back of the saddle, continuing
to release the fleshy part of the meat from the carcass.
When finished, you should have 2 pieces of meat
from each saddle. Trim off any fleshy remains from
each carcass and chop finely for the stuffing.

☙ To make the stuffing, in a bowl, combine the
ground meats, shallot, garlic, lemon zest, sage, olives,
and reserved kidneys and rabbit trimmings. Mix well,
then add the egg and mix well again. Season with salt
and pepper.

☙ Lay the meat flat on a work surface. Using a meat
pounder, shape each piece into a rough oval about
7 inches (18 cm) long and 3½–4 inches (9–10 cm)
wide. Line each piece with 2 spinach leaves, if using,
and then spread with the stuffing, dividing it evenly
among the 4 pieces. Working from a narrow end, roll
up each piece into a cylinder and wrap with 2 pieces
of the ham. Tie each parcel with kitchen string at
3 intervals along its length.

☙ In a deep frying pan, warm the olive oil. Add the
parcels, neatest side down, and brown, turning once,
until lightly browned on both sides, 5–8 minutes.
Add the white wine, sage, and thyme and bring to a
boil. Season lightly with salt and pepper, then reduce
the heat to low, cover, and simmer slowly until tender
when pierced with the point of a knife, 15–20 minutes. Transfer the parcels to a cutting board, tent
loosely with aluminum foil, and let rest for 5 minutes.

☙ Cut the parcels into slices ½ inch (12 mm) thick.
Slide a spatula under the slices of each parcel and
transfer to warmed individual plates. Return the pan
to high heat, add the water, bring to a boil, and deglaze the pan, stirring to scrape up any browned bits
from the pan bottom. Boil until reduced slightly, then
taste and adjust the seasoning with salt and pepper.
Spoon the sauce over the slices and serve.

serves 4

Le Gigot de Sept Heures

seven-hour leg of lamb

The nearer you get to a lamb-producing community—in this case the foothills of the Alps, near Sisteron—the more you find the people talking about the virtues of eating older lamb. These sheep, twelve to eighteen months old, are considered more succulent and richer in flavor than their younger counterparts and ideal for use in this classic recipe.

1 leg of lamb, 5–5½ lb (2.5–2.75 kg) (see note)

2 tablespoons unsalted butter

1 tablespoon olive oil

3 tablespoons brandy

2 heads garlic, separated into cloves and peeled (about 40 cloves)

⅔ cup (5 fl oz / 160 ml) dry red wine

⅔ cup (5 fl oz / 160 ml) chicken stock (page 251)

4 large fresh thyme sprigs

salt and freshly ground pepper to taste

♛ Fill a large stockpot three-fourths full of water and bring to a boil. Plunge the lamb into the boiling water and allow the water to return to a boil. Then reduce the heat to medium and simmer for 15 minutes. Drain and pat dry.

♛ Preheat an oven to 250°F (120°C).

♛ In a heavy Dutch oven over high heat, melt the butter with the olive oil. Add the lamb and brown on all sides, about 15 minutes. Add the brandy and ignite it with a long match. When the flames subside, add the garlic cloves, wine, stock, and thyme. Season lightly with salt and pepper. Cover, place in the oven, and cook, turning twice, until the lamb is tender, about 7 hours.

♛ Remove the pan from the oven and, using a slotted utensil and balancing the leg with a fork, transfer to a warmed platter and keep warm. Pass the contents of the pan through a sieve, pressing firmly on the garlic to extract the cooked flesh. Return the liquid to the pan over high heat and bring to a boil, scraping up any browned bits from the pan bottom. Reduce the liquid to a sauce consistency. Taste and adjust the seasoning. Strain into a small warmed bowl. Carve the lamb, then pass the sauce at the table.

serves 6

Vaucluse

Canard aux Olives

duckling with olives

Slow roasting, a classic technique of French cuisine, yields moist poultry and is an excellent way to prepare duck. While cooks in the north of France add turnips, the Provençaux make the dish their own by using large, fleshy green olives to give an appealing tinge of bitterness to the accompanying sauce.

1 duck, 3½ lb (1.75 kg)

¼ cup (2 oz/60 g) unsalted butter

1 yellow onion, chopped

1 small carrot, peeled and sliced

¾ cup (6 fl oz/180 ml) beef stock (page 251)

½ cup (4 fl oz/125 ml) dry white wine

½ celery stalk, sliced

½ beef bouillon cube, crumbled

bouquet garni (page 246)

salt and freshly ground pepper to taste

¼ teaspoon tomato paste

½ lb (250 g) large, brine-cured green olives

beurre manié *made with 2 tablespoons unsalted butter, at room temperature, and 1 tablespoon all-purpose (plain) flour (optional)*

1–1½ teaspoons brandy or Madeira

⚜ Use poultry shears to cut the duck into 4 pieces: Cut alongside the breastbone, then gently force the bird open and cut down either side of the backbone. Remove and discard the backbone. Cut each bird half in half again, following the rounded line of the leg bones so that each person getting a wing section also gets a little extra breast. Cut off the wing tips and set aside along with the neck.

⚜ In a large Dutch oven or large, heavy, deep sauté pan over high heat, melt the butter. Add the duck pieces, wing tips, and neck and brown well on all sides, about 15 minutes. Transfer the duck pieces, wing tips, and neck to a platter. Add the onion and carrot to the pan and cook until caramelized, about 4 minutes. Return the duck pieces, wing tips, and neck to the pan. Add the stock, wine, celery, bouillon cube, and bouquet garni. Season lightly with salt and pepper and add the tomato paste. Bring to a boil, reduce the heat to low, cover, and simmer gently until the duck is opaque throughout, about 1½ hours.

⚜ Meanwhile, fill a saucepan three-fourths full of water, add the olives, and bring to a boil. Reduce the heat to low and simmer for 1 minute. Drain and then pit if desired.

⚜ Using a slotted utensil, transfer the duck pieces to a warmed platter and keep warm in a low (225°F/110°C) oven with the door ajar. Pass the contents of the pan through a sieve, pressing on the solids with the back of a spoon. Discard the vegetable remnants, wing tips, and neck. Skim the fat from the juices and return the juices to the pan. Place over high heat and boil to reduce by about one-third. The sauce will become more syrupy. If you want to thicken it a little, make a *beurre manié* by working together the butter and flour to form a paste. Return the sauce to a boil and gradually add the *beurre manié,* stirring after each addition, until the sauce is the desired consistency. You may not need all of the paste. Add the olives and brandy or Madeira, then taste and adjust the seasoning with salt and pepper.

⚜ Place the duck on individual plates and spoon a little sauce over each serving. Pour the remaining sauce into a serving bowl and pass at the table.

serves 4

Alpes-de-Haute-Provence

Côtelettes de Veau en Petit Ragoût

veal chop ragout

In Provence, veal cutlets and chops are often pot-roasted. Here, their aromatic quality is enhanced with the addition of fresh mint.

3 tablespoons unsalted butter

1 tablespoon olive oil, plus more if needed

6 thick-cut young veal chops

1 yellow onion, cut into 8 thin wedges

¾ cup (6 fl oz/180 ml) dry white wine

4 slender carrots, peeled and sliced

3 large fresh mint sprigs, tied with kitchen string

salt and freshly ground pepper to taste

1¼ lb (625 g) young fava (broad) beans, shelled and peeled (page 247)

½ cup (4 fl oz/125 ml) water

½ cup (4 fl oz/125 ml) heavy (double) cream

about 1 teaspoon fresh lemon juice, or to taste

2 tablespoons shredded fresh mint leaves

In a deep sauté pan over high heat, melt the butter with the 1 tablespoon olive oil. Add the veal and brown on both sides, 10–12 minutes total. Transfer to a plate. Reduce the heat to medium, add the onion, and sauté for 1½–2 minutes, adding more oil if needed. Add the wine, raise the heat to high, and deglaze the pan, scraping up any bits from the bottom. Return the chops to the pan, add the carrots and tied mint, season with salt and pepper, cover, reduce the heat to low, and cook for 20 minutes.

Turn the chops, add the fava beans, and stir once. Add the water, re-cover, and simmer until the veal is tender, about 20 minutes longer.

Transfer the chops and vegetables to individual plates and keep warm. Discard the tied mint. Add the cream to the pan, raise the heat to high, and boil, stirring, to reduce to a sauce consistency. Adjust the seasoning. Add the lemon juice, stir in the shredded mint, and spoon the sauce over the chops.

serves 6

Bouches-du-Rhône

Poularde aux Dragées

capon with sugared almonds

This is an updated version of an ancient recipe dating from when mead, or honey wine, was a customary beverage. Mead can still be found, and if several styles of the beverage are available in your community, use a spicy one, which tends to counteract the innate sweetness of the drink.

Dragées are the colored candied almonds used for christenings and communions in countries all along the Mediterranean. In France, the city of Nancy in the northeast is famous for making dragées. But the almonds themselves come from Provence, as does this recipe from Marseilles, in which fennel and olives also figure prominently.

Although the combination may seem strange, it is actually quite delicious. The vinegar in the sauce counteracts the sweetness of the mead, and the sauce, in turn, offers good contrast with the earthy flavors of the fennel stuffing. A recipe not to be ignored.

STUFFING

4 tablespoons (2 oz/60 g) unsalted butter

1 large or 2 small fennel bulbs, trimmed and finely sliced, then chopped

2 tablespoons water

⅔ cup (3 oz/90 g) large, fleshy black olives, pitted and coarsely chopped

3 tablespoons chopped fresh cilantro (fresh coriander)

grated zest of 1 lemon

1 capon, 5 lb (2.5 kg)

2 tablespoons unsalted butter

2 tablespoons olive oil

½ lb (250 g) candied almonds

salt and freshly ground pepper to taste

ground allspice to taste

SAUCE

2½ cups (20 fl oz/625 ml) mead, or light chicken stock (page 251) plus 1 tablespoon honey

1½ tablespoons white wine vinegar

salt and freshly ground pepper to taste

ground allspice to taste

1 tablespoon unsalted butter

⚜ Preheat an oven to 400°F (200°C).

⚜ To make the stuffing, in a small frying pan over medium heat, melt 2 tablespoons of the butter. Add the fennel and sauté, stirring constantly, until beginning to soften, about 2 minutes. Add the water, cover, and continue to cook until softened, about 3 minutes longer. Drain in a colander and let cool completely.

⚜ In a large bowl, combine the fennel, olives, cilantro, and lemon zest. Mix well. Rinse the capon and pat dry with paper towels. Spoon the stuffing into the cavity and truss or skewer closed.

⚜ Smear a roasting pan with a little of the butter and oil. Place the capon in the pan and rub the remaining butter and oil over the bird. Roast until the juices run clear when a knife tip is inserted into the thigh joint, about 1½ hours. An instant-read thermometer inserted into the thickest part of the thigh away from the bone should register 180°F (82°C).

⚜ Meanwhile, place the candied almonds in a paper bag and crush with a rolling pin or a mallet. Alternatively, place in a food processor and pulse to break them up into small pieces, some almost a powder. Pour into a small bowl.

⚜ Remove the roasting pan from the oven and raise the oven temperature to 425°F (220°C). Snip and remove the trussing string or pull out the skewers. Spoon 3 tablespoons of the pan juices from the roasting pan onto the candied almonds and season with salt, pepper, and allspice. Stir, then spoon all but 2 tablespoons of the almonds over the breast of the capon and return the bird to the oven. Roast for 10 minutes to melt the candied coating.

⚜ Transfer the capon to a warmed platter and keep warm. Spoon the fat off the pan juices.

⚜ To make the sauce, in a small saucepan, bring the mead or the stock and honey to a boil. Add the reserved 2 tablespoons sugared almonds, the pan juices, and the vinegar, and stir to blend. Season with salt, pepper, and allspice. Remove from the heat and stir in the butter. Strain the sauce into a warmed serving bowl.

⚜ Carve the capon at the table, spooning a little stuffing from the cavity alongside each serving. Pass the sauce at the table.

serves 6–8

Les Marrons

Throughout Provence, chestnuts are a familiar sight in the winter months. At busy intersections, even in the smallest towns of the region, one finds mitten-clad men, woolen scarves doubled around their necks and caps pulled tight onto their heads, selling hot, charred chestnuts—*les marrons*—from street-corner braziers. One by one, they count them into paper cones for passersby, who buy them in hope of warding off the winter chill. The women clutch the hot chestnuts between their hands while the men push them deep into the pockets of their trousers.

Fresh chestnuts are also a hearthside winter treat enjoyed by families at home. A slit is cut into the shell, and the nuts are placed in the hollow indentations of a specially designed long-handled metal pan. The pan is set on the hot embers of the fireplace and left until the shells begin to open and lift free from the meat. Once peeled, they are spread with butter and eaten piping hot.

These popular nuts are also blanched and shelled and then boiled for an hour to soften, for adding to many regional braised dishes, especially those based on wild duck, venison, pheasant, and other game. At Christmastime, chestnuts are not only traditional but de rigueur. A cupful of tender boiled ones are folded into the stuffing for the turkey served at the holiday meal, and then a second, larger amount is boiled until soft enough to mash, puréed with cream and butter, and served alongside the carved bird.

Chestnuts are transformed into wonderful sweets as well. The valley around Collobrières, on the *route des vins* northeast of Toulon in the Var, is a sea of chestnut trees. The township not only sells the harvest, but, following the traditions of Provençal craftsmanship, local companies candy the nuts, wrap them individually, and pack them in gift boxes labeled *marrons glacées.* Although fewer small businesses are now involved—once even the nuns in the nearby convent sold their own fabrication—a handful of operations continue to market both the candied nuts and *crème de marrons,* a delectable sweetened purée.

Alpes-Maritimes

Entrecôte Mirabeau

double-thick sirloin steak with
anchovy butter

*In Provençal restaurants, the steaks are usually
presented topped by a grid of anchovies, with a
stuffed-olive slice decorating each space in the pattern.
The home version is less formal and uses anchovy
butter. It is a thick steak, a luxury in France.*

ANCHOVY BUTTER

*¾ cup (6 oz / 185 g) unsalted butter, at room
temperature*

*2 or 3 salt-packed anchovies, filleted and rinsed
(page 246), then finely chopped, or 6–8 olive
oil–packed anchovy fillets, finely chopped*

fresh lemon juice to taste

freshly ground pepper to taste

*2 tablespoons finely chopped fresh flat-leaf
(Italian) parsley (optional)*

1 tablespoon finely chopped shallot (optional)

olive oil for oiling pan

*3 sirloin or porterhouse steaks, each about
12 oz (375 g) and 1½ inches (4 cm) thick*

salt and freshly ground pepper to taste

To make the anchovy butter, place the butter in a
bowl and cream with a whisk until well softened. Stir
in the anchovies, then add the lemon juice and pepper, and the parsley and shallot, if using.

Oil a ridged stove-top grill pan with the olive oil
and place over medium heat. When the pan is hot,
place the steaks on it. After about 2 minutes, rotate the
steaks 90 degrees to sear the grid pattern on them.
After about 2 minutes, turn the steaks, season with salt
and pepper, and cook on the second side. Ideally, the
meat is served rare; the exact timing will depend on
the thickness of the steaks. They should be ready in
8–9 minutes total. Transfer to a cutting board, cover
loosely with aluminum foil, and let rest for 2 minutes.
Slice each steak on the diagonal across the grain, then
lay the 3 steaks side by side on a platter. Top generously
with the anchovy butter and serve at once.

serves 6

Vaucluse

Carré d'Agneau Colette

rack of lamb colette

This recipe employs a common Provençal technique: a large amount of garlic is boiled, puréed, and used to thicken the sauce. Garlic loses much of its strength when boiled, and you'll be amazed to find that the two cloves studding the meat are more evident than the twenty cloves cooked and puréed for the sauce. The purée goes well with other lamb dishes and is used in sauces for roast lamb, too. To make the job easier, ask the butcher to french the rib chops for you.

2 large lamb racks, with 9 chops each,
or 6 individual racks, with 3 chops each

22 cloves garlic

salt to taste

¼ cup (2 oz/60 g) unsalted butter, cut into small pieces

2 fresh rosemary sprigs, each broken into several small pieces

6 tablespoons (3 fl oz/90 ml) dry white wine

½ cup (4 fl oz/125 ml) water

1 cup (8 fl oz/250 ml) chicken stock (page 251)

2 tablespoons chopped fresh flat-leaf (Italian) parsley

freshly ground pepper to taste

2 teaspoons brandy

✤ Preheat an oven to 475°F (245°C). Ideally, your butcher will have frenched the rib chops (trimmed away the meat from the end of each chop). If not, then trim the racks as needed for them to stand without toppling. Protect the stripped tips of the bones from burning by folding aluminum foil across the top. Cut 2 of the garlic cloves into slivers. Using a sharp knife, make shallow slits in the meatiest part of the chops and slip a garlic sliver into each slit. Stand the racks in a roasting pan and rub salt into the fattier side of the meat. Dot the butter over the surface and place the rosemary sprigs here and there.

✤ Roast the lamb for 10 minutes. Add the wine to the pan and continue to roast until an instant-read thermometer inserted into the thickest part of the lamb registers 145°F (63°C) for medium-rare, about 20 minutes longer for larger racks and 10–15 minutes for smaller ones. The lamb should remain pink in the center. If the pan dries out before the lamb is ready, add a few spoonfuls of water.

✤ Meanwhile, in a saucepan, combine the remaining 20 garlic cloves with salted water to cover and bring to a boil. Boil until very soft, about 15 minutes. Drain, then push through a sieve or purée in a small food processor. Set aside.

✤ Transfer the racks to a warmed platter and keep warm. Spoon off any fat from the pan juices and place the pan over high heat.

✤ Add the water to the pan, bring to a boil, and deglaze the pan, scraping up any browned bits from the pan bottom. Continue to boil until the juices are reduced to the point that they begin to fry onto the bottom of the pan. (This step reinforces the browning of the sauce, because well-seared meats that are eaten rare exude few juices into the pan.)

✤ Add the stock to the pan and bring to a boil, scraping up the browned bits from the pan bottom. Mix in the puréed garlic and the parsley. Season with salt and pepper and stir in the brandy. Pour the sauce into a warmed bowl.

✤ Serve the small racks on warmed individual plates, or carve the larger racks and divide among warmed plates. Pass the sauce at the table.

serves 6

Local sheep graze on a fragrant forest of bushes—wild thyme, rosemary, savory, fennel—that perfumes their meat.

Vaucluse

Poussins à la Clamart

poussins with peas and shallots

This dish is served in the Vaucluse around Cavaillon. Clamart, outside Paris, is known for growing peas. Cornish hens may also be used.

6 poussins, about 1 lb (500 g) each

6 tablespoons (3 oz/90 g) unsalted butter, or as needed

1 tablespoon olive oil

2½ oz (75 g) thick-cut sliced slab bacon, cut crosswise into pieces ½ inch (12 mm) wide

1½ lb (750 g) English peas, shelled

12 shallots

2 teaspoons sugar

salt and freshly ground pepper to taste

2 or 3 large lettuce leaves

3 tablespoons dry white wine

½ chicken bouillon cube, crumbled

Rinse the poussins and pat dry. Truss with kitchen string. In a large Dutch oven over medium heat, melt 4 tablespoons (2 oz/60 g) of the butter with the olive oil. Add the poussins and brown on all sides, about 15 minutes. If the butter burns, discard it and add a little more. As the poussins are browned, transfer to a platter. Add the bacon and fry until crisp, about 2 minutes. Add the peas and shallots, stir, and then sprinkle with the sugar. Cook, stirring, for 1–1½ minutes. Season lightly with salt and pepper.

Return the poussins to the pan. Cover the peas and shallots with the lettuce leaves, add the wine, reduce the heat to low, cover, and simmer until the juices run clear when the thigh of a poussin is pierced, 35–40 minutes. Transfer the poussins to warmed individual plates. Discard the lettuce leaves and, using a slotted spoon, arrange the peas, shallots, and bacon around the poussins.

Return the pan to high heat and reduce the liquid to a light sauce, stirring constantly and adding the crumbled bouillon. Season with salt and pepper, whisk in the remaining 2 tablespoons butter, and then spoon over the poussins. Serve immediately.

serves 6

Vaucluse

Lapin aux Herbes
de la Garrigue

rabbit with wild herbs

*The garrigue is the sparse scrubland that covers the
undulating foothills, including those at the base
of the Lubéron mountain range, in the lower Alps.
Ideal hunting territory, the garrigue is at once great
shooting grounds for rabbits and a source of wild
herbs such as thyme, savory, rosemary, and lavender.*

1 large rabbit, about 3½ lb (1.75 kg)

¼ cup (2 fl oz/60 ml) olive oil

salt and freshly ground pepper to taste

2 large fresh thyme sprigs

2 tablespoons chopped fresh rosemary

2 fresh sage leaves, chopped

1 cup (8 fl oz/250 ml) dry white wine

1½ cups (12 fl oz/375 ml) water

2 English (hothouse) cucumbers, peeled if desired

2 tablespoons unsalted butter

2 teaspoons sugar

20 small white onions, each 1 inch (2.5 cm) in
diameter

10 cloves garlic

⅔ cup (5 fl oz/160 ml) crème fraîche

2 tablespoons chopped fresh flat-leaf (Italian)
parsley

❦ Place the rabbit, belly side down, on a cutting
board. Run a sharp knife around the outline of each
leg, slice away from the tail area of the carcass, then
remove the legs. Using a cleaver or heavy knife, sever
the front legs from the saddle (loin) section. Cut the
saddle crosswise into 3 pieces, then the large back legs
into 2 pieces each. Cut off and discard the small triangle containing the tail. You should have 9 pieces,
plus the ribcage area, which you may use or discard.

❦ In a large Dutch oven over medium heat, warm
the olive oil. Add the rabbit pieces and brown well
on all sides, about 15 minutes. Season lightly with salt
and pepper and add the thyme, rosemary, and sage.
Toss to disperse evenly and then add the wine and
1 cup (8 fl oz/250 ml) of the water. Bring to a boil,
reduce the heat to low, cover, and simmer gently,
turning the rabbit pieces once, until tender when
pierced with a knife, about 35 minutes.

❦ Meanwhile, halve the cucumbers lengthwise and
remove any seeds. Cut each half lengthwise into
thirds. Then, using a small knife, shape uniform long,
oval pieces from the fleshy part, forming them as
neatly as possible.

❦ In a saucepan over medium heat, melt the butter.
Add the sugar and cook until it starts to brown,
about 1 minute. Add the onions and sauté, tossing,
until they turn brown, about 2 minutes. Add the
remaining ½ cup (4 fl oz/125 ml) water, cover,
reduce the heat to low, and cook until the onions are
almost tender, about 5 minutes. Add the cucumber
ovals, re-cover, and continue until both vegetables are
tender and the water is nearly evaporated, about
2 minutes longer. At the same time, fill a small saucepan three-fourths full of water, add the garlic cloves,
and bring to a boil. Boil until softened, 10–15 minutes. Drain and press through a sieve set over a small
bowl, to purée the cloves.

❦ When the rabbit is ready, using a slotted utensil
or tongs, transfer to a bowl and keep warm. Add the
crème fraîche, the onions and cucumbers, and the
garlic purée to the pan, raise the heat to high, and
boil down to a sauce consistency. Taste and adjust the
seasoning with salt and pepper. Return the rabbit
pieces to the pan and stir to coat with the sauce. Add
the parsley, mix well, and transfer to a warmed platter. Serve immediately.

serves 4

Alpes-de-Haute-Provence

Carré de Porc aux Feuilles de Sauge

roast pork loin with sage

Both the standing rack of lamb and that of pork are often served persillé *style in Provence. Lines are scored across the back of the rack, and the classic* persillade *mixture of olive oil, garlic, and parsley is pressed against the scored surface. I find that sage suits pork better than any other herb, so I was happy to find that people in the foothills of the Alps, with sage typically just beyond their doorsteps, appreciate the combination as much as I do. Throughout Provence, you will find the same enthusiasm for adding fruits to pork found elsewhere in the world. I have had roast pork surrounded by panfried figs or by orange sections, or sprinkled with cinnamon and served with grapes, but the affinity of apples, sage, and pork is special, and I still prefer this simplest of farmhouse recipes.*

1 pork loin, about 2½ lb (1.25 kg) and with 6 or more chops

3 large fresh sage sprigs, each with 12–14 leaves

1 yellow onion, cut into wedges

3 cloves garlic, crushed

3 tablespoons olive oil

2 tablespoons lavender honey or other honey

3 tablespoons unsalted butter

2 Granny Smith apples, peeled, halved, cored, and cut into medium-thick slices

salt and freshly ground pepper to taste

¾ cup (6 fl oz / 180 ml) water

❧ The night before serving, run a sharp, thin-bladed knife along the lower part of the bone behind the base of the chop meat. Remove 2 or 3 sage leaves from 1 of the sprigs and push them into the cavity from each side of the loin. Stand the loin in a roasting pan. Press 2 of the sage sprigs across the top and back of the pork, splaying them out to cover the surface. Place the third sprig on the bottom of the pan. In a bowl, toss the onion wedges and garlic with the oil and then spill the contents of the bowl over the meat. Cover and refrigerate overnight. Bring to room temperature before proceeding.

❧ Preheat an oven to 400°F (200°C).

❧ Place the roasting pan in the oven and roast for 15 minutes. Reduce the oven temperature to 375°F (190°C) and continue to roast the pork, without basting, until the juices are no longer pink when the pork is pierced, about 45 minutes longer. An instant-read thermometer inserted into the pork should register 160°F (71°C). About 10 minutes before the end of the cooking time, raise the oven temperature again to 400°F (200°C), remove the pan from the oven, and drizzle the honey over the pork. Return the loin to the oven for 10 minutes to glaze the meat. Transfer the pork loin to a warmed serving platter and keep warm. Set the pan aside, unwashed.

❧ In a large frying pan over high heat, melt the butter. Just as the butter begins to brown, add the apple slices in a single layer and fry until well browned on the first side, about 3 minutes. Turn the slices and brown on the second side, about 2 minutes longer. Season with salt and pepper and transfer the slices to the platter, arranging them around the pork. Keep warm in a low (225°F/110°C) oven with the door ajar.

❧ Place the roasting pan with the onion wedges and honey flavoring on the stove top over high heat. Add the water to the pan, bring to a boil, and deglaze the pan, stirring to scrape up any browned bits from the pan bottom. Season with salt and pepper.

❧ Spoon 2 tablespoons of the sauce over the apples, and pour the remainder into a warmed serving bowl. Carve the pork loin at the table. Serve accompanied with the sauce.

serves 6

In rugged Haute Provence, austerity and simplicity, tradition and hard work are part of daily life.

Vaucluse

Suprêmes de Volaille aux Asperges

chicken breasts with asparagus

Near the ramparts of Avignon, just through a gateway into the old city from the banks of the Rhône River, is the restaurant of my friend Jean-Marc. He has repeatedly invited me into the kitchen of his restaurant, Le Jardin de la Tour, and into his home, as well as to the markets of Avignon and Cavaillon and the truffle markets of Carpentras. One day, after returning from the market with a handful of the first spring asparagus, he made me this simple dish, handling two pans at once and deftly transferring the flavorful liquid from cooking the asparagus to the chicken, to marry the two with a light sauce. The dish made an unbeatable springtime lunch.

4 skinless, boneless chicken breasts

3 tablespoons chopped fresh flat-leaf (Italian) parsley

2 tablespoons chopped fresh cilantro (fresh coriander)

2 tablespoons chopped fresh mint

1 tablespoon chopped fresh thyme or winter savory

20 asparagus spears

¼ cup (2 oz/60 g) unsalted butter

salt and freshly ground pepper to taste

1 cup (8 fl oz/250 ml) water

3 tablespoons olive oil

☙ Rinse the chicken breasts and pat dry.

☙ Combine the parsley, cilantro, mint, and thyme or savory on a cutting board or large platter. Mix well, then roll the chicken breasts in the herbs and leave to stand for about 1 hour before cooking. (They can be left longer but must be refrigerated and then returned to room temperature before cooking.)

☙ Meanwhile, if the asparagus stalks are thick, peel them to within about 2 inches (5 cm) of the tips and then snap off the tough ends. Place the asparagus in a frying pan, add the butter, season lightly with salt and pepper, and pour in the water. Cover and set the pan aside.

☙ In a large frying pan over high heat, warm the olive oil. When the pan is hot enough to sear the chicken, add the chicken breasts, and cook until browned on the first side, about 3 minutes.

☙ Turn the chicken breasts, season with salt and pepper, reduce the heat to medium-low, and cook until the second side is browned and the chicken is opaque throughout, about 3 minutes longer.

☙ When the chicken is half cooked, place the pan holding the asparagus over high heat and bring to a boil. Move the lid slightly ajar and boil until the water is reduced by half and the asparagus is cooked, about 3 minutes. Using tongs or a slotted utensil, transfer the asparagus to warmed individual plates, reserving the pan juices.

☙ Transfer the chicken breasts to the plates, placing them alongside the asparagus, and keep warm. Place the pan used to cook the chicken over medium-high heat, add the asparagus water, and boil, stirring constantly and scraping up any browned bits from the pan bottom, until the liquid is reduced to a light sauce consistency. Taste and adjust the seasoning. Spoon the sauce over the chicken and serve immediately.

serves 4

The fortified villages of the Vaucluse harbor medieval castles and churches with bell towers.

Alpes-de-Haute-Provence

Chou Fassum

stuffed cabbage

Sometimes known simply as fassum, *this beautiful stuffed-cabbage dish is fast disappearing as the younger generation looks to spend less time in the kitchen. Yet few who have tasted this great rustic classic would fail to appreciate its depth of flavor, nor the wonderful sense of hearth and home that is conjured up by this style of cookery. Any leftover broth can be seasoned with salt and pepper and served as a first course, or it can be used as stock for making soup.*

1 head savoy cabbage, about 5 lb (2.5 kg)

1 lb (500 g) Swiss chard

3½ oz (105 g) fresh pork rind, diced

olive oil as needed

½ lb (250 g) thick-cut sliced slab bacon, cut crosswise into pieces ½ inch (12 mm) wide

3 yellow onions, chopped

3 tomatoes, peeled, seeded, and neatly diced

2 cloves garlic, finely chopped

1½ lb (750 g) medium-grind pork sausage meat

2 cups (10 oz / 310 g) cooked long-grain white rice, cooled

salt and freshly ground pepper to taste

6–8 cups (48–64 fl oz / 1.5–2 l) beef stock or chicken stock (page 251), or as needed

Dijon mustard

Trim the stalk of the cabbage, then discard any wilted or damaged outer leaves. Bring a large saucepan about two-thirds full of salted water to a boil and add the cabbage. Parboil for about 15 minutes, then lift the cabbage from the pan and refresh it under running cold water to set the color. Place the cabbage upside down in a colander to drain until fully cooled. As the cabbage begins to cool, squeeze it gently between your palms (protected with kitchen gloves) to release excess water.

Fill the same saucepan about two-thirds full of salted water and bring to a boil. Add the Swiss chard and parboil for 5 minutes, lift it out with a wire skimmer, and refresh under running cold water to set the color. Drain and squeeze to release as much water as possible. Chop the chard and place in a bowl. Return the water to a boil, add the pork rind, and boil for 2 minutes, then drain and add to the bowl.

❧ Oil a small frying pan and place over high heat. Add the bacon and fry until crisp, about 1 minute. Transfer to the bowl holding the Swiss chard. Add a little more oil to the pan if necessary, reduce the heat to medium, add the onions, and sauté until softened, about 2 minutes. Add to the bowl along with the tomatoes and garlic.

❧ Place the cabbage, core end down, on a work surface. Gently spread the leaves apart to reveal the center, then cut out a piece about the size of a tennis ball. Chop this piece and add to the bowl. Fold the sausage meat and the rice into the vegetables, mixing carefully so as not to mash the other ingredients. Season with salt and pepper.

❧ To stuff the cabbage, place it upright on a board and again gently spread open the leaves from where the center has been removed. Fill this cavity with the stuffing, then, working outward, spread some stuffing between each of the outer leaves, gently easing them back around the center and using the stuffing between the leaves to mold the cabbage back into its original shape.

❧ Some cooks tie the finished stuffed cabbage—around the girth and around the top and bottom—suggesting that it is easier to remove from the pot later. Many, however, find that the string pulls through the flesh of the cabbage when it is cooked and tender. Alternatively, press the cabbage into shape with your palms. Transfer the cabbage, core side down, to a large saucepan in which it fits snugly. Add enough stock to cover the cabbage fully. Bring to a boil over medium heat, reduce the heat to low, cover, and simmer gently until tender to the core when pierced with a skewer, about 3 hours.

❧ If you have used string, grab the ties, lift the cabbage out, and place in a large, shallow bowl. Otherwise, lift the cabbage gently with 2 slotted spoons angled away from each side (if you have a helper, 3 spoons is even better) and transfer to the bowl.

❧ Present the cabbage whole at the table, with a few ladlefuls of the broth spooned around it. Pour some of the broth into a warmed serving bowl and pass it at the table. Cut the cabbage into wedges and serve. Accompany with the mustard.

serves 8

Les Saucissons de Provence

Sausages in Provence come in all types. In general, the frying sausages (*saucisses*) have a lower bread or cereal content than their counterparts in Anglo-Saxon countries, and their flavors are bold. The great sausages of Provence, however, are neither *saucisses* nor the boiling sausages one finds sliced thickly into stews and daubes. Instead, they are the air-cured sausages that are sliced and eaten alone, appreciated for their unique flavor. These are the *saucissons*.

The alpine regions are the source of these specialties. The sausages, hung in the mountain air, are primarily of pure pork, heavy with lard and flavored with peppercorns, fennel seed, cumin, and sometimes even chestnuts. Most interesting of the various *saucissons* available is the *saucisson d'Arles,* whose flavor and texture result from a mixture of 60 percent pork and 40 percent "selected cuts" of beef and donkey, additions that make this sausage different from all others. Saverus de Provence, located in Tarascon, is responsible for most of the production of this prized sausage, just as it is for another unusual sausage made with 40 percent meat from the famed little black bulls (*les taureaux*) of the Camargue.

Bouches-du-Rhône

Daube de Canard

duck daube

Recipes such as this were undoubtedly developed to tenderize wild duck. The daube, one of the most masterly, complete recipes I know, works its alchemy by using a marinade, aromatic vegetables and herbs, and a gentle simmering of the meat. There is no better way to cook domestic or wild birds.

4 tablespoons (2 oz/60 g) unsalted butter

3 tablespoons olive oil

1 duck, 4 lb (2 kg)

1½ cups (12 fl oz/375 ml) dry white wine

1 clove garlic, finely chopped

3 fresh sage leaves

3 oz (90 g) thick-cut sliced slab bacon, cut crosswise into pieces ½ inch (12 mm) wide

2 yellow onions, chopped

2 carrots, peeled and sliced

1 turnip, peeled and cut into large dice

2 tablespoons all-purpose (plain) flour

1 cup (8 fl oz/250 ml) beef stock or chicken stock (page 251)

½ cup (4 fl oz/125 ml) fresh orange juice

1 piece fresh pork rind, 6 by 4 inches (15 by 10 cm)

2 orange zest strips, about ½ inch (12 mm) wide

½ celery stalk, cut into 4 equal pieces

bouquet garni (page 246)

5 oz (155 g) fresh white mushrooms, brushed clean and sliced

⅔ cup (3 oz/90 g) Niçoise olives

salt and freshly ground pepper to taste

2 tablespoons Madeira or port

2 tablespoons tomato paste, or to taste

❧ In a large Dutch oven over high heat, melt 2 tablespoons of the butter and 1 tablespoon of the olive oil and brown the duck on all sides, 15–20 minutes. Transfer the duck to a cutting board. Set aside the pan without washing it. Use poultry shears or sturdy kitchen scissors to cut the duck into 8 pieces: 2 drumsticks, 2 thighs, 2 wings, and 2 breasts. Lay the pieces in a rectangular dish and add the wine, the remaining 2 tablespoons oil, the garlic, and the sage. Cover and marinate in the refrigerator for 4 hours.

❧ Place the Dutch oven over medium heat and, when it is hot, add the bacon and fry until crisp, about 1 minute. Add the onions, carrots, and turnip to the pan and fry for about 2 minutes. Add the flour, stir to distribute, and cook until it browns lightly, about 45 seconds. Add the stock and orange juice, bring to a boil, reduce the heat to low, cover, and simmer until thickened, about 10 minutes. Carefully pour the liquid in the pan into a bowl. Preheat an oven to 350°F (180°C).

❧ Place the piece of pork rind, skin side up, in the bottom of the pan, pushing the bacon and vegetable pieces above the rind. Place the duck pieces, one slightly overlapping the other, into the pan, then pour in the liquid from the cooked vegetables and the marinade from the duck. Add the orange zest, celery, bouquet garni, mushrooms, and olives and season with salt and pepper. Cover, place in the oven, and cook until the duck is tender, 2–2¼ hours.

❧ Transfer the pan to the stove top. Using a slotted utensil, remove the duck pieces and vegetables to a warmed platter and discard the bouquet garni and orange zest. Taste the pan juices, and if they are not too salty, boil down to a sauce consistency, stirring often and adding the Madeira or port. Adjust the seasoning with salt, pepper, and tomato paste. Spoon the sauce over the duck and serve immediately.

serves 6

Alpes-Maritimes

Paillard d'Agneau au Pistou

grilled lamb shoulder with pesto

The word paillard *literally means "bawdy," but when used to describe meat, it refers to a cut that has been butterflied to provide a thin, flat surface, a necessary procedure to bring a thick cut to the grill. Ask your butcher to bone and butterfly the lamb for you.*

5 lb (2.5 kg) lamb shoulder, boned and butterflied

Pistou *for Vegetable Broth with Pesto (page 43)*

2 cloves garlic, finely chopped

1 tablespoon freshly cracked pepper

5 tablespoons (2½ fl oz/75 ml) olive oil

salt to taste

❦ The night before grilling, using a sharp knife, trim any excess fat from the butterflied shoulder. Slice any thicker parts open horizontally without cutting them completely free, and lay them open to achieve a similar thickness at all points. A meat pounder helps to thin out any remaining thicker areas. The meat should measure about 12 by 6 by 2 inches (30 by 15 by 5 cm). Lay in a large, shallow dish and brush both sides with the *pistou*. Sprinkle both sides with the garlic and pepper and drizzle with the olive oil. Cover with plastic wrap and refrigerate overnight.

❦ Prepare a fire in a grill.

❦ Spoon any liquid that has collected in the bottom of the dish over the meat, making sure the surface of the meat is oily. Place the meat on the grill rack over a hot fire and grill, turning once, for 20–25 minutes total for medium-rare. It is best to cook the meat more than halfway through on the first side, which later becomes the side that faces up when carving. Be sure to salt the meat only after it is turned, to prevent the loss of juices.

❦ Transfer the lamb to a cutting board, tent loosely with aluminum foil, and let stand for 5 minutes before carving. Carve the meat on the diagonal across the grain and serve directly from the board, or place on warmed individual plates and serve.

serves 6

LES LÉGUMES

Vegetables are eaten in season—braised in olive oil and garlic, baked in a gratin.

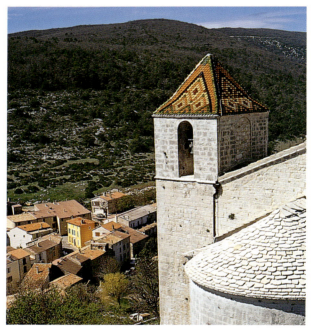

Preceding pages: Colorfully printed table linens, in profuse array at a market in Arles, are bordered with motifs inspired by two eminent elements of the Provençal landscape, the olive and the sunflower. **Top:** A favorite vegetable combination savored in the Alpes-Maritimes is artichokes with fava (broad) beans, or *artichauts aux fèves.* **Above:** The medieval church of Saint-André, built in the twelfth century, watches over the village of Comps-sur-Artuby in the Var. **Right:** If space allows in the *potager*—the kitchen garden—a gardener can bring to the table a splendid homegrown pumpkin in the form of a layered *tian de potiron.*

IN THIS SOUTHERN, SUNNY LAND, the market-garden capital of France, the colorful profusion of vegetables on offer is breathtaking, and Provençal cooks know just how to make the most of them. No meal is complete without vegetables, whether they come at the beginning of the repast, where they appear both raw and cooked in prepared dishes and in soups; in their more traditional place alongside meat or fish at the main course; or served separately following the main dish, where the most elaborate vegetable dishes can be appreciated for their own beauty. It is even common to find a dish of baked vegetables as the centerpiece of the evening supper, a legacy perhaps of the fact that meat traditionally has been expensive (for vegetarianism as an ethic is rare in France). A plate of baked fennel or whole stuffed onions, or a dish of layered vegetables, seasoned perhaps with just a little ham, bits of bacon *(lardons),* or salt cod, is considered ideal for this lighter meal of the day.

The favorite vegetables of Provence are those of the brightest color, maybe to match the sun-emblazoned landscape and the vivid blue sky. Deep purple eggplants (aubergines); brazenly red tomatoes; red, green, and yellow

Below: The folk-art figurines known as *santons* are meticulously handcrafted and costumed to depict traditional Provençal villagers. At Christmastime, these "little saints" join the Nativity scene, bearing their homely country gifts. **Right:** In the Bouches-du-Rhône, much of the arable land of the northern Camargue is given over to the cultivation of rice, which has its own tradition of fairs and festivals. The September harvest is celebrated for five days in nearby Arles, while year-round in Le Sambuc visitors can also enjoy a tour of the Musée du Riz.

bell peppers (capsicums); and green and yellow zucchini (courgettes) come first to mind. Simmered together with onion and garlic, they become ratatouille, the seminal dish through which most foreigners first learn what it means to cook a vegetable Provençal style.

Strangely, the peppers, squashes, and tomatoes that are so indelibly a part of Provençal cuisine today had to wait for Columbus to arrive in the New World to find their way into the pantry of the Midi. They serve to remind us that the table of Provence has developed over time due to successive colonization and to the region's role as a hub for international trade routes for over two thousand years. Less known to outsiders is the local love of fennel, globe artichokes—the Provençaux prefer the tiny, pointed-leaved purple-tinged ones—Jerusalem artichokes, green beans, peas, and

asparagus, and the particular penchant of the Niçois for Swiss chard, cardoons, fava (broad) beans, and chickpeas (garbanzo beans).

Behind this affection for vegetables is a peasant's almost symbiotic relationship with the land. Farmers, especially in the isolated regions of the Alpes-de-Haute-Provence, have long grown vegetables in the stretches of land behind their flat-roofed one-story *mas* (homesteads), and life without these subsistence plots is unthinkable. Almost anyone in the Midi with a scrap of backyard has a vegetable patch. Even the small balconies of the most cramped apartment dwellers typically boast pots containing a bevy of herbs, tomatoes, arugula (rocket), and small salad leaves. Until recently, municipal governments provided land on the outskirts of their communities for *potagers* (vegetable gardens) for those with lesser incomes.

If people are unable to grow vegetables themselves, the growers are never far away. Bustling local markets transform the narrow streets, wide boulevards, town squares, or riverbanks of every village, town, and city at least twice a week, bringing sparkling fresh produce right to the doorstep. This keeps cooks acutely aware of the passing of the seasons, as each vegetable comes to market in its first burst of beauty, continues to appear through its various stages of maturity, and then gradually passes out of season and out of the market, to be replaced by something else.

When I was a young bride, my mother-in-law never tired of taking me to the market, lecturing me en route as to what we might expect and on what she planned to make in the following days depending on what she found. Leading me by the hand, she would introduce me to Madame So-and-So, who paid particular attention to the cultivation of her leeks, or picked her zucchini flowers in the flush of dawn, or piled the dirt around her asparagus high and tight, making them the whitest specimens in the market.

In the marketplaces of Provence, cooks forge personal relationships with the growers of their food, sympathizing with them when a lack of rain means the beans are going to be late this year, or when a lack of sun yields only a meager crop of red-ripe tomatoes for the stall this week. Shoppers discuss the merits of the newest variety of late-season leeks and, the next week, report back on the dish they made and how it tasted. If fibrous strings have begun to circle turnips, shoppers understand that they are suitable only for a pot-au-feu or for soup and can no longer be simply boiled and

glazed. They also know to pay less, of course, than the price asked in the previous week. While they chat, they swap a recipe or two for making the most of the cardoons recently returned to the market, or argue over whether or not their grandmothers added rice to a *tian de courges* (*tian* of squash).

This closeness to the marketplace brings into force an inescapable logic that dictates the rhythm of what is eaten and how and when. If something is out of season, it is off the dinner plates, to be welcomed back with joy when it appears again the next year.

The care at the market continues in the kitchen. The Provençal cook never simply steams or boils a vegetable and dumps it on a plate with a knob of butter. Instead, vegetables are invariably given a local touch, braised in olive oil and garlic, or cooked with onion, tomato, and garlic to ensure a pungent saucy residue in which to serve them. The adventurous Provençaux also combine vegetables better than any cooks I know: English peas with mushrooms, fava beans with haricot verts, carrots with baby onions or cucumbers, asparagus with peas and/or fava beans, globe artichokes with Jerusalem artichokes, and tomatoes with just about anything. Nowhere else does one find baby carrots in a cream sauce with basil, or haricots verts with anchovies. Interesting textures and contrasting flavors are central themes in vegetable preparation.

Winter vegetables are cooked in a hearty, gutsy manner in large earthenware gratin dishes *(les tians)*. Cardoons, carrots, turnips, Belgian endive (chicory/witloof), cauliflower, cabbage, pumpkin, or potatoes are seasoned with garlic and olive oil, sprinkled with herbs from bouquets that have been drying, and intensifying in flavor, since the summer harvest, and then baked, with or without cheese, or folded into a white sauce and gratinéed.

The excitement is palpable as the new season's produce appears in the market. The first vegetables of spring, the most eagerly awaited, have a special name, *les primeurs*—"the first ones"—and are sold as such to proclaim their arrival. Among them are baby peas and haricots verts, first from Pertuis, then from all across the Var and the Vaucluse; the prized

Left: Gothic ornamentation frames a casual café in Aix-en-Provence. Such anachronistic scenes are commonplace in this city, whose history spans twenty-two centuries. Today, Roman ruins mix with Romanesque splendor, and medieval mingles with modern. **Below:** In Aix, a pair of lions repose at each corner of the stately fountain of the Rotonde, at the foot of fashionable Cours Mirabeau. **Bottom:** Serious shoppers arrive early for fresh-picked greens and herbs at the Cours Saleya market in Nice.

Below: Ruins of the Roman empire serve a modern-day function in Arles. In summer, the Théâtre Antique holds open-air concerts, while in fall, the well-preserved amphitheater draws capacity crowds for bullfights as part of the festivities celebrating the local rice harvest. **Bottom:** The heartland of Provence's olive culture lies at the foot of the Alpilles, the bare limestone "little Alps" in the northern Bouches-du-Rhône.

asparagus from the village of Lauris on the banks of the Durance; fava beans from Carpentras; *cocos* (creamy white shell beans, thinner but not unlike the fava) from Cadenet; and baby carrots, baby beets, baby spring turnips, and baby onions.

Combinations will change again in summer, as tomatoes and the summer's leafy greens are harvested. The tomatoes will be baked with chopped spinach or mushrooms stuffed in their centers; artichokes will be braised with chopped carrots, onions, and mushrooms; and cucumbers will be peeled, halved, and seeded, and then braised with tomatoes, onions, and fresh herbs. The *tian* dish will come off the cupboard shelf again, and the creative cook will form all sorts of patterns and colors by layering in it the best of the summer market: tomatoes, eggplant, zucchini, fennel. Oil and garlic will still prevail, but this time they will

be enlivened by basil and other fresh herbs. Baked in less time than their winter counterparts, the season's *tians* are redolent with the sweet aromas of a summer garden.

In the fall, no self-respecting local drives into the countryside without a bucket in the back of the car for toting the mushrooms he hopes to spot. If he does find some, he will return again the next day, and maybe the day after, but the place will remain a well-kept secret. The lucky hunter will share the bounty with you, frying the mushrooms with a *persillade;* grilling them stuffed with *lardons,* garlic, and the chopped stems; or simmering them in white wine and stock and thickening the juices with a knob of butter. The meal will be shared with pleasure, but even a best friend will never know where the treasured patch of *sanguins* (pine mushrooms), chanterelles, or cèpes was found.

Come November, winter has arrived again, and the most prized fungus of all is in the market. But this one is found only underground, and only with the help of the olfactory powers of specially trained dogs or pigs. The truffles of the Lubéron, among the finest in France and distributed at special markets like those of Carpentras and Richerenche, are finely sliced and used sparingly, since they are extremely expensive (the best truffles were selling at 3,000 francs a kilo in 2001). Stored buried in the egg basket or embedded in rice, so the aroma does the work even before the truffle graces a dish, they are preferred above all with eggs, potatoes, celery root (celeriac), and pasta.

This bounty of vegetables is nature's gift to the cuisine of Provence. The following are just some of the ways in which the Provençaux take this gift to the table.

Alpes-Maritimes

Artichauts aux Fèves

artichokes with fava beans

The Niçois are so fond of artichokes that they eat the small, tender early-spring ones raw. These delicate specimens are also pickled so they can grace salads in the months ahead. Larger artichokes are cut into halves or quarters and are typically paired with another favorite Mediterranean vegetable, the fava bean. A recipe like this one is often the result.

5 medium artichokes

3 tablespoons olive oil

6 tablespoons (3 fl oz/90 ml) dry white wine

2 cloves garlic, finely chopped

3 fresh thyme sprigs

salt and freshly ground pepper to taste

2 lb (1 kg) fava (broad) beans, shelled and peeled (page 247)

3 tablespoons chopped fresh flat-leaf (Italian) parsley

☙ Trim and quarter the artichokes as directed on page 246.

☙ In a sauté pan or wide, shallow saucepan over medium heat, warm the olive oil. Add the artichoke sections and toss to coat them well with the oil. Do not allow them to brown.

☙ Add the wine, garlic, and thyme and season with salt and pepper. Stir once, bring to a boil, cover, reduce the heat to low, and simmer slowly until the artichokes are almost tender, 15–18 minutes.

☙ Add the fava beans to the pan and simmer, covered, until the artichokes and fava beans are tender, 6–8 minutes.

☙ Taste and adjust the seasoning with salt and pepper. Add the parsley and stir it through the artichokes and fava beans to distribute evenly. Transfer to a warmed serving bowl and serve immediately.

serves 4–6

Alpes-Maritimes

Salade de Fenouil à l'Orange

fennel salad with orange segments

Some of the best citrus found in France grows around the Riviera town of Menton. Terraced hillsides behind the town are full of lemon and orange trees, and the beautiful Biovès gardens in the town center are bordered by lemon and palm trees. Although Menton is better known for its sought-after lemons— there is even a lively lemon festival on Shrove Tuesday—my memory of the town is also associated with this simple and refreshing salad.

1 large or 2 baby fennel bulbs

2 green (spring) onions, including tender green tops, sliced

1 orange

5 fresh mint leaves, shredded

4 large, fleshy black olives, pitted (optional)

¼ cup (2 fl oz/60 ml) olive oil

1 tablespoon red wine vinegar, or to taste

salt and freshly ground coarse pepper to taste

☙ Trim off the base of the fennel bulb(s), then cut away the feathery fronds and most of the stem portions. Reserve the fronds. If using a large bulb, cut in half lengthwise and then cut each half crosswise into thin slices. If using baby fennel, slice the bulbs lengthwise as finely as possible. Include any stem portions that remain intact. Place the slices in a salad bowl and add the green onions.

☙ Using a sharp knife, cut a thin slice off the top and the bottom of the orange to expose the flesh. Place the orange upright on a cutting board and thickly slice off the peel in strips, cutting around the contour of the orange to expose the flesh. Holding the orange in one hand over the bowl of fennel, cut along either side of each section to free it from the membrane, allowing the sections and any juice to fall into the bowl.

☙ Add the mint and the olives, if using, to the bowl. In a small bowl, whisk together the olive oil and vinegar and season with salt and pepper. Drizzle over the salad, toss, and serve.

serves 6

Alpes-de-Haute-Provence

Oignons Blancs Farcis

baked stuffed onions

Stuffed and baked vegetables, along with vegetables in white sauce, are commonplace in Provence, particularly in rustic areas where time-consuming cooking remains part of family life. Lunch is still the main meal, with something lighter for supper the rule, so that stuffed vegetables, especially those with a small portion of meat, are served not only as accompanying vegetables but also as a light meal. Variations on this onion recipe exist for fennel (halved lengthwise and with the stuffing placed over the bulb rather than discarding a portion of it), for large mushrooms, for bell peppers (capsicums), and in the scooped-out centers of zucchini (courgettes) or eggplants (aubergines).

8 large white onions, each about 3 inches (7.5 cm) in diameter

4 tablespoons (2 fl oz/60 ml) olive oil

2 tomatoes, peeled, seeded, and roughly chopped

2 cloves garlic, finely chopped

salt and freshly ground pepper to taste

2 slices coarse country bread, crusts removed

6 tablespoons (3 fl oz/90 ml) milk

¼ lb (125 g) each ground (minced) veal and pork, or ½ lb (250 g) ground (minced) beef

2 oz (60 g) air-cured ham (page 247) or prosciutto, chopped

1 teaspoon herbes de Provence

1 tablespoon chopped fresh flat-leaf (Italian) parsley

flesh of 4 large black olives, chopped (optional)

1 egg

½ cup (4 fl oz/125 ml) chicken stock (page 251)

♔ Cut a slice ½ inch (12 mm) thick off the top of each onion, then peel the onions without cutting through the root ends. Bring a large saucepan of salted water to a boil, add the onions, reduce the heat to medium, and cook until softened, about 20 minutes. Drain the onions and, when cool enough to touch, scoop out the centers and discard, leaving only 3 or 4 outer layers of the flesh intact.

♔ In a small frying pan over medium heat, warm 2 tablespoons of the olive oil. Add the tomatoes and garlic and sprinkle lightly with salt and pepper. Simmer gently, stirring frequently, until the tomatoes release their juice, about 10 minutes. Raise the heat to high and cook, stirring constantly, until thickened, about 2 minutes.

♔ Preheat an oven to 375°F (190°C). Oil a baking dish large enough to accommodate the onions in a single layer.

♔ In a small bowl, combine the bread and milk and let stand for 2 minutes. Drain the bread, squeezing out the excess moisture, chop, and place in a bowl. Add the tomato mixture, the ground veal and pork or ground beef, the ham, the *herbes de Provence*, the parsley, the olives (if using), and the egg. Mix thoroughly, then season with salt and pepper.

♔ Fill the onions with the ground meat mixture, dividing it evenly, and place the stuffed onions in the prepared baking dish. Add the chicken stock to the bottom of the dish, and drizzle the onions with the remaining 2 tablespoons olive oil.

♔ Bake the onions, basting from time to time with the liquid in the bottom of the dish, until tender throughout when pierced with a skewer, about 45 minutes. Serve the onions hot, spooning any liquid in the bottom of the dish over them.

serves 8

In spring, the Valensole Plain is white with almond blossoms; come summer, the dusky violet of lavender prevails.

Bouches-du-Rhône

Riz au Safran

saffron rice

*Historically, saffron was an important plant through-
out the Mediterranean and was cultivated in France
just south of Paris in the Gatinais. The Provençaux
like to use it primarily in soups. There is hardly a
fish soup, including the famous bouillabaisse of
Marseilles, that does not include the spice. An interesting recipe that I found in Cannes calls for poaching
potatoes in saffron-infused chicken stock, lending
them an aromatic pungency and turning them bright
orange-yellow. Much more commonly, saffron is coupled
with rice, and in this recipe from the rice-growing
region of the Camargue, the combination is superlative.
Serve the rice with Nougat of Beef (page 129)
from the same area.*

2 tablespoons unsalted butter

1 small yellow onion, chopped

2 cups (14 oz/440 g) long-grain white rice

4 cups (32 fl oz/1 l) boiling water

¼ teaspoon powdered saffron

salt and freshly ground pepper to taste

pinch of freshly grated nutmeg

❦ Preheat an oven to 400°F (200°C).

❦ In a heavy ovenproof saucepan over medium
heat, melt the butter. Add the onion and sauté until
softened but not colored, about 1 minute.

❦ Add the rice and stir until the kernels are well
coated with butter and shiny. Add the boiling water,
raise the heat to high, and return to a boil. Stir once
or twice, season with the saffron, salt, pepper, and
nutmeg, cover, and transfer to the oven. Bake the rice
for 18 minutes. By this time, the liquid will have been
absorbed and the rice will be tender.

❦ Remove from the oven and set aside without lift-
ing the cover for a further 5 minutes to absorb any
remaining moisture. Uncover the pan, fluff the rice
with a fork, transfer to a warmed serving bowl, and
serve at once.

serves 6

La Camargue

Windswept and treeless, the Camargue, the triangle of land caught between the two major tributaries of the Rhône River, is a fascinating, if somewhat desolate place. For years the flat, marshy area penetrated by arms of salty water and a giant salt lake, l'Étang de Vaccarès, was home only to birds, small herds of sheep and cattle that grazed the patches of meager grasses dotted across the landscape, and vast white expanses of salt harvested from the sea and spread to dry. A remarkable protected reserve harbors thousands of pink flamingos.

After World War II, money from the United States–financed Marshall Plan helped harness the waters of the Rhône, channeling them into an irrigation system that has seen the Camargue develop into the premium rice-growing area of France. Today, three hundred farmers cultivate rice on small plots that together amount to forty square miles (10,000 ha), only one-third of the land cultivated in the 1960s. The rice is harvested in September and October and provides the country—never a significant rice-eating nation—with most of its needs. The majority of the harvest is from a smaller-husked long-grain variety (*le riz Vaccarès*), sold both polished and as brown rice, but there are also farmers growing basmati, short-grain, and jasmine rice, as well as a nutty-textured red variety (*le riz Flamade*). I buy the last at roadside stalls on every visit, so much do I love it for pilafs and poultry and seafood stuffings, or simply boiled, buttered, and served with a daube.

But the Camargue leaves its most indelible impression as the marshy playground of great white horses and little black bulls (*les taureaux*) and of the *gardians* (cowboys) who oversee them. Although now sold for meat locally, the *taureaux* were bred originally for bullfighting, and small bullrings and riding huts give the area an atmosphere somewhere between the American Wild West and the bullfighter's Spain. *Gardians* are the equestrians of France, riding proudly into the ring at competitions and circuses. Many give riding lessons on their *manades* (small ranches) for bread-and-butter money.

As in the French Basque country, bullfighting is legal here, but not for the kill. The bullfighter's task is to use courage and agility to get close enough—in a fifteen-minute bout—to pull a series of ribbons, rosettes, and strings from the bull's head.

Var

Chou-fleur Toulonnaise

cauliflower in tomato sauce

It is said that any dish à la toulonnaise contains tomatoes, and if the dish is a seafood recipe, it has tomatoes and mussels. In this Toulon-style dish, cauliflower is paired with a delicious tomato–bell pepper sauce in a particularly lovely presentation.

1 head cauliflower

5 tablespoons (2½ fl oz/75 ml) olive oil

1 yellow onion, chopped

½ small red bell pepper (capsicum), seeded and sliced

½ small green bell pepper (capsicum), seeded and sliced

3 large tomatoes, peeled, seeded, and roughly chopped

2 cloves garlic, finely chopped

2 fresh thyme sprigs or 2 large fresh oregano sprigs

salt and freshly ground pepper to taste

¼ cup (2 fl oz/60 ml) water

about 1 heaping teaspoon tomato paste

small black olives (optional)

1 tablespoon chopped fresh flat-leaf (Italian) parsley

♨ Divide the cauliflower into large, chunky florets with a good length of stalk intact, so that the head can be reassembled for serving. Peel the stems to remove the bitter skin.

♨ In the pan of a steamer over medium heat, warm the olive oil. Add the onion and sauté until softened, about 2 minutes. Add the bell peppers, stirring to coat with the oil. Add the tomatoes, garlic, thyme or oregano, salt, pepper, and water, stir, and then reduce the heat to low.

♨ Arrange the cauliflower florets on the steamer rack and place over the tomato mixture. Cover and steam the florets until just tender, 4–5 minutes. Remove the steamer from the heat. Scoop up the cauliflower florets from the rack and stack them on a round, shallow serving dish, re-forming them loosely into a mound that resembles the original shape and size of the cauliflower head.

♨ If the vegetable mixture in the steamer pan is watery, raise the heat to high and reduce, stirring constantly, until thickened. Taste and adjust the seasoning, then add the tomato paste to reinforce the tomato flavor. Add the olives, if using, and heat through.

♨ Spoon the tomato mixture over the cauliflower, sprinkle with the parsley, and serve immediately.

serves 6

The forested massifs of the southern Var give way to the terraced vineyards of Bandol.

Vaucluse

Flageolets au Thym

flageolets with thyme

In the street markets of Cavaillon and Carpentras, farmers' wives bring in flageolets for sale. My mother-in-law, who was born in northern France, took her marketing seriously, including her search for the best of these popular and special beans. She was not alone in her pursuit. In Provence, as in all of France, cooks consider flageolets the aristocrats of the dried bean world, preparing them in a variety of ways, especially as an accompaniment to roast leg of lamb.

1¾ cup (12 oz/375 g) dried flageolets

leaves from 2 fresh thyme sprigs

1 bay leaf

¾ cup (6 fl oz/180 ml) heavy (double) cream

salt and white pepper to taste

⚜ Pick over the beans, discarding any grit or mis-shapen beans. Rinse the beans, place in a large bowl, add water to cover generously, and let soak overnight.

⚜ Drain the beans. Bring a large saucepan three-fourths full of salted water to a boil. Add the thyme and bay leaf and then pour in the beans in a steady stream. Return the water to a boil, reduce the heat to medium, cover, and simmer until just tender, about 1¼ hours. Drain, discarding the bay leaf and reserving ½ cup (4 fl oz/125 ml) of the cooking water.

⚜ Combine the cream and the reserved cooking water in a sauté pan large enough to accommodate the beans. Add the beans, stirring to distribute the cream and water evenly, then place over medium heat. Bring slowly to a boil, stirring occasionally. Season with salt and white pepper, reduce the heat to low, and simmer until the beans "soften" into the sauce, the elements are bound together, and the cream has thickened slightly, about 10 minutes. Transfer to a warmed bowl and serve.

serves 6

Var

Paillasson aux Courgettes et Pommes

potato and zucchini cake

The Provençaux go into raptures about the beautiful blossoms of the zucchini plant. Cooks turn them into fritters or stuff them with goat cheese or whatever strikes their fancy. My friend Arlette grows zucchini in her garden in Hyères just for the flowers. Although she appears to regard the rest of the vegetable as a ubiquitous leftover, she shared with me this marvelous potato dish with julienned zucchini.

1 zucchini (courgette), about 6 oz (185 g), trimmed

3 waxy potatoes, no more than 1 lb (500 g) total weight

5 oz (155 g) large fresh white mushrooms, brushed clean and cut into julienne about 2 inches (5 cm) long

salt and freshly ground pepper to taste

3 tablespoons olive oil

2 tablespoons unsalted butter, cut into small pieces

✤ Using a food processor fitted with the larger shredding disk, julienne the zucchini and potatoes separately. Do not rinse the starch from the potatoes, but pat dry with paper towels. Place the zucchini and potatoes in a large bowl, add the mushrooms, and season with salt and pepper. Mix well.

✤ In a nonstick 9- or 10-inch (23- or 25-cm) frying pan over medium heat, warm the olive oil. Add the vegetable mixture, spreading it evenly, and press down on it with a spatula. Scatter about 1 tablespoon of the butter pieces over the top. Reduce the heat to medium-low and cook slowly, pressing occasionally against the vegetables to compact the cake, until the underside is well browned, about 15 minutes.

✤ Place a plate upside down over the frying pan and, holding the plate and pan together, invert them, allowing the cake to fall onto the plate. Slide the cake back into the pan, browned side up. Scatter the remaining 1 tablespoon butter pieces over the top and again press on the top. Cook until the second side is browned, about 15 minutes longer.

✤ Slide the cake onto a serving plate, cut into wedges, and serve immediately.

serves 4–6

Alpes-Maritimes

Tomates Ménagère

baked tomatoes, home style

The word ménagère, *which translates as "housewife," usually indicates a simple home-style way of cooking. Such dishes are rarely lacking in flavor, however, particularly in Provence. Garlic is one of the first ingredients that the housewife reaches for when preparing a recipe such as these baked tomatoes. She also turns to her garden patch or windowsill pots to select an array of aromatic fresh herbs.*

6 large, ripe tomatoes

6 tablespoons (3 fl oz/90 ml) olive oil

6 tablespoons (½ oz/15 g) chopped fresh flat-leaf (Italian) parsley

18 fresh basil leaves, shredded, plus 12 whole leaves or small sprigs

½ cup (2 oz/60 g) grated Parmesan cheese, plus a small wedge (optional)

3 cloves garlic, finely chopped

salt and freshly ground pepper to taste

✤ Cut each tomato in half horizontally. Holding each half upside down over the sink, press gently to expel most of the seeds and water. In a nonstick frying pan large enough to hold all 12 tomato halves, warm 4 tablespoons (2 fl oz/60 ml) of the olive oil over medium heat. Add the tomatoes, cut sides down, reduce the heat to medium-low, and cook slowly for 5 minutes to intensify their flavor. Carefully transfer the tomato halves, cut side up, to a work surface and let cool until they can be handled.

✤ Preheat an oven to 350°F (180°C). Oil a baking dish large enough to hold the tomatoes in a single layer. In a small bowl, combine the parsley, shredded basil, grated cheese, and garlic. Mix well, adding the remaining 2 tablespoons olive oil to bind the mixture. Season with salt and pepper. Fill each of the tomato halves with an equal amount of this mixture, and place the tomatoes in the prepared baking dish.

✤ Bake the tomatoes until lightly browned, about 25 minutes. Remove from the oven and transfer to a serving platter. If desired, using a vegetable peeler, shave thin shards from the wedge of Parmesan, allowing them to drop onto the tomato halves. Garnish with the basil leaves or sprigs and serve at once.

serves 6

Auguste Escoffier

In the small, peaceful village of Villeneuve-Loubet in the Cannes hinterland, in a narrow street halfway up the hill overlooking the lower part of the town, stands the house in which Auguste Escoffier (1846–1935), the man whose name is synonymous with French haute cuisine of the early twentieth century, was born. At the age of thirteen, the young Escoffier left this comfortable, two-story home, now a museum to his talents, to apprentice in the kitchen of his uncle's restaurant in Nice.

Within a few years, the gifted Provençal native would be behind the stoves in restaurants in Paris, Monte Carlo, and London, where he was teamed with César Ritz at the Savoy and later at the equally renowned Carlton, as well as the Ritz in Paris. Most culinary scholars credit Escoffier with creating the dominance of French cuisine in the kitchens of the world's greatest hotels.

He attained this supremacy by taking the classic recipes of the Gallic table, studying them closely, and then refining their preparation without any loss of elegance or extravagance. Master, teacher, and icon, he recorded his ideas in a trio of books, *Livre des menus, Guide culinaire,* and *Ma cuisine,* the last an exhaustive twenty-five-hundred-recipe compendium that remains required reading in many professional kitchens.

Bouches-du-Rhône

Petits Fenouils Braisés

braised baby fennel

Nowhere in the world is fennel taken more seriously than it is in Provence. The large bulb of the vegetable is commonly baked or used raw in salads, and the feathery tops are used raw as an herb in salads or are cooked in braised dishes, particularly with fish. In this recipe from the town of Salon-de-Provence, the fennel bulbs are small enough to be served whole.

12–16 baby fennel bulbs

5 tablespoons (2½ fl oz/75 ml) olive oil

1 small yellow onion or 4 shallots, cut into thin rings

1 long, slender carrot, peeled and sliced

2 cloves garlic, finely chopped

½ red bell pepper (capsicum), diced

2 tomatoes, peeled, seeded, and cubed

1 scant teaspoon tomato paste

5 tablespoons (2½ fl oz/75 ml) water

salt and freshly ground pepper to taste

chopped fresh chervil or flat-leaf (Italian) parsley

❧ Trim off the feathery tops and the stalks from each fennel bulb, leaving about 1½ inches (4 cm) of the stalks intact. Discard the stalks and tops or reserve for another use. Remove any bruised areas and trim the base of the core.

❧ In a wide saucepan or deep frying pan over medium heat, warm the olive oil. Add the onion or shallots and the carrot and sauté for about 2 minutes. Add the fennel bulbs, stir to coat with the oil, and then add the garlic and bell pepper. Toss the vegetables, then add the tomatoes, tomato paste, water, salt, and pepper. Stir well, cover, reduce the heat to low, and simmer gently until the fennel bulbs are tender when pierced with a knife, 12–15 minutes. If the saucepan is deep, it is wise to butter a piece of parchment (baking) paper the diameter of the pan and place it, buttered side down, over the vegetables to keep the steam in and lessen the chance of scorching.

❧ Transfer the contents of the pan to a warmed serving dish and sprinkle with the chervil or parsley. Serve immediately.

serves 6–8

Tian de Légumes

layered vegetable gratin

One of the most important characteristics of tians *is the effect obtained from the layering of different vegetables. This dish, typical of those from the hinterlands behind the Riviera, combines tomato sauce and Swiss chard, which is grown in nearly every* potager. *The top layer of zucchini is often replaced with a layer of panfried eggplant (aubergine) slices.*

4 zucchini (courgettes), each about 1½ inches (4 cm) in diameter, trimmed and sliced

Grandmother's Swiss Chard (page 194)

Tomato Sauce for Egg, Onion, and Tomato Gratin (page 37)

¾ cup (3 oz/90 g) shredded Gruyère cheese

2 tablespoons fine dried bread crumbs

2 tablespoons unsalted butter, cut into small pieces

¼ cup (2 fl oz/60 ml) olive oil

☙ Position a rack in the upper third of an oven and preheat to 400°F (200°C). Oil a gratin dish about 12 inches (30 cm) long and 7 inches (18 cm) wide.

☙ Bring a saucepan three-fourths full of salted water to a boil. Add the zucchini and blanch for 1½ minutes. Drain and set aside.

☙ Place the Swiss chard in the prepared gratin dish, spreading it evenly. Spread a layer of the tomato sauce on the chard. Arrange the zucchini slices, overlapping them slightly, in an attractive pattern on top. Sprinkle evenly with the Gruyère cheese and then with the bread crumbs. Dot the top with the butter and drizzle with the olive oil.

☙ Bake the gratin until heated through and the top is a deep golden brown, 20–25 minutes. If the top has not browned sufficiently, and you have used a flameproof gratin dish, slip the gratin under the broiler (griller) until nicely browned. Remove from the oven or broiler and serve immediately.

serves 6–8

Vaucluse

Salade d'Épinards

salad of baby spinach

Spinach, a popular vegetable in Provence, is often boiled, chopped, and reheated with cream or white sauce. When tender, young spinach is available, the Provençaux like to eat the leaves raw, as in this well-crafted salad. Since Provence produces few cow's milk cheeses, Parmesan cheese from Italy is the likely choice for this dish. Cantal from the Auvergne and Beaufort, a slightly softer, Emmentaler-style cheese from the Savoy, are also excellent.

2 tablespoons pine nuts

5 tablespoons (2½ fl oz/75 ml) olive oil

2 tablespoons sherry vinegar or red wine vinegar

salt and freshly ground coarse pepper to taste

½ lb (250 g) young, tender spinach leaves, stems removed

small wedge of Parmesan, Cantal, or Beaufort cheese

2 tablespoons chopped fresh chervil

♛ Preheat an oven to 325°F (165°C). Spread the pine nuts in a small pan and toast in the oven, shaking the pan occasionally, until crisp and golden, about 10 minutes. Alternatively, toast the pine nuts in a small, lightly oiled frying pan over medium-low heat, stirring constantly, until crisp and golden, about 2 minutes. Pour onto a plate to cool.

♛ In a small bowl, whisk together the oil and vinegar. Season with salt and pepper.

♛ Place the spinach in a salad bowl or spread in a large, two-handled porcelain dish. Scatter with the pine nuts and drizzle with the dressing.

♛ Using a small, sharp knife or a vegetable peeler, shave pieces of the cheese over the top. Sprinkle with the chervil and serve immediately without tossing.

serves 6

Alpes-de-Haute-Provence

Endives Poêlées

caramelized belgian endive

I sampled this dish at a small café overlooking the Durance River in the wine-making town of Tallard, where the endives accompanied a panfried trout.

8–10 green (spring) onions

3–4 tablespoons (1½–2 oz/45–60 g) unsalted butter

1 teaspoon sugar

3 large or 4 smaller heads Belgian endive (chicory/witloof), leaves separated

salt and freshly ground pepper to taste

2 tablespoons chopped fresh flat-leaf (Italian) parsley

❦ Trim the root end and strip away the outer leaves from the green onions but leave them whole. In a frying pan, melt 3 tablespoons of the butter over medium heat and add the sugar. When the sugar begins to caramelize lightly, after about 1 minute, add the green onions and sauté for about 30 seconds. Toss in the endive leaves and stir until coated, adding more butter if necessary to prevent sticking.

❦ Cover, reduce the heat to low, and cook, stirring twice, until softened, about 3 minutes. Season with salt and pepper, add the parsley, and serve.

serves 4

Alpes-de-Haute-Provence

Ragoût d'Artichauts et Topinambours

ragout of two artichokes

This dish highlights the complementary flavors and contrasting textures of two similarly named but unrelated vegetables.

3 globe artichokes

6 Jerusalem artichokes

6 tablespoons (3 fl oz/90 ml) olive oil

salt and freshly ground pepper to taste

chopped fresh flat-leaf (Italian) parsley

❦ Trim and quarter the globe artichokes as directed on page 246. Bring a saucepan three-fourths full of salted water to a boil. Add the artichokes and boil until tender, 10–15 minutes. Drain and transfer to a bowl. Peel and slice the Jerusalem artichokes about ¼ inch (6 mm) thick. Bring a saucepan three-fourths full of water to a boil. Add the Jerusalem artichokes and boil until tender, about 8 minutes. Drain well.

❦ In a frying pan over high heat, warm the olive oil. Add both types of artichokes and toss well to coat with the oil. When the vegetables are heated through and nicely glazed, season with salt and pepper and stir in the parsley. Transfer to a warmed serving bowl and serve at once.

serves 6–8

Alpes-Maritimes

Carottes et Courgettes à la Vapeur

steamed carrots and zucchini

If there is one place where your figure matters more than elsewhere in France, it is around the pleasure playground of the Riviera. That is why I wasn't surprised to find this light, bright treatment of carrots and zucchini in Cannes.

10 oz (315 g) carrots, peeled and cut into julienne 2 inches (5 cm) long

2 zucchini (courgettes), about 10 oz (315 g) total weight, trimmed and cut into julienne 2 inches (5 cm) long

1 tablespoon unsalted butter

salt and freshly ground pepper to taste

1 teaspoon fresh lemon juice, or to taste

1 tablespoon chopped fresh flat-leaf (Italian) parsley

❦ Spread the carrots on a steamer rack, place over boiling water, cover, and steam for 1½ minutes. Add the zucchini and continue to steam until both vegetables are tender, 1½ minutes longer. Drain well.

❦ In a frying pan over medium-high heat, melt the butter. Add the steamed vegetables and toss to mix well and coat with the butter, 1–1½ minutes. Season with salt, pepper, and lemon juice. Stir in the parsley and serve at once.

serves 6

Alpes-Maritimes

Haricots Verts à la Niçoise

green beans with garlic and anchovy

For thirty-five years, a friend of mine in Provence has been married to a man from northern France. Olive oil, anchovies, and garlic are truly alien to his palate, so my Niçoise friend waits until her husband leaves town on one of his business trips to buy anchovies and garlic so she can make traditional recipes such as this one.

¼ cup (2 fl oz/60 ml) olive oil

2 yellow onions, sliced

3 cloves garlic, finely sliced

3 tomatoes, peeled, seeded, and roughly chopped

1 large fresh thyme sprig

1 bay leaf

2 lb (1 kg) haricots verts, trimmed

salt and freshly ground pepper to taste

3 salt-packed anchovies, filleted and rinsed (page 246), or 8 olive oil–packed anchovy fillets

In a frying pan over medium heat, warm the olive oil. Add the onions and garlic and sauté until golden, about 3 minutes.

Add the tomatoes, thyme, and bay leaf, stir to mix well, cover, reduce the heat to low, and simmer until the tomatoes soften and release their juice, 6–8 minutes.

Add the haricots verts and mix thoroughly. Season lightly with salt and pepper. Re-cover and continue to simmer until the beans are tender, 5–6 minutes.

If using salt-packed anchovies, cut each fillet into 3 or 4 pieces; if using oil-packed anchovy fillets, cut each into 3 pieces. Add the anchovies to the pan and stir well. Using a slotted spoon, transfer the vegetable mixture to a warmed serving plate. Raise the heat to high and boil, stirring constantly, to reduce the pan juices by half, about 3 minutes.

Spoon the sauce over the vegetables, stirring to combine, and serve.

serves 4–6

Alpes-Maritimes

Poireaux Côte d'Azur

leeks with tomatoes

In France, leeks are generally panfried in a little butter or are boiled. Here, the addition of tomatoes, onions, and herbs gives this commonly more subtly seasoned vegetable a strong Mediterranean profile. The combination allows leeks, normally an accompaniment to fish and light meats, to stand alongside rich meats such as lamb and pungent fish dishes such as sea bass grilled with fennel. If only large leeks are available, use half as many.

12 young leeks, as small as possible, including tender green tops

½ cup (4 fl oz/125 ml) olive oil, plus more for drizzling

3 yellow onions, chopped

5 large, ripe tomatoes, peeled, seeded, and roughly chopped

3 tablespoons dry white wine

6 fresh sage or basil leaves or 2 fresh oregano sprigs

salt and freshly ground pepper to taste

tomato paste to taste (optional)

2 tablespoons chopped fresh flat-leaf (Italian) parsley

Bring a saucepan three-fourths full of salted water to a boil. Add the leeks and cook until tender, 4–6 minutes, depending on their size. Drain well.

In a saucepan over medium heat, warm the ½ cup (4 fl oz/125 ml) olive oil. Add the onions and sauté until golden, 4–5 minutes. Add the tomatoes, white wine, and sage or other herb and season lightly with salt and pepper. Cook, stirring occasionally, until the tomatoes have softened, about 15 minutes. Mash lightly with a wooden spoon, then add a little tomato paste, if desired, to intensify the tomato flavor.

Reduce the heat to low, add the leeks to the tomato sauce, and turn to coat with the sauce. Remove the oregano sprigs, if used, and transfer the leeks and sauce to a serving platter, with the white ends of the leeks all facing the same direction. Sprinkle with the parsley, drizzle olive oil over the top, and serve at once.

serves 6

Le Marché

The market in the sunny, sleepy town of Arles has always been my favorite street market in Provence. Running a kilometer or two along the Boulevard des Lices, the town's main thoroughfare, it continues around the stony rampart wall at the Tour des Mourgues in the shadow of the old Roman theater and forum. For well over a thousand years, shoppers have been coming here to seek out a bargain in seafood, an extra artichoke or two in the bag, or the finest, plumpest chicken.

The market is held on Wednesdays and Saturdays, but the latter is the much larger of the two. Magnificent, colorful vegetables, standing straight, heads held high, juices ready to burst, are piled in boxes at stall after stall. Brought in by both merchants and local farmers, they never have a shriveled leaf or a wilted head. Specialized vans bring butchers selling Provençal lamb, *charcutiers* with their terrines and sausages, and cheese merchants displaying local cheeses and those from afar.

Standing under an umbrella, a woman cuts slices from a large air-dried ham of wild boar for prospective buyers to taste. A vendor presides over a dozen open bowls of olives, while another offers jars of honey and confectionery. A teenaged girl ladles fresh yogurt from a huge bucket, another uses a wire string to cut slices from a mound of farm butter, and still another stands before a bench of her family's homemade fresh goat cheeses.

In a huge, black iron pan, a man sautés *tellines*—dwarf clams unique to Arles and the Camargue—in garlic and parsley, spooning them into containers for passersby. Today's special at the seafood trestle is mussels, which lie in huge bins on the street—bins large enough to accommodate ten or twelve varieties of local rock fish alongside the bivalves. There's a stall for sharpening knives, and one selling powdered spices mounded into lovely, material-clad baskets.

I spot *tielle*, the tomato-squid pie specialty from Sète; a baker's table piled high with crusty loaves; and a merchant selling paella. And I'm just at the corner. The clothing and bric-a-brac stalls are still ahead.

Bouches-du-Rhône

Émincé de Pommes de Terre

baked sliced potatoes

In the Camargue, where the gardians *(cowboys) live in stone houses with rudimentary kitchens and boast unsophisticated tastes, these homely but flavorful potatoes sit alongside grilled fish, steaks, and one-pot stews. The rich olive oil of the south, the garlic, and the rosemary have proved to be such a magnificent combination that the dish has migrated to many areas around the French Mediterranean.*

5 waxy potatoes, about 2½ inches (6 cm) in diameter, peeled

8 cloves garlic, unpeeled

2 teaspoons fresh rosemary leaves

¾ cup (6 fl oz / 180 ml) olive oil

salt and freshly ground pepper to taste

Preheat an oven to 400°F (200°C). Oil a baking dish large enough to hold the fanned potato slices in a single layer.

Slice the potatoes about ⅛ inch (3 mm) thick, keeping each potato in its original shape as the slices fall from the knife. Using a metal spatula, lift each sliced potato in one piece and transfer it to the prepared baking dish, then press down to fan out the slices. Arrange all the potatoes around the dish in the same way, placing them side by side but not touching one another.

Tuck the garlic cloves here and there, slipping them slightly under the potatoes to help prevent them from scorching. Tuck the rosemary leaves under the potatoes as well. Drizzle the oil over the top and season with salt and pepper.

Bake the potatoes, basting 2 or 3 times with the olive oil in the bottom of the dish (tilt the dish and scoop it up with a spoon), until tender and the exposed edge of each slice is browned and crisp, about 35 minutes. To test, pierce the potatoes with the tip of a small knife.

Bring the potatoes to the table and serve directly from the baking dish.

serves 6

Alpes-Maritimes

Primeurs Provençaux Braisés à l'Huile d'Olive

new season's vegetables braised
in olive oil

The term les primeurs, *literally "the first ones,"
is used for the baby vegetables that grace French
markets at the start of the season. Here, they are
braised in olive oil, resulting in a vegetable dish that
complements strong-flavored meat dishes. Use the
smallest vegetables you can find.*

*about 3 lb (1.5 kg) mixed baby vegetables such
as carrots, turnips, eggplants (aubergines), zucchini
(courgettes) with or without flowers attached,
green beans, snow peas (mangetouts), pattypan
squashes, artichokes, fennel bulbs, large shallots,
ears of corn, and asparagus tips*

olive oil for braising

salt and freshly ground pepper to taste

*3 tablespoons chopped fresh flat-leaf (Italian)
parsley*

✾ Prepare the vegetables: Peel the carrots and
turnips. Trim off the ends of the eggplants and zucchini. Trim the stem ends from the green beans and
string the snow peas, if necessary. Halve or quarter
the pattypan squashes; trim and halve or quarter the
artichokes as directed on page 246. Trim the fennel
bulbs and halve lengthwise if large. Peel the shallots
but leave whole. Shuck the ears of corn and remove
the silk. Trim the asparagus tips as necessary.

✾ Pour the olive oil to a depth of ¼ inch (6 mm)
into a large, wide frying pan and place over medium
heat until hot but not sizzling hot. First, add the
carrots, turnips, fennel, and artichokes and toss well
until evenly coated with the oil. Reduce the heat to
low, cover the pan, and braise gently until beginning
to soften, about 5 minutes. Add the eggplants,
zucchini, green beans, pattypan squashes, shallots, corn,
and asparagus and stir to coat with the oil. Re-cover
and continue to cook, stirring from time to time, until
the vegetables are tender, 13–15 minutes longer.

✾ Add the snow peas and stir and toss for about
45 seconds until just tender. Season with salt and
pepper, remove from the heat, and stir in the parsley.
Transfer to a warmed platter and serve.

serves 6

Alpes-de-Haute-Provence

Salade de Concombres et Fenouil

cucumber and fennel salad

The textures and flavors of fennel and cucumber are combined in this light salad. The fennel can also be sliced even more finely and used raw.

2 large, round fennel bulbs

12 tablespoons (6 fl oz / 180 ml) olive oil

6 cloves garlic, unpeeled

1 large English (hothouse) cucumber, peeled

1 heaping tablespoon salt-packed capers, rinsed

juice of 1 lemon, or to taste

salt and freshly ground coarse pepper to taste

2 tablespoons chopped fresh flat-leaf (Italian) parsley

Preheat an oven to 375°F (190°C). Lightly oil a baking sheet. Trim off the feathery tops and the stalks from each fennel bulb. Remove any bruised areas and trim the base of the core. Stand the bulb on its base and cut vertically into slices ⅛ inch (3 mm) thick. The stalks may be sliced on the diagonal and baked with the sliced bulbs, or they may be reserved for another use along with the tops.

Place the fennel slices in a single layer on the prepared baking sheet, then drizzle with 4 tablespoons (2 fl oz/60 ml) of the olive oil. Rub the garlic cloves with 2 tablespoons of the oil and place on top of the fennel. Bake, turning the fennel slices 2 or 3 times, until they soften slightly, about 20 minutes. Remove the garlic and set aside. Transfer the fennel to a platter and let cool.

Halve the cucumber lengthwise. Scoop out any seeds. Cut the flesh into small, even dice. Place in a bowl, add the capers, and spoon over the fennel.

Squeeze the roasted garlic cloves, forcing out the soft garlic into a bowl. Discard the skin. Mash with a fork. Add the remaining 6 tablespoons (3 fl oz/ 90 ml) olive oil and the lemon juice and whisk together. Season with salt and pepper and stir in the parsley. Drizzle the dressing over the cucumber and fennel. Toss in the kitchen or at the table and serve.

serves 6

Alpes-de-Haute-Provence

Aubergines en Éventail

eggplant fans

Eggplant is a favorite vegetable of the Provençaux. This particularly popular dish can be served as an accompanying vegetable, as an appetizer, or as an attractive addition to a buffet table, where it is offered hot or cold. The dish lends itself to many variations. One of the most common is to add cheese, sometimes goat cheese but more often tomme de Savoie or Gruyère, both of which are good melting cheeses. The olives are always used when the "fans" are served as an appetizer, but are less critical when the dish is presented as a vegetable accompaniment.

6 tablespoons (3 fl oz / 90 ml) olive oil

3 yellow onions, chopped

½ red bell pepper (capsicum), seeded and chopped

½ green bell pepper (capsicum), seeded and chopped

salt and freshly ground pepper to taste

4 eggplants (aubergines), each about 1½–2 inches (4–5 cm) in diameter

3 tomatoes, sliced

2 cloves garlic, finely chopped

8 fresh basil leaves, roughly torn, plus 2 leaves, chopped

few small black olives (optional)

2 tablespoons chopped fresh flat-leaf (Italian) parsley

In a 10- or 11-inch (25- or 28-cm) ovenproof cast-iron or double-handled copper frying pan that can be taken to the table, warm 3 tablespoons of the olive oil over medium heat. Add the onions and sauté until well softened without coloring, about 5 minutes. Add the bell peppers and stir to coat with the oil. Season with salt and pepper and set the pan aside.

Preheat an oven to 400°F (200°C).

Working on a cutting board, trim off the stem end of each eggplant, leaving as much of the end as possible. Slice each eggplant lengthwise into 6 or 7 slices each about ⅓ inch (9 mm) thick; stop just short of the stem end so that the slices remain attached to one another.

Fan open the slices of each eggplant and stuff the tomato slices here and there between them. Scatter the garlic and torn basil leaves into the cuts alongside the tomato slices.

Using a wide spatula, carefully transfer each eggplant to the top of the onion mixture in the pan, arranging the eggplants in a spiral pattern with the stem end toward the center. Press the slices with the palm of the hand to fan them open slightly, sprinkle with salt and pepper, and drizzle with the remaining 3 tablespoons olive oil. If desired, dot the olives among the eggplants.

Bake until the eggplants are tender when pierced with a skewer, about 35 minutes.

Remove from the oven, scatter the parsley and chopped basil over the top, and serve immediately directly from the pan.

serves 6–8

Var

Blettes Grand-mère

grandmother's swiss chard

In the Var and in the countryside behind the Riviera, Swiss chard is a common vegetable in the garden. It has more bitterness than its less rustic counterpart, spinach, and cooks of the area tend to choose one of two ways to handle this characteristic—by capitalizing on it with lemon juice and cracked pepper or by counteracting it with the addition of raisins. Those inclined to cook chard this latter way also usually add pine nuts, raw or toasted. Roasted hazelnuts (filberts), halved or sliced (flaked), are also delicious.

Although the white stems are removed from the leaves for better presentation, they are rarely discarded. Expect that same grand-mère to bring them out a few days later boiled, drained, and then baked in white sauce as a gratin. Spinach can be substituted for the chard in this recipe with no modifications.

1 bunch Swiss chard

3 tablespoons unsalted butter

1 tablespoon olive oil

1 tablespoon sugar

1 tablespoon chopped fresh rosemary

⅓ cup (2 oz/60 g) dark raisins, roughly chopped, or golden raisins (sultanas)

2 tablespoons pine nuts (optional)

salt and freshly ground pepper to taste

❧ Remove the stems from the Swiss chard leaves, along with the thicker part of each stem that runs into the leaves. Roughly slice the leaves.

❧ In a large frying pan over high heat, melt the butter with the oil until it is sizzling. Add the sugar and stir until the sugar just begins to brown, about 1 minute. Immediately add the Swiss chard and rosemary and stir well to coat the chard with the butter. Continuing to stir, cook until the chard wilts to about half of its volume, 1–1½ minutes. Add the raisins and stir to distribute evenly. Add the pine nuts, if using, and continue to cook over high heat to evaporate any moisture. The total cooking time is about 3 minutes.

❧ Season with salt and pepper, transfer to a warmed serving plate, and serve immediately.

serves 4

Alpes-Maritimes

Artichauts à la Barigoule

braised artichokes

This recipe is said to be named for the shape of the artichokes after they are trimmed, as the bottoms resemble the sanguin mushroom, known colloquially as barigoule in Provence. In this version, the artichokes are cut into pieces and cooked with sliced mushrooms.

6 medium to large artichokes

7 oz (220 g) thick-cut sliced slab bacon, cut crosswise into pieces ½ inch (12 mm) wide

1 large yellow onion, chopped

4–5 tablespoons (2–2½ fl oz/60–75 ml) olive oil

2 carrots, peeled and chopped

3 oz (90 g) fresh sanguin mushrooms or white mushrooms, brushed clean and sliced

6 tablespoons (3 fl oz/90 ml) dry white wine

2 cloves garlic, chopped

salt and freshly ground pepper to taste

3 tablespoons chopped fresh flat-leaf (Italian) parsley

❧ Trim the artichokes and quarter medium ones or cut large ones into sixths as directed on page 246.

❧ In a frying pan over high heat, fry the bacon until it is crisp and renders its fat, about 1 minute. Reduce the heat to medium and add the onion to the bacon and rendered fat, adding 1 or 2 tablespoons of the olive oil if the pan seems too dry. Sauté the onion until softened, about 2 minutes. Add the carrots and mushrooms, turn them in the fat to give them a sheen, and add the remaining 3 tablespoons olive oil. Place the artichoke pieces in the pan, top with the white wine and garlic, and season with salt and pepper. Cover, reduce the heat to low, and simmer until the artichokes are tender, about 30 minutes.

❧ Using a slotted spoon, transfer all the vegetables to a plate and keep warm. Taste the pan juices, and if they are not too salty and you want a thicker sauce, boil over high heat until reduced to a sauce consistency. Taste and adjust the seasoning.

❧ Return the vegetables to the sauce and stir gently to coat well. Transfer to a warmed serving bowl, top with the parsley, and serve.

serves 6

Alpes-de-Haute-Provence

Tian de Potiron

pumpkin gratin

This hearty pumpkin gratin, typical of the tians served in the cold regions of Provence, comes from the mountains behind Manosque. I first tasted the dish in the kitchen of a family that raised sheep. They prepared the gratin in the oven of an old combustion stove and served it alongside a wonderful aromatic Seven-Hour Leg of Lamb (page 141).

1 pumpkin, about 2 lb (1 kg), halved, seeded, peeled, and cut into 1-inch (2.5-cm) cubes

¾ cup (4 oz/125 g) cooked white rice

1 scant cup (3½ oz/105 g) shredded Gruyère cheese

¼ cup (1½ oz/45 g) all-purpose (plain) flour

2 cloves garlic, finely sliced

¼ cup (½ oz/15 g) mixed chopped fresh thyme and winter savory

salt and freshly ground pepper to taste

pinch of freshly grated nutmeg

3 tablespoons fine dried bread crumbs

3 tablespoons olive oil

❦ Preheat an oven to 325°F (165°C). Oil a 7-inch-by-12-inch (18-cm-by-30-cm) baking dish.

❦ Place the pumpkin cubes in a large bowl. Scatter the rice, cheese, flour, and garlic over the top. Sprinkle with the thyme and savory, salt, pepper, and nutmeg. Using a large spoon or your hands, toss together all of the ingredients, making sure the pumpkin cubes are well coated with the flour. Spoon the pumpkin mixture into the prepared baking dish, spreading it evenly. Scatter the bread crumbs over the top and drizzle with the olive oil.

❦ Bake the gratin until the pumpkin is tender when pierced with the tip of a knife and the top is a deep golden brown, about 30 minutes. If the top has not browned sufficiently, raise the oven temperature to 425°F (220°C) and bake for 5 minutes longer, or slip the gratin under a broiler (griller), first making sure the baking dish is flameproof, until browned.

❦ Remove from the oven or broiler and serve.

serves 6

Les Tians

The *tian*, a shallow-sided, glazed, brown earthenware Provençal baking dish, popular since the days of wood-fired stoves, has proved its staying power as an attractive vessel used for vegetable gratins. Over time, recipes cooked and presented in these rectangular dishes have themselves become known as *les tians*.

Common to all vegetable *tians* is some form of layering. They may be as simple as the potato *tian* of Apt, which uses only potatoes with bacon, garlic, and thyme, ending with grated cheese to form a crusty top. More complicated versions have three, even four layers of vegetables posed one above the other. The choice of vegetables can vary considerably, with eggplants (aubergines), zucchini (courgettes), fennel, pumpkin, and Jerusalem and globe artichokes among the selections. The creative cook can compose a *tian* with almost anything on hand. Some *tians* include rice and some add small pieces of leftover fish, particularly salt cod, as in Carpentras. But one can usually expect a *tian* to be a vegetable dish. All come from the oven with the top browned, crisp, and crusty—the true glory of the *tian*.

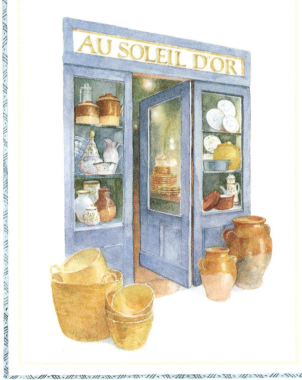

Vaucluse

Papetons d'Aubergines au Coulis de Tomates

eggplant custards with tomato sauce

From Avignon, City of the Popes, comes this traditional recipe for serving eggplant. Legend has it that when the popes first came to Avignon from Rome, they had difficulty adapting to the local cuisine. One of the papal chefs, determined to gain papal approval, created this elegant eggplant dish in the form of the papal tiara. He evidently succeeded, as it became a classic of Avignon gastronomy. It makes an impressive accompaniment to a roast leg of lamb or sirloin of beef.

2 lb (1 kg) eggplants (aubergines), peeled and diced

about 1 tablespoon salt, plus salt to taste

¼ cup (2 fl oz/60 ml) olive oil

¼ cup (1 oz/30 g) shredded Gruyère cheese

1 tablespoon fresh lemon juice

⅔ cup (5 fl oz/160 ml) milk

½ teaspoon grated lemon zest

2 whole eggs, plus 2 egg yolks

3 tablespoons crème fraîche

freshly ground pepper to taste

boiling water, as needed

about 1½ cups (12 fl oz/375 ml) Tomato Sauce for Stuffed Vegetables (page 67), heated

6 fresh basil leaves, shredded (optional)

♆ Place the diced eggplant in a colander, sprinkle with the 1 tablespoon salt, and let stand for about 30 minutes to drain off the bitter juices. Pat dry with paper towels.

♆ In a nonstick frying pan over medium heat, warm the olive oil. When the oil is hot, add the eggplant, then reduce the heat to low, cover partially, and cook until tender, 20–30 minutes. Remove from the heat and let cool.

♆ Preheat an oven to 375°F (190°C). Butter six ½-cup (4–fl oz/125-ml) ramekins.

♆ In a blender or food processor, purée the cooled eggplant until smooth. Transfer the eggplant to a bowl and add the cheese and lemon juice. In a small saucepan over medium heat, combine the milk and lemon zest and heat until bubbles appear along the edges of the pan. Place the whole eggs and yolks in a bowl. While whisking constantly, slowly pour the hot milk into the eggs. Stir the egg mixture into the eggplant purée, then fold in the crème fraîche.

♆ Season with salt and pepper, and spoon the mixture into the prepared ramekins, dividing it evenly. Place the ramekins in a baking pan, place the baking pan on an extended oven rack, add boiling water to the pan to reach nearly to the rims of the ramekins, and carefully slide the rack into the oven.

♆ Bake until the custards are set and a skin has formed on top, about 25 minutes. Carefully transfer the baking pan to a work surface and remove the ramekins. Let the ramekins stand for 2–3 minutes.

♆ Run the blade of a knife around the inside edge of each ramekin and invert it onto a warmed individual plate. Spoon 3–4 tablespoons of the tomato sauce around each custard and garnish with the basil, if desired. Serve immediately.

serves 6

Var

Salsifis à la Persillade

salsify with garlic and parsley

Sometimes known as oyster plant, salsify is a root vegetable that comes in two forms. True salsify has gray skin and is thick, dividing at the base into a number of rootlets that are usually discarded before the vegetable is sold. Black salsify is longer and thinner and is cultivated for canning. The two forms are interchangeable in recipes. Soaking the roots in water for about an hour facilitates peeling. They are also available canned, in which case they have been peeled, boiled, and cut to the thickness of asparagus tips. If you are using canned salsify roots, they need only be reheated and tossed with the garlic, butter, and parsley. The Provençaux also like to boil salsify and then serve it au gratin.

6–8 gray salsify or 4–6 black salsify (see note)

4 cups (32 fl oz / 1 l) water or vegetable stock

salt to taste

⅓ cup (3 oz / 90 g) unsalted butter

2 cloves garlic, finely chopped

2 tablespoons chopped fresh flat-leaf (Italian) parsley

freshly ground coarse pepper to taste

❧ Place the salsify in a large bowl and add water to cover. Let stand for 1 hour. Drain and, using a sharp knife or vegetable peeler, peel the roots. Cut into 2-inch (5-cm) lengths.

❧ Place the salsify in a saucepan and add the water with salt to taste or the vegetable stock. Bring to a boil, reduce the heat to medium-low, and simmer until tender, about 45 minutes. Drain well.

❧ In a large frying pan over medium heat, melt the butter. Add the garlic and sauté until softened but not colored, about 15 seconds. Add the salsify and stir to coat with the butter. Allow it only to color lightly, or it might lose its texture. Add the parsley and stir to coat the salsify. Season with salt and pepper. Transfer to a warmed serving dish and serve.

serves 4–6

Var

Salade de Tomates

fresh tomato salad

Nothing reflects the sun-drenched image of Provence more than the ubiquitous tomato, which is at its best in the sunniest season of all. This simple salad from Saint-Raphaël shows off the tomato in its natural state, adorning it with two of the south's other gifts: sweetly pungent basil and rich, golden extra-virgin olive oil.

1 tablespoon small capers, preferably salt packed

4 large tomatoes or 6 plum (Roma) tomatoes, sliced

1 small English (hothouse) cucumber, peeled or unpeeled and sliced

1 celery stalk, sliced

1 small white onion, sliced paper-thin

8–10 small black olives (optional)

leaves from 1 large fresh thyme sprig

¼ cup (2 fl oz/60 ml) extra-virgin olive oil

1½ tablespoons red wine vinegar or sherry vinegar

salt and freshly ground coarse pepper to taste

1 tablespoon chopped fresh flat-leaf (Italian) parsley

⚜ If you are using salt-packed capers, rinse the capers and pat dry.

⚜ Place the tomatoes, cucumber, celery, onion, and capers in a wide, shallow bowl. Scatter the olives, if using, and the thyme over the top. Drizzle with the olive oil and vinegar and season with salt and pepper. (The salad can be made up to this point, covered, and left at room temperature for 2 hours.)

⚜ Just before serving, sprinkle with the parsley. Toss at the table and serve at once.

serves 6

Alpes-de-Haute-Provence

Ragoût de Champignons

mushroom ragout

Nearly everyone in Provence likes to forage for mushrooms. As soon as the spring or autumn rains come, clusters of wild mushrooms seem to push up through the damp soil almost overnight, and the locals head out immediately to gather them for preparations like this ragout. In the autumn, the dish is served alongside pigeons, woodhens, guinea fowl, or quail brought home by hunters living in the rural alpine areas. During the rest of the year, cooks use large cultivated mushrooms in the recipe.

3 lb (1.5 kg) fresh portobello mushrooms or 1½ lb (750 g) each portobello mushrooms and a mixture of fresh wild mushrooms such as cèpe, chanterelle, black trumpet, morel, and sanguin

½ cup (4 fl oz / 125 ml) olive oil, or as needed

4 cloves garlic, finely chopped

3 shallots, finely chopped

⅓ cup (3 fl oz / 80 ml) dry white wine

½ cup (4 fl oz / 125 ml) chicken stock (page 251)

2 tablespoons dried bread crumbs

¼ cup (⅓ oz / 10 g) chopped fresh flat-leaf (Italian) parsley

salt and freshly ground pepper to taste

3 tablespoons unsalted butter

☙ Trim the stems from all the mushrooms, then brush the caps clean. If some of the wild mushrooms are particularly sandy or gritty, rinse briefly in water. Cut the larger mushrooms into halves, quarters, or sixths, depending on their size. The pieces should be about 1½ inches (4 cm) wide at the widest point.

☙ In a large, heavy frying pan (at least 14 inches/ 35 cm in diameter), warm the ½ cup (4 fl oz / 125 ml) olive oil over high heat. Add the mushrooms, reserving any small ones for adding later, and sauté, stirring and tossing continually, until the mushrooms are well glazed and have reduced a little in size, and any liquid they release has evaporated, about 5 minutes. Add the garlic and shallots and sauté for 1 minute until fragrant, adding a little more oil if the pan is dry.

☙ Pour in the wine and stock and deglaze the pan, stirring to scrape up any browned bits on the pan bottom. Bring the liquid to a boil, reduce the heat to medium, cover, and simmer, stirring occasionally, until the liquid reduces a little and the mushrooms are tender, 6–8 minutes longer.

☙ Uncover the pan and sprinkle the bread crumbs over the mushrooms (they will thicken the sauce slightly). Add the parsley, season with salt and pepper, and stir to combine. Remove from the heat and add the butter, stirring until it melts and binds the sauce. Transfer to a warmed serving dish and serve.

serves 6

Seasoned mushroom foragers, armed with buckets, pursue their prey with passion.

Le Mesclun

It is likely that the contemporary idea of *mesclun*, mixed salad leaves picked when small, young, and tender, was born long ago with the custom of foraging for wild greens in the fertile Provençal countryside. The word itself comes from *mescla*, local dialect for "to mix," and although the term *mesclun* has spread far beyond its original borders, this distinctive blend of salad makings remains an integral part of the regional table.

The mix varies with the season, but most combinations include frisée, arugula (rocket), red and green oak leaf lettuce, *mâche* (also known as lamb's lettuce), radicchio, *trévisse* (a small oval leaf reminiscent of arugula), and herbs like chervil, cress, and purslane. In the spring, when gardens are at their most bountiful, *mesclun* may contain up to ten or more different greens.

Mesclun typically appears as the salad course. It is usually dressed with a good olive oil and a fine wine vinegar and nothing more. But *mesclun* has assumed an important second role as well, in which the delicate leaves serve as the base for such familiar first courses as smoked or air-dried meats or broiled goat cheese.

Alpes-de-Haute-Provence
Salade de Pissenlits
dandelion salad

The Provençaux forage for dandelions in the wild for this simple salad, looking for the youngest greens, since the leaves can be bitter and tough. Perhaps this explains why the salad is always served with a hot dressing, which softens the leaves and tempers their flavor. In the dressing, bacon contrasts with the sharp acidity of the vinegar, both of which enhance the peppery dandelion leaves.

If dandelions are unavailable, use other strong-textured leaves, so the greens do not wilt when the hot dressing is poured over the salad. I have substituted the outer dark green leaves of curly endive. The salad also works well with spinach.

6 oz (185 g) young dandelion leaves, tough stems and base ends removed

2 tablespoons blanched hazelnuts (filberts), coarsely chopped (optional)

3 oz (90 g) thick-cut sliced slab bacon, cut crosswise into pieces ½ inch (12 mm) wide

1½ tablespoons sherry vinegar or red wine vinegar

2–3 tablespoons olive oil

salt and freshly ground coarse pepper to taste

❧ Pick over the dandelion leaves, tearing the larger ones in half. Place in a wooden salad bowl. Add the hazelnuts, if using.

❧ In a small frying pan over high heat, fry the bacon until crisp and its fat has been rendered, about 1 minute. Using a slotted spoon, transfer the bacon to the bowl holding the dandelions, leaving the fat in the pan.

❧ Return the pan to high heat, add the vinegar, and swirl the pan or stir with a wooden spoon to pick up the sediment on the bottom.

❧ Pour in as much additional oil as will be necessary to dress the salad, swirl once to heat a little, and then pour the contents of the pan over the salad. Season with salt and pepper, toss, and serve immediately.

serves 6

Alpes-de-Haute-Provence

Pois Chiches Braisés

braised chickpeas

If you do not have time to soak dried chickpeas, use 2 cans (1 lb/500 g each) chickpeas, drained and rinsed. Reduce the cooking time to about 15 minutes.

2 cups (14 oz/440 g) dried chickpeas (garbanzo beans)

5 tablespoons (2½ fl oz/75 ml) olive oil

2 large yellow onions, sliced

3 large fresh tomatoes, peeled, seeded, and chopped

2 cloves garlic, finely chopped

1 tablespoon tomato paste, or as needed

3 fresh thyme or winter savory sprigs

1½ teaspoons chopped fresh rosemary

1 fresh oregano sprig

¼ red bell pepper (capsicum), seeded and cut into short, narrow strips

salt and freshly ground pepper to taste

♛ Pick over the chickpeas, discarding any grit or misshapen chickpeas. Rinse well, place in a bowl, and add water to cover generously. Let stand overnight, changing the water once. Drain.

♛ In a large, heavy saucepan over medium heat, warm the olive oil. Add the onions and sauté until softened, about 2 minutes. Add the tomatoes and garlic and stir briefly. Add the chickpeas, 1 tablespoon tomato paste, herbs, and bell pepper. Season with salt and pepper and add 2 cups (16 fl oz/500 ml) water. Bring to a boil, cover partially, reduce the heat to low, and simmer until the chickpeas are tender, about 45 minutes.

♛ Using a slotted spoon, scoop out the solids from the pan and transfer to a warmed serving bowl. Taste the liquid, and if it is not too salty, raise the heat to high and boil, uncovered, to reduce the liquid. There should only be enough to keep the chickpeas looking moist. Remove the herb sprigs, then adjust the seasoning with salt, pepper, and tomato paste. Spoon over the chickpeas and serve.

serves 6

Alpes-Maritimes

Ratatouille

In France, the word ratatouille, *meaning "tossed" or "tumbled together," not only is the name of this well-known dish, but also is used as an exclamation when one gets into an awkward situation: quelle ratatouille! (what a mess!).*

8–10 tablespoons (4–5 fl oz / 125–160 ml) olive oil

2 yellow onions, chopped

3 large or 4 small zucchini (courgettes), cut into slices ⅜ inch (1 cm) thick

1 large eggplant (aubergine), unpeeled, cut into chunks about the same size as the zucchini slices

5 large tomatoes, peeled, seeded, and chopped

1 green bell pepper (capsicum), seeded and chopped or cut into short, narrow strips

1 red bell pepper (capsicum), seeded and chopped or cut into short, narrow strips

2 or 3 cloves garlic, finely chopped

salt and freshly ground pepper to taste

tomato paste to taste (optional)

In a large frying pan over medium heat, warm 5–6 tablespoons (2½–3 fl oz/75–90 ml) of the olive oil. Add the onions and sauté until softened but not colored, about 1 minute. Add the zucchini and eggplant and sauté until lightly browned, about 2 minutes. The eggplant will absorb much of the oil, so add a little more if necessary. Stir in the tomatoes, bell peppers, and garlic. Cover, reduce the heat to low, and simmer gently until the tomatoes have softened into a chunky sauce and the vegetables are cooked through, about 20 minutes.

Uncover, raise the heat to high, and cook rapidly for 2–3 minutes, stirring constantly, to evaporate any excess liquid. Season with salt and pepper and, if necessary, reinforce the tomato flavor with tomato paste. Spoon into a serving dish and serve immediately, or let cool and stir in a little olive oil before serving.

serves 6

LES DESSERTS

Fresh fruits, raw and unadorned, are the everyday dessert of the family table.

WHEN THE BEEHIVES ARE NEAR bursting with honey, the tree branches are heavy with fruit, and the weather is too hot to do much cooking, it is little wonder that the Provençaux most often turn to cheese and fresh fruit to end a meal.

A perusal of old Provençal cookbooks may amaze sweet-toothed foreigners, for most of them do not even include a chapter for desserts. They are more likely to finish with recipes on how to preserve fruit for when it is no longer in season, how to make jams and conserves—the most uniquely Provençal are watermelon and melon, fig, and pumpkin— and how to make alcohol from fruits.

Homemade liqueurs continue to be a tradition in many households. Walnut liqueur, anisette, orange liqueur made by studding an orange with cloves and leaving it to macerate in alcohol—forty cloves, forty days, instruct the old recipes—and fresh fruit *ratafias,* made by crushing fresh fruit, simmering it with wine, filtering it, and then fortifying it with rum or other spirits, are longtime favorites. Nearly every family also has a large preserving

jar filled with alcohol and fruits for *confiture de vieux garçons* (bachelors' jam). Berries, cherries, apricots, and other fruits of summer are the first to go in the jar. The buckle-down lid is easily opened to accommodate additions as the seasons change. The resulting fruit, fully matured after a year or so, is ladled into glasses along with the fruit-infused alcohol, for the pleasure it gives after a good meal.

Most meals are concluded with just a piece of fresh fruit, however. This is not only the case at family tables. I remember being in restaurants in my teens and finding that inexpensive prix fixe meals usually finished in this simple way. To this day, I blush when I recall the first time I had to eat a pear with a knife and fork. I have vivid memories of that pear tossing and turning while I figured out just how to hold it down with the fork in one hand and struggle my way through peeling and coring it with the knife in the other.

A perfect peach is a thing of beauty. When it is in the first flush of the season, no one would dream of denying nature by doing anything but eating it raw. The first nectarine, the first juicy pear, the magnificent melons of Cavaillon—all are best uncooked. The melons are served with their hollowed-out center doused with port; with Muscat-de-Beaumes-de-Venise, one of the sweet white muscat wines of the region just north of Carpentras in the Vaucluse; or with a local *vin cuit* (fortified "cooked" wine made from must). Only when those exquisite first tastes have been abated does anyone think of cooking the fruits, and then only in a simple manner that will not spoil their inherent beauty. Hence, the penchant for lightly poached fruit desserts.

As with vegetables, combinations designed to create interesting flavors and contrasting textures are preferred: a mix of stone fruits, the first autumn figs poached with the last of summer's raspberries, a perfectly poached pear half baked into puff pastry, or poached quinces sitting between layers of thin, crunchy *tuiles dentelées*. Whole or in segments, poached fruits may be served with ice cream or with a purée of contrasting fruit, such as a fresh raspberry *coulis*. Raspberry purée is also a delight in the cavity of a melon or spooned over lightly

Left: Cherry orchards surround the town of Apt, proudly dubbed the Capitale Mondiale du Fruit Confit, "World Capital of Candied Fruit." **Below:** Pastis, the aniseed-flavored aperitif of the Provençaux, is clear amber in the bottle but turns cloudy and pale when mixed with ice-cold water, the common way it is drunk. **Bottom:** Generations of *confiseurs* in Apt have preserved fresh fruits for year-round enjoyment. The time-honored method calls for repeatedly plunging the fruits in syrup baths of successively higher sugar concentration.

Below: Hefty bars of lavender soap carry the heady perfume of Provence from field to bath. **Bottom:** Trompe l'oeil marzipan fruits fool the eye and tempt the sweet tooth. **Right top:** Visitors to the glassworks of La Verrerie de Biot, in the valley below the village of Biot on the Côte d'Azur, can observe the artisans close-up as they demonstrate their craft. **Right bottom:** Distinctive Biot glassware—*verre à bulles*—is flecked with tiny bubbles to capture the light.

poached Cotignac figs from the Var or small, whole Bartlett (Williams') pears from the Bouches-du-Rhône.

Fresh cheeses are as close to a creamy taste as the Provençaux get with their desserts, for they are not lovers of dairy cream. Brousse du Rove and brousse de Vésuble from the Vésuble Valley northeast of Nice in the Alpes-Maritimes, along with the other well-known fresh cheese of the region, la faiselle de chèvre (also goat), are fresh curd cheeses given to children as dessert. Sometimes they are sprinkled with sugar, but most likely they are treated to a drizzle of honey, and then, when the season permits, with a mixture of berries.

When cheese is offered as a course in its own right, it is served by presenting two or three cheeses, chosen for contrasting effect, on a platter. They arrive before the dessert and after the main dish, while the red wine is still on the table. Local goat and ewe cheeses are the favorites, in all stages of maturity, but this is France and a gourmet feast will call in cheeses of different personality from all over the country.

Cream may not be popular, but ice cream definitely is. Most *pâtissiers* sell house-made ice cream, and occasionally small specialist shops sell nothing but their own production. One day in Sisteron, I saw a sign outside a shop that showed just how *local* ice cream specialties can be. The large square sign announced, with small detachable labels, the flavors of the day, proclaiming a choice of six. Taken together, they epitomized all that is Provençal: *macaron* (almond macaroon), lavender, melon, *marron glacé* (candied chestnut), nougat, and *réglisse* (licorice). Inside the shop, the merchant may have sold an ice cream as everyday as vanilla.

If the local housewife sets herself to cook dessert, the result will most likely be a tart. In Provence, one learns to make shortcrust pastry from one's mother, and it is rare to find a housewife that cannot deliver a satisfying, eye-appealing tart, her filling varying with the fruits of the season. Most common are the single-fruit tarts, but those that combine fruit with nuts are typical for festive occasions.

Top: The Jouvaud family of Carpentras runs a prosperous *confiserie,* where father and son honor the old-fashioned methods of slowly candying fruits in small batches. Connoisseurs especially prize the perfection of the Jouvauds' whole fruits, including melons, pears, and pineapples.
Above: In the orchards of the Vaucluse, bees pollinate the blossoms of cherry, apricot, and almond trees, ensuring a large spring harvest. **Right:** The interplanting of vines and fruit trees is a custom dating from Roman times. As one crop surges with growth, the other takes its seasonal rest.

Interestingly, the French have no generic word for nuts. Considered "fruits of the tree," they are distinguished in the language by the addition of the word *dried (fruits secs).* If one looks closely into their marriage with fresh fruits in Provençal confectionery—*calissons d'Aix,* or nougat—it is not surprising to find that the Alpes-de-Haute-Provence is home to the almond tree, nor that pine nuts have been grown along the littoral since Roman times, and that the French production of both walnuts and hazelnuts (filberts) is centered here, too.

Given the fact that the housewife can make her own tarts, her own bavarian creams, her own crepes, and even her own soufflés if she is a gourmet cook, it is interesting to reflect on just how often people turn to the local *pâtissier.* The *pâtissier* adds a little luxury to the Sunday meal or any larger, more festive occasion. Something from a shop is considered better than what can be made within the family, and a large boxed cake or decorative tart will always find its place at the table. Most *pâtissiers* also have their own specialty to tempt buyers. One in Arles displays no less than eighteen differently flavored large loaves of fruit-studded nougat in the window.

Regional cake specialties abound as well. Carpentras is known for *La Christine,* a jelly-roll-shaped cake enveloping *fruits confits* (candied fruits) mixed with an almond stuffing, while Tarascon has its *pan pèri* (pear bread). *La Tropézienne,* a brioche-based pastry filled with pastry cream, originated in the 1950s at Alexandre Micka's *pâtisserie* in the Place de la Mairie in Saint-Tropez and is now seen everywhere along the coast. Found at carnival time in Nice, carnival fritters *(les ganses)* are deep-fried ribbons of shortcrust pastry that have been twisted and tied into loose bows. In late December and for Christmas, everyone buys *pompe à l'huile,* also known as *pompe de Noël,* an olive oil–based disklike brioche. By Twelfth Night, it is replaced by a *galette des rois,* a ring-shaped brioche topped with *fruits confits,* which continues to sell until the end of January. The candied fruits identify it as a product of the south and very different from the puff pastry, almond-frangipane-filled *galettes des rois* of northern France.

Vaucluse

Tarte Moelleuse aux Pommes

apple tart with almonds and pine nuts

Since the days of the Roman Empire, pine nuts have been harvested along the coastline of Provence, and since medieval times, Digne and Aix-en-Provence have been at the heart of a thriving almond industry. Here, the two are combined in a simple apple tart.

PASTRY

1¼ cups (6½ oz/200 g) all-purpose (plain) flour

7 tablespoons (3½ oz/105 g) unsalted butter, at room temperature, cut into small pieces

1 egg yolk

3 tablespoons superfine (caster) sugar

3 tablespoons water

ALMOND CREAM

6 tablespoons (3 fl oz/90 ml) milk

1 whole egg, plus 1 egg yolk

2 tablespoons granulated sugar

2 tablespoons cornstarch (cornflour)

½ teaspoon vanilla extract (essence)

3 tablespoons unsalted butter, at room temperature

½ cup (2 oz/60 g) ground almonds

¼ cup (1 oz/30 g) confectioners' (icing) sugar

1 tablespoon dark rum

¼ cup (2 oz/60 g) fig or apricot jam

3 tablespoons water

1 large Granny Smith apple, peeled, cored, and cut into ½-inch (12-mm) dice

1 cup (5 oz/155 g) pine nuts

♛ To make the pastry, in a food processor, combine the flour and butter and pulse until uniformly blended. Add the egg yolk, superfine sugar, and 1 tablespoon of the water and pulse until the pastry gathers in a mass on the blade, adding some of the remaining 2 tablespoons water if the mixture is too dry. Transfer to a floured work surface and form into a ball. Cover the pastry with plastic wrap and refrigerate for at least 30 minutes or for up to 2 hours.

♛ On a floured work surface, roll out the pastry into a round 12 inches (30 cm) in diameter and ⅛ inch (3 mm) thick. Drape it around the rolling pin and transfer to an 11-inch (28-cm) tart pan with a removable bottom. Ease the pastry into the bottom and sides of the pan and make a small lip of pastry at the top edge. Cut away the excess pastry, then use your fingers to round the top edge attractively.

♛ To make the almond cream, pour the milk into a saucepan and heat over medium heat until small bubbles appear along the edges of the pan. Remove from the heat. In a bowl, whisk together the whole egg and egg yolk until well blended. Whisk in the granulated sugar, and then whisk in 1 tablespoon of the cornstarch. Pour about half of the hot milk over the egg mixture while whisking constantly. Then pour the egg-milk mixture into the saucepan holding the remaining milk, place over medium heat, and cook, stirring constantly, until the mixture thickens and comes to a boil, 1½–2 minutes. Remove from the heat, stir in the vanilla, and immediately pour back into the bowl and set aside to cool.

♛ Preheat an oven to 375°F (190°C).

♛ In another bowl, using a wooden spoon, beat the butter until creamy. Stir in the ground almonds. Using a fine-mesh sieve, sift in the confectioners' sugar and then stir to mix. Whisk in the rum and the remaining 1 tablespoon cornstarch. Fold the cooled custard into the almond mixture until fully combined.

♛ In a small saucepan, combine the fig or apricot jam and the water. Place over low heat and stir constantly until the jam dissolves and is fluid. Brush a thin layer of the dissolved jam on the bottom of the pastry-lined pan. Spread the almond cream over the jam layer, smoothing the top to cover evenly. Spread the diced apple over the custard layer, again distributing evenly. Press the apple pieces lightly so they sit well in the custard, but do not sink. Cover the entire surface with the pine nuts, again making sure they adhere but not immersing them in the cream.

♛ Place the tart in the oven and immediately reduce the heat to 350°F (180°C). Bake until the top is golden, about 40 minutes, rotating the pan 180 degrees after about 30 minutes to ensure even browning. Transfer to a rack and let cool completely. Remove the pan sides, slide the tart onto a serving plate, and serve at room temperature, cut into wedges.

serves 8

Les Calissons d'Aix

For more than four centuries, the *calisson d'Aix* has been the unrivaled champion of Provençal confectionery. Nowadays, the diamond-shaped sweetmeat is manufactured in fewer than half a dozen local factories, although a handful of artisans, laboring in spaces behind their family *pâtisseries,* continue to make *calissons* by hand in the time-honored manner.

Georges Touzet is a fourth-generation *pâtissier* from Maison Béchard on Cours Mirabeau, the beautiful plane tree–lined main street of Aix-en-Provence. Each day, Georges and his octogenarian father, Raymond, oversee the production of 100 to 110 pounds (50 to 60 kg) of the classic confection, shaping them in cast-iron molds that hold just thirty-six at a time.

Following rules that guarantee both quality and regional integrity, the Touzets painstakingly build the *calissons.* First they prepare the traditional paste center, a mixture of ground blanched almonds, at least 40 percent of which must come from Mediterranean trees; the famed candied Presco melon of Apt; candied orange peel; honey; and orange flower water. The almond mixture is molded upon a thin rice-paper base, the top is lightly brushed with apricot jam, and then a snow-white fondant is applied. Once the finished confections are slipped from their molds, they are briefly dried and then carefully packed for sale.

Vaucluse
Figues Sèches au Marzipan
figs stuffed with marzipan

When people think of the foods associated with Provence, the olive surely comes first to mind. Second would likely be garlic, though in my opinion it is the fig. Fig trees are nearly as dominant in the landscape as olive trees. The recipe for these little marzipan-stuffed delicacies from the papal city of Avignon includes two versions, a moister one for use as a dessert and a sweeter and stickier one for use as a sweetmeat to accompany coffee.

3 cups (24 fl oz/750 ml) water

1 cup (8 oz/250 g) sugar

3 whole cloves

3 orange zest slices

18–20 dried figs, moister if for dessert and drier if for a sweetmeat

4 tablespoons (2 fl oz/60 ml) Cognac or Armagnac

1 package (6½ oz/200 g) marzipan paste

In a small saucepan over medium heat, combine the water, sugar, cloves, and orange zest. Bring to a boil, stirring to dissolve the sugar. Add the figs and 3 tablespoons of the Cognac or Armagnac. Reduce the heat to as low as possible and simmer gently for 2 hours to plump the figs. Let cool for 30–45 minutes.

Remove the figs from the cooking liquid, reserving the liquid. Using a small knife, make a slit at the center of each fig. Using a small spoon or your fingers, press a scant teaspoon of marzipan into each fig, smoothing the surface of the marzipan. Pinch the slit closed, but leave a little marzipan visible. Return the figs to the liquid in the saucepan. Stir in the remaining 1 tablespoon Cognac or Armagnac, mixing well, and then stir the figs to coat them with the liquid. Using a slotted spoon, transfer the figs to a bowl.

To serve the figs as a dessert, boil the liquid in the pan, stirring often, until it is a good sauce consistency, then pour over the figs. To use the figs as a sweetmeat, reduce the liquid to a thick syrup, stirring constantly. Transfer the figs and syrup to a bowl or jar, cover, and store in the refrigerator for up to 4 weeks. Remove from the refrigerator at least 1 hour before serving.

serves 6 as a dessert, or 10 as a sweetmeat

Bouches-du-Rhône

Ratafia de Framboises aux Beaumes-de-Venise

raspberry liqueur

As the primary port of southern France, Marseilles has served as an entry point for people of far-flung départements *such as Martinique and Guadeloupe in the Caribbean, who introduced their food traditions to Provence. Ratafia, a rum-based liqueur, originated from a Creole drink said to have been imbibed after a business agreement was reached—literally,* rata fiat, *"let the deal be sealed." Muscat-de-Beaumes-de-Venise, the most renowned sweet wine of the area, is made from muscatel grapes and is excellent for ratafia. Another sweet wine may be used.*

1 lb (500 g) raspberries

1⅔ cups (12 oz/375 g) superfine (caster) sugar

2 cups (16 fl oz/500 ml) Muscat de Beaumes-de-Venise or other sparkling white wine

5 tablespoons (3 fl oz/80 ml) light rum

☙ In a saucepan, combine the raspberries and sugar. Place the saucepan in a larger saucepan and add hot water to the larger pan to reach halfway up the sides of the smaller pan. Place over medium-high heat and bring the water to a simmer. Reduce the heat to low and simmer gently until the raspberries have liquefied and their juice is syrupy, about 1¼ hours, adding hot water to the larger pan as needed to maintain the original water level. Remove the inner saucepan from the pan holding the water, let cool, cover, and refrigerate overnight.

☙ The following day, strain the raspberries through a medium-mesh sieve, pressing against the contents of the sieve with the back of a wooden spoon to extract the juices. You need 2 cups (16 fl oz/500 ml) juice. Mix in the wine, stir in the rum, and then strain through a fine-mesh sieve.

☙ Sterilize two 1-pt (16–fl oz/500-ml) bottles or carafes by washing well in hot, soapy water, rinsing well, and then boiling in fresh water to cover for about 5 minutes. Drain. Pour the strained liqueur into the sterilized containers, cover, and store in a cool, dark place or refrigerate for up to 1 month.

makes 1 qt (1 l)

Vaucluse

Pêches Gratinées au Pain d'Épices

gratinéed peaches with honey cake

This dessert is ideal at the beginning of the peach season, when the fruits are more likely to need cooking. Pain d'épices is a soft, gingerbread-like loaf cake sold internationally by Dutch companies under the name "honey cake." Each cake weighs about 1 pound (500 g). If it is unavailable, pound cake, plain or flavored with lemon, nuts, or dried fruit, may be substituted. Nectarines or pears can be used in place of the peaches. Peel the pears prior to cooking and allow up to 15 minutes of poaching for most varieties, 20 minutes for Bosc pears.

4 cups (32 fl oz/1 l) water

1½ cups (12 oz/375 g) granulated sugar

6 medium-ripe peaches

½ loaf pain d'épices *(see note)* or pound cake

2 egg yolks

2 tablespoons brown sugar, plus more for topping

1 cup (8 fl oz/250 ml) heavy (double) cream, whipped until stiff

1 tablespoon ground toasted hazelnuts (filberts) *(page 248)*

1½–2 tablespoons amaretto or peach liqueur

6 tablespoons (2 oz/60 g) hazelnuts (filberts), toasted and chopped

⚜ Select a saucepan large enough to hold the peaches snugly. Combine the water and granulated sugar in the pan and place over high heat, stirring constantly to dissolve the granulated sugar before the water comes to a boil. Add the peaches (they should be fully immersed) and bring to a boil over high heat. Reduce the heat to low and simmer, uncovered, until the peaches are just tender, 5–8 minutes. Do not overcook, or the peaches will be difficult to slice neatly.

⚜ Drain the peaches and, when cool enough to handle, peel, halve, and remove the pits. Cut the halves lengthwise into slices ¼ inch (6 mm) thick.

⚜ Preheat a broiler (griller) or preheat an oven to 450°F (230°C). Roughly crumble the *pain d'épices* or pound cake onto the bottom of individual dessert dishes, ideally small oval or round white porcelain dishes. The dishes must be flameproof or ovenproof. Arrange the peach slices concentrically, overlapping the slices slightly.

⚜ In a bowl, beat together the egg yolks and 2 tablespoons brown sugar until creamy. Fold in the whipped cream and the ground hazelnuts. Flavor to taste with the liqueur. Spread the mixture thickly over the peach slices, leaving a border ½–¾ inch (12 mm–2 cm) wide uncovered.

⚜ Sprinkle the cream topping with the chopped hazelnuts and then with a light coating of brown sugar. Slip under the broiler until the tops are lightly browned, about 1 minute, or bake in the oven for 2–3 minutes. Serve at once.

serves 4

Sun-kissed peaches of the Vaucluse fill summer market baskets.

Alpes-Maritimes

Feuilleté de Poires

pears in puff pastry

The pear halves look beautiful framed in their puff pastry casings. These pastries are usually served with a custard, often one perfumed with lavender (right).

3 pears, with stems intact

2 cups (1 lb/500 g) sugar

4 cups (32 fl oz/1 l) water

3 tablespoons sweet white wine

1 vanilla bean, split lengthwise

6 teaspoons marzipan or 6 pitted dates or prunes (optional)

¾ lb (375 g) puff pastry, homemade (page 249) or purchased

1 egg beaten with 1 tablespoon milk

¼ cup (2 oz/60 g) apricot jam

3 tablespoons water

❦ Peel the pears, leaving the stems intact. In a saucepan large enough to hold the pears snugly, combine the sugar, 4 cups (32 fl oz/1 l) water, wine, and vanilla. Bring to a boil over high heat, stirring to dissolve the sugar. Add the pears, reduce the heat to low, and simmer until the pears are tender, 15–20 minutes. Let the pears cool in the liquid, then transfer to paper towels to drain well. Split each pear in half lengthwise, splitting the stem, if possible. Remove the cores gently without disturbing the stems. If you like, place 1 teaspoon of the marzipan or a date or prune in the hollow left in each half after the removal of the core.

❦ Make a template by tracing a pear half, including its stem, on a piece of cardboard. Cut out the shape, leaving an extra ¾ inch (2 cm) outside the tracing.

❦ Preheat an oven to 400°F (200°C).

❦ On a floured work surface, roll out the puff pastry into a large rectangle no more than ⅛ inch (3 mm) thick. Using the template, cut out 6 pieces of pastry and transfer to 2 ungreased baking sheets. Dry the pear halves well on paper towels and place a pear half, rounded side up, in the center of each piece of pastry. Brush the exposed pastry edges with the egg-milk mixture. Place 1 sheet in the oven and bake, rotating the sheet 180 degrees after 15 minutes to ensure even coloration, until the pastry is puffed up and golden brown, 20–25 minutes.

❦ Meanwhile, in a small saucepan, combine the apricot jam and 3 tablespoons water. Place over low heat and stir constantly until the jam dissolves.

❦ Remove the pastries from the oven, slide onto a rack, and brush with half of the apricot glaze. Repeat the process with the second baking sheet of pastries. Serve warm or at room temperature.

serves 6

Alpes-de-Haute-Provence

Crème Anglaise à la Lavande

lavender custard

This perfumed custard, an edible reminder of the purple fields around Sault, the center of the French lavender industry, can be served with the Pears in Puff Pastry (left), Apricot Flan (page 228), or Poached Quinces (page 238).

2 cups (16 fl oz/500 ml) milk

4 egg yolks

½ cup (4 oz/125 g) sugar

1 tablespoon pesticide-free fresh or dried lavender flowers, without stems

❦ Pour the milk into a saucepan and place over medium heat until small bubbles appear along the edges of the pan. In a bowl, beat together the egg yolks and sugar until creamy. Pour about ½ cup (4 fl oz/125 ml) of the hot milk into the egg mixture while whisking constantly. Return the milk-egg mixture to the saucepan and stir constantly over medium heat with a wooden spoon until the mixture thickens and lightly coats the back of the spoon, about 1 minute. Do not allow it to boil. An instant-read thermometer inserted into the custard should read 180°F (82°C).

❦ Remove from the heat and immediately stir in the lavender flowers. Pour into a pitcher, cover with plastic placed directly on the surface to prevent a skin from forming, and refrigerate overnight.

❦ The next day, pour the custard through a sieve. Return the custard to the pitcher, cover with clean plastic wrap again pressed directly on the surface, and refrigerate for up to 2 days before serving.

serves 8

Vaucluse

Tarte aux Mendiants

fruit and nut tart

Raisins, dried figs, hazelnuts, and almonds symbolically represent the mendicant religious orders at the Christmas ritual of le Gros Souper (page 242) and give this tart its name. The tart has a wonderful chewy consistency, and although it is popular at Christmastime, it can be served for special occasions throughout the year.

SHORTCRUST PASTRY

1¼ cups (6½ oz/200 g) all-purpose (plain) flour

7 tablespoons (3½ oz/105 g) unsalted butter, at room temperature, cut into small pieces

pinch of salt

1 egg yolk

1 tablespoon honey

3 or 4 drops vanilla extract (essence) (optional)

3 tablespoons water

FILLING

1 cup (4 oz/125 g) plus 2 tablespoons ground walnuts, plus ¾ cup (3 oz/90 g) walnut pieces

½ cup (3½ oz/105 g) plus 1 tablespoon firmly packed brown sugar

1 whole egg, plus 3 egg whites

1½ teaspoons cornstarch (cornflour)

½ cup (2½ oz/75 g) hazelnuts (filberts), toasted and skinned (page 248)

½ cup (2½ oz/75 g) blanched almonds

⅓ cup (2 oz/60 g) unsalted roasted cashews

3½ tablespoons pine nuts

3½ tablespoons blanched unsalted pistachio nuts

2 tablespoons raisins, coarsely chopped

2 dried figs, chopped

1 tablespoon candied orange peel

1 tablespoon candied lemon peel

3 tablespoons lavender or other honey, heated

❦ To make the pastry by hand, mound the flour on a work surface. Make a well in the center and add the butter, salt, egg yolk, honey, and vanilla (if using). Using your fingertips, mix the ingredients in the well, then begin to incorporate the flour. When the mixture has the consistency of coarse meal, add 1½ tablespoons of the water and continue to blend and

encourage the pastry into a ball. Add the remaining 1½ tablespoons water as needed to create a workable dough. Taking care not to knead in too much elasticity, lightly flour the work surface and push the ball of pastry forward and away from you with the heel of your hand, then gather into a ball. Repeat 2 or 3 times, stopping as soon as the pastry has a light springiness. Cover the ball of pastry with plastic wrap and refrigerate for at least 30 minutes or for up to 2 hours.

❦ To make the pastry in a food processor, combine the flour, butter, and salt in the processor and pulse until uniformly blended. Add the egg yolk, honey, vanilla (if using), and 1 tablespoon of the water and continue to pulse until the pastry gathers in a mass on the blade, gradually adding the remaining 2 tablespoons water if the mixture is too dry. Transfer to a floured work surface, form into a ball, and refrigerate as directed for the hand method.

❦ Preheat an oven to 375°F (190°C).

❦ On a floured work surface, roll out the pastry into a round 12 inches (30 cm) in diameter and ⅛ inch (3 mm) thick. Drape it around the rolling pin and transfer to an 11-inch (28-cm) tart pan with a removable bottom. Ease the pastry into the bottom and sides of the pan and make a small lip of pastry at the top edge. Use the rolling pin to cut away the excess pastry, then use your fingers to round the top edge attractively. Set aside.

❦ To make the filling, in a saucepan over low heat, combine the ground walnuts, brown sugar, whole egg, 1 egg white, and cornstarch. Stir until the mixture is warm but not hot. Transfer to a bowl.

❦ In a bowl, using a whisk or a handheld electric mixer, beat the remaining 2 egg whites until stiff peaks form. Using a rubber spatula, fold the egg whites into the ground nut mixture. Spread the mixture evenly in the pastry-lined tart pan.

❦ Bake the tart until the mixture has firmed slightly, 15–20 minutes. Remove from the oven and, while still hot, cover with the walnut pieces, hazelnuts, almonds, cashews, pine nuts, pistachios, raisins, figs, and orange and lemon peels, distributing them evenly and covering the surface completely. Return the tart to the oven and bake until golden and a knife inserted into the center comes out moist but clean, 15–20 minutes longer.

❦ Transfer to a rack, immediately drizzle the top evenly with the honey, and let cool. Remove the pan rim and slide the tart onto a serving plate. Serve at room temperature, cut into wedges.

serves 8–10

Alpes-de-Haute-Provence
Oranges Épicées

hot spiced oranges

This easy dessert highlights the wonderful navel oranges of the Mediterranean coastline. The French name comes from the cinnamon-and-clove-scented rum that spices the oranges.

½ cup (3 oz/90 g) dried apricots, halved and soaked in 1 cup (8 fl oz/250 ml) boiling water for 30 minutes

5 tablespoons (2½ fl oz/75 ml) dark rum

3 or 4 whole cloves

2 small orange zest pieces

1 cinnamon stick, about 3 inches (7.5 cm) long

pinch of ground cinnamon

small piece of star anise

5 tablespoons (2½ oz/75 g) sugar

5 navel oranges

❦ Place the apricots and their soaking water in a saucepan and add the rum, cloves, orange zest, cinnamon stick, ground cinnamon, and star anise. Spoon the sugar over the mixture, then place the pan over medium heat. Bring to a simmer, stirring until the sugar dissolves, then continue to simmer until the apricots are just tender, 8–10 minutes. Remove from the heat and set aside. (This can be done up to 12 hours before serving.)

❦ Working with 1 orange at a time, and using a sharp knife, cut a thin slice off the top and bottom of the orange to expose the flesh. Stand the orange upright and thickly slice off the peel in strips, following the contour of the orange and removing all the white pith and membrane. Cut the oranges crosswise into slices ¼ inch (6 mm) thick. Place the orange slices in a large bowl.

❦ Return the saucepan holding the apricot mixture to medium heat and bring to just under a boil. Remove from the heat and pour over the orange slices. Serve immediately directly from the bowl or in individual bowls.

serves 6

Les Fruits Frais

Provence is so richly blessed with fruit trees, plants, and vines that it almost single-handedly produces all the fruits that go into the jams, jellies, breads, and desserts of France. With the arrival of spring comes the first of the plums, including the Greengage and the Mirabelle. April brings the joy of the sweet-smelling Cavaillon melons. Stone fruits lead into summer, especially the sun-kissed peaches, apricots, and nectarines of the Vaucluse and the Var.

The warmest months are also the time of the cherry harvest, centered at Brignoles and the Gapeau Valley. Strawberries abound—those of Carpentras always the first—as do raspberries, loganberries, and "fruits of the forest" (mulberries, blueberries, and red, black, and white currants). Sometimes the berries are wild, but now most are cultivated for availability in the markets, making mixed berries one of the most anticipated summer pleasures of the Provençal table.

By autumn, grapes are plump with juice, and the ubiquitous fig—as representative of Provence as the piercingly noisy cicada—becomes the fruit to eat raw, poached, and later dried. The season sees plums being transformed into prunes as well, including the beloved *violettes* of Brignoles. Fall is also the time for apples, and the Bouches-du-Rhône is second only to the better-known Normandy in their production. But it is second to no region when it comes to pears, boasting the largest harvest in the country.

As the weather cools, citrus fruits appear. From Hyères east along the Côte d'Azur—the citrus belt of France—lemons, grapefruits, and oranges flourish, and connoisseurs seek out the tangerines of Cagnes and Cannes, the mandarins of Antibes, and the wonderful bitter oranges of Nice. In Grasse, workers extract orange flower water from orange blossoms, a flavoring used in many local pastries.

This bounty is critical to the French meal. Without question, fresh, ripe fruits, eaten raw and unadorned, are the customary dessert of the Midi. In fact, only when the hardworking cook has a bit of time is this rich harvest fashioned into something more—a simple fresh or cooked compote—for an everyday meal.

Vaucluse

Croûte d'Abricots

apricot flan

From Saint-Saturnin-les-Apt, deep in the country that produces the best stone fruits in France, comes this interesting "almost-cake." Although the consistency is a little firmer than that of a clafoutis, the result is not unlike that well-known rustic dessert of the Limousin. The addition of 2 tablespoons all-purpose (plain) flour and ½ teaspoon baking powder to the cream will turn the mixture into a cake, but try it this authentic way first. The combination of luscious fresh apricots and lavender flowers is totally seductive.

about 2 teaspoons unsalted butter, plus 6 table-spoons (3 oz/90 g), melted and cooled

confectioners' (icing) sugar for dusting tart dish, plus 3 tablespoons

1¾ cups (7 oz/220 g) ground almonds

3 eggs

pinch of salt

¼ cup (3 oz/90 g) lavender honey

1 teaspoon pesticide-free fresh lavender flowers, without stems

12 large apricots, halved, pitted, then each half halved again

♛ Preheat an oven to 350°F (180°C). Butter a 9-inch (23-cm) fluted white porcelain tart dish or a metal tart pan with about 2 teaspoons butter. Dust with the confectioners' (icing) sugar and tap out the excess.

♛ In a bowl, combine the ground almonds, eggs, 6 tablespoons (3 oz/90 g) melted butter, 3 table-spoons confectioners' sugar, salt, honey, and lavender flowers and stir to mix well. Spread the mixture in the bottom of the prepared dish or pan.

♛ Arrange the apricots in concentric circles on top of the almond mixture, pressing lightly to embed them but leaving their edges protruding above the surface. Bake the flan until it is bubbling and the edges of the apricots are brown, about 45 minutes, rotating the dish 180 degrees after 20 minutes and then again after another 15 to ensure even browning.

♛ Transfer to a rack and use a paper towel to blot up some of the moisture from the top of the flan. Let cool and serve warm or at room temperature.

serves 8

Alpes-Maritimes

Madeleines au Miel

honey madeleines

In Provence, the rich, golden interiors of madeleines, one of the classic small cakes of France, are made more succulent by the addition of a choice local honey. My preference is honey from orange flowers, augmented with a little grated orange zest. Lavender honey is the most recognizably Provençal of all.

5 tablespoons (3 oz / 90 g) unsalted butter, at room temperature, plus melted butter for greasing molds

scant ⅓ cup (2½ oz / 75 g) superfine (caster) sugar

2 teaspoons light brown sugar

pinch of salt

1 tablespoon honey (see note)

½ cup plus 2 tablespoons (3 oz / 90 g) all-purpose (plain) flour

scant 1 teaspoon baking powder

2 eggs

1 teaspoon grated orange zest

confectioners' (icing) sugar (optional)

✽ In a bowl, using a wooden spoon, beat the 5 tablespoons (3 oz / 90 g) butter until creamy. Beat in the superfine and brown sugars. Stir in the salt and honey. Sift the flour and baking powder into a bowl. Add the eggs to the butter mixture one at a time, beating well after each addition. Then add the flour mixture and orange zest.

✽ Preheat an oven to 375°F (190°C). Brush a tray of 12 standard madeleine molds or 24 miniature molds with melted butter and place in the refrigerator for 2 minutes. Brush again with melted butter and coat with flour, tapping out the excess.

✽ Spoon the batter evenly into the prepared molds; do not overfill. Bake until golden, 6–7 minutes for miniature madeleines, 8–9 minutes for standard. Let rest for a few seconds, and then invert the pan and tap on a work surface. Transfer the madeleines to a rack to cool. If desired, dust with confectioners' sugar.

makes 12 large or 24 miniature madeleines

Var

Petits Pots de Crème
à l'Orange

little pots of orange cream

I have had petits pots de crème all over France made with every flavor from vanilla to passionfruit to chocolate. But there are none I remember more vividly than those I ate under an orange tree in full fruit, on the patio of a friend's house in Saint-Raphaël. This town is said to have been a holiday resort since Roman times and in the mid-nineteenth century was the haunt of such writers as Alexandre Dumas.

This dessert is such a popular one that French porcelain factories make dainty individual pots with lids expressly designed for the cream. Ramekins that hold a scant ½ cup (3½ fl oz/105 ml) are an alternative. A few small orange segments can be placed alongside each serving, or the pots may be served with Caramelized Oranges with Orange Flower Water (page 244).

1 orange

2 cups (16 fl oz/500 ml) milk

6 tablespoons (3 oz/90 g) sugar

3 eggs

few drops of vanilla extract (essence)

boiling water, as needed

1 cup (8 fl oz/250 ml) water

1 cup (8 fl oz/250 ml) heavy (double) cream, whipped until stiff (optional)

♛ Using a small knife with a flexible blade, remove the zest from the orange in strips ¾ inch (2 cm) wide and as long as possible. Reserve 3 of the strips to infuse the custard. Turn the other strips over and, using a small, sharp knife, remove any residual white pith. Cut the strips into fine julienne for the garnish and set aside. (Reserve the orange flesh for another use.)

♛ Pour the milk into a saucepan and add the reserved zest strips. Let stand for 30 minutes.

♛ Preheat an oven to 400°F (200°C). Select a baking dish large enough to hold 8 small pots or ramekins (see note). Set the molds in the dish.

♛ Add 4 tablespoons (2 oz/60 g) of the sugar to the saucepan holding the milk, place over medium heat, and stir to dissolve the sugar. Bring just to a boil and remove from the heat.

♛ In a bowl, whisk the eggs until blended. Pour half of the hot milk over the eggs, whisking constantly.

Then pour the egg-milk mixture into the saucepan of milk, place over medium heat, and cook, stirring constantly, until the mixture coats the back of a spoon, about 2 minutes. Do not let boil. An instant-read thermometer inserted into the custard should read 180°F (82°C).

♛ Add the vanilla, whisk to blend, and then quickly pour the custard through a sieve into the pots or ramekins, dividing it evenly. Discard the zest strips. Place the baking dish on an extended oven rack, add boiling water to the dish to reach nearly to the rims of the pots or ramekins, and carefully slide the rack into the oven.

♛ Bake the custards until set, about 20 minutes. To test, insert a metal skewer into the center of a custard; it should come out clean. Transfer the baking dish to a work surface and remove the pots or ramekins. Let cool and refrigerate until set, 2–3 hours.

♛ Meanwhile, place the reserved julienned zest in a small saucepan with the 1 cup (8 fl oz/250 ml) water. Add the remaining 2 tablespoons sugar and bring to a boil, stirring to dissolve the sugar. Boil rapidly until the zest becomes flexible and shiny from the sugar, about 2 minutes. Drain and spread out on a plate.

♛ To serve, top each custard with whipped cream, if using, and a few strands of the julienned zest.

serves 8

Les Fruits Confits

Candying fruit is the art of gently bathing flawless fruits in up to a dozen basins of successively more dense sugar syrup until the original water content of the fruits has been replaced with the sugary liquid. Apt, in the Lubéron, is now the world capital of this six-centuries-old art, closely followed by Carpentras and Oraison, both important centers with a reputation for high-quality handmade *fruits confits*.

But the Provençaux love to champion artisans who make things by hand, where the eye, rather than the machine, is in charge, and the Jouvauds are an excellent example of such an artisanal tradition. Each year, the family produces more than four thousand pounds (2,000 kg) of the preserved fruits in its small *pâtisserie* in Carpentras. They create some of the most beautifully symmetrical candied fruits imaginable, each revealing no change in texture when cut through to the center, each firm and with no crystallization. Frédéric Jouvaud, with his "retired" father, Gilbert, and son Pierre by his side, uses only fruit from his *département*, except for the large Corsican melons and whole pineapples he loves to spend up to four months completing.

Alpes-Maritimes

Nougat Glacé aux Figues et Gingembre

iced terrine of fig and ginger

The frozen terrine may be served as is, but looks beautiful garnished with fresh berries, orange slices, or fresh figs or cherries.

7 tablespoons (3½ oz / 105 g) superfine (caster) sugar

5 tablespoons (2½ fl oz / 75 ml) water

4 egg yolks

6 plump, moist dried figs, each cut into 3 or 4 pieces

2 tablespoons candied ginger, coarsely chopped

1 tablespoon each candied orange peel and candied lemon peel

6 candied red cherries, halved

⅓ cup (2 oz / 60 g) pistachios

½ teaspoon ground cinnamon

¼ teaspoon ground cardamom

1¼ cups (10 fl oz / 310 ml) heavy (double) cream, whipped

2 tablespoons kirsch

In a saucepan over medium heat, combine the sugar and water. Heat, stirring to dissolve the sugar, then raise the heat to high and bring to a boil. Boil without stirring until the mixture reaches 240°F (116°C), the soft-ball stage, on a candy thermometer.

Meanwhile, in a bowl, beat the egg yolks with a handheld electric mixer. When the sugar mixture is ready, pour onto the eggs in a slow stream while beating constantly. Beat until the mixture has cooled and has doubled in volume. Fold in the figs, ginger, citrus peels, cherries, pistachios, and spices, then carefully fold in the whipped cream. Fold in the kirsch.

Pour the mixture into a 4-cup (32–fl oz/1-l) rectangular ceramic terrine or loaf pan. Cover with plastic wrap and freeze for at least 8 hours or up to 4 days. Run a knife blade around the sides of the mold and invert the mold onto a plate. Soak a kitchen towel with hot water, wring out, place on the bottom of the mold to release the nougat, and lift off the mold. Return to the freezer to refirm. Cut into slices ½ inch (12 mm) thick and serve.

serves 8–10

Alpes-de-Haute-Provence

Pain Perdu

bread and butter pudding

Meaning "lost" or "hidden" bread, pain perdu was originally invented as a way to use up stale bread. It has become such a favorite, however, that it rivals only crème caramel *as the most popular cooked family dessert in France. This real country household recipe comes from Digne, northeast of Marseilles. Other flavors of jam may be used, but raspberry is probably the most common. More sophisticated versions substitute a raspberry coulis (sauce of puréed sweetened raspberries) for serving as a sauce at the table.*

about 20 thick slices day-old bread from a square-cornered loaf

⅓ cup (3 oz/90 g) unsalted butter, at room temperature

about 5 tablespoons (3 oz/90 g) raspberry jam or red currant jelly

2 cups (16 fl oz/500 ml) milk

1 vanilla bean, split lengthwise

3 whole eggs, plus 2 egg yolks

½ cup (4 oz/125 g) plus 2 tablespoons granulated sugar

boiling water, as needed

confectioners' (icing) sugar (optional)

♛ Preheat a broiler (griller). Spread 1 side of each bread slice with butter and cut in half on the diagonal. Working in batches if necessary, arrange the slices, buttered side up, on a baking sheet and slip under the broiler close to the heat source to brown. This should take only 30–45 seconds. Remove from the broiler and turn the oven to 400°F (200°C).

♛ Arrange the toasted slices, buttered side up, points of the triangles facing the same direction, and each slice slightly overlapping another, in a rectangular gratin dish 12 inches (30 cm) long and 8 inches (20 cm) wide. The dish should hold 2 or 3 slices across and 6–8 slices along the length. As the dish is being filled, spoon or spread a little raspberry jam or red currant jelly here and there among the slices.

♛ Pour the milk into a saucepan, add the vanilla bean, and place over medium heat until small bubbles appear along the edges of the pan. Remove from the heat and let cool. While the milk is cooling, in a bowl, whisk together the whole eggs, egg yolks, and granulated sugar until creamy and the mixture lightens.

♛ Remove the vanilla bean from the cooled milk and discard. Whisk the milk into the egg mixture until well blended, then pour it over the bread slices.

♛ Place the gratin dish in a large baking pan and add hot water to the pan to reach halfway up the sides. Place the pan on an extended oven rack, add boiling water to the pan to reach almost to the rim of the gratin dish, and carefully slide the oven rack into the oven.

♛ Bake the pudding for 5 minutes, then, using a wide metal spatula, press on the bread slices to embed them in the custard fully before it sets. Continue to bake until the custard is set and the top is golden, about 25 minutes longer.

♛ Carefully remove the baking pan from the oven and let stand for 30 minutes. Remove the gratin dish from the pan. If desired, dust the top of the pudding with confectioners' sugar before serving.

serves 6

Vaucluse

Granité de Vin Rouge aux Fruits Rouges

red wine granita with berries

Summer in Provence would not be summer without fresh berries. I've rarely tasted strawberries as pungent as the small, vividly colored berries from Carpentras, which are always labeled as such. Here they are mixed with other berries atop a cool granita.

GRANITA

¾ cup (6 oz / 185 g) sugar

¾ cup (6 fl oz / 180 ml) water

2 cups (16 fl oz / 500 ml) dry red wine

juice of 1 orange

about 4 cups (1 lb / 500 g) mixed berries such as raspberries, blueberries, blackberries, loganberries, and small strawberries

1 tablespoon sugar

8 fresh mint sprigs

To make the granita, in a saucepan over medium heat, combine the sugar and water. Bring to a boil, stirring to dissolve the sugar. Remove from the heat, pour the syrup into a bowl, and refrigerate until cold, about 30 minutes.

Add the red wine and orange juice to the sugar syrup and mix well. Pour into a nonreactive metal pan about 8 by 12 inches (20 by 30 cm) and 1 inch (2.5 cm) deep. The mixture should be about ½ inch (12 mm) deep. Place in the freezer until the mixture starts to thicken, 1½–2 hours. Remove from the freezer, stir with a fork to break up the crystals, and then return to the freezer. Repeat this process every 30 minutes until the mixture begins to firm, then every 15 minutes until all of the liquid has turned into well-separated granules. The granita should be ready in 4–5 hours.

Place the berries in a bowl, sprinkle with the sugar, and stir gently to combine. Set aside.

To serve, chill individual bowls in the freezer. Spoon some of the granita into each chilled bowl and top with the berry mixture. Garnish with the mint sprigs.

serves 8

Alpes-Maritimes

Tourte aux Blettes

apple and swiss chard pie

*All of France loves an apple tart, but this very
typical southern version, known in the dialect
of Nice as* tourta de bléa, *is surely the most unusual
one. The filling contains apples, raisins, pine nuts,
and that most beloved vegetable of the locals,* blettes,
*or Swiss chard. The combination is sublime. Marc
de Provence is a spirit distilled from the must, or
pulp and skins, of Provençal grapes.*

SHORTCRUST PASTRY

2¾ cups (14 oz/440 g) all-purpose (plain) flour

*1 cup (8 oz/250 g) unsalted butter, cut into
small pieces*

1 egg yolk

¼ cup (2 oz/60 g) superfine (caster) sugar

4–5 tablespoons (2–2½ fl oz/60–75 ml) water

FILLING

*½ cup (3½ oz/105 g) firmly packed
brown sugar*

2 eggs

*2 heaping tablespoons golden raisins (sultanas),
plumped in 3 tablespoons dark rum*

¼ cup (1½ oz/45 g) pine nuts

pinch of freshly ground pepper

2 tablespoons marc de Provence, brandy, or kirsch

1 tablespoon olive oil

*8 leaves Swiss chard, stems removed and leaves
roughly shredded*

3 Granny Smith apples, peeled, cored, and sliced

1 egg beaten with 1 tablespoon milk

To make the pastry by hand, mound the flour on a work surface. Make a well in the center and add the butter, egg yolk, superfine sugar, and 3 table-spoons of the water. Using your fingertips, mix the ingredients in the well, then begin to incorporate the flour. When the mixture has the consistency of coarse meal, add 1 tablespoon of the water and continue to blend and encourage the pastry into a ball. Add more water, ½ tablespoon at a time, as needed to create a workable dough. Taking care not to knead in too much elasticity, lightly flour the work surface and push the ball of pastry forward and away from you with the heel of your hands, then gather into a ball. Repeat 2 or 3 times, stopping as soon as the pastry has a light springiness. Cover with plastic wrap and refrigerate for at least 30 minutes or for up to 2 hours.

To make the pastry in a food processor, combine the flour and butter in the processor and pulse until uniformly blended. Add the egg yolk, superfine sugar, and 2 tablespoons of the water and continue to pulse until the pastry gathers in a mass on the blade, adding 1½–2 tablespoons water if the mixture is too dry. Transfer to a work surface, form into a ball, and refrigerate as directed for the hand method.

To make the filling, place the brown sugar in a bowl and add the eggs, one at a time, stirring well after each addition to dissolve the sugar and blend well. Drain the raisins, reserving the rum, and add the raisins to the bowl along with the pine nuts, pepper, brandy or liqueur, and olive oil. Stir until well mixed. Add the Swiss chard leaves and stir well.

Preheat an oven to 400°F (200°C).

Divide the pastry in half. On a floured work surface, roll out half the pastry into a round 12 inches (30 cm) in diameter and ⅛ inch (3 mm) thick. Drape it around the rolling pin and transfer to an 11-inch (28 cm) tart pan with a removable bottom. Ease the pastry into the bottom and sides of the pan. Spoon half of the Swiss chard filling into the lined pan. Arrange half of the apple slices on top. Add the remaining chard mixture, then top with the remaining apple slices, arranging them neatly in concentric circles to create an even top. Drizzle the reserved rum over all. The filling will reach higher than the rim of the tart pan.

On a floured surface, roll out the remaining pastry half into a round 12 inches (30 cm) in diameter. Drape it around the pin and transfer to the tart pan, laying it evenly over the filling. Tuck the edges of the top pastry inside the bottom pastry, pressing to seal the pastry edges and contain the filling, and cutting off any excess pastry.

Brush the top pastry with the egg-milk mixture. Prick the top with a fork, in 2 concentric circles. Bake until the pastry is a rich brown, 45–50 minutes, rotating the pan 180 degrees after about 30 minutes.

Transfer to a rack and let cool. Remove the pan sides and slide onto a serving plate. Serve warm or at room temperature, sliced into wedges.

serves 8

Alpes-de-Haute-Provence

Coings Pochés

poached quinces

Quince trees thrive in hundreds of household gardens in the south of France. Although quinces may be cooked much more quickly, here they are slowly poached to a glorious deep hue the color of carnelian, destined to prompt envy in all other cooks. The technique is one passed on by the wise grandmothers of Provence. The poached quinces can also be used for making a tart, in which case you should cut them into thick wedges rather than quarters.

4 large quinces

2¼ cups (18 oz / 560 g) sugar

4 cups (32 fl oz / 1 l) water

zest from 1 large lemon, cut into strips ¾ inch (2 cm) wide

1 orange zest strip, ¾ inch (2 cm) wide

❦ Peel, quarter, and core the quinces. Place the cores and peelings on a piece of cheesecloth (muslin), bring the corners together, and tie with kitchen string. In a large nonaluminum saucepan, combine the sugar and water. Bring to a boil, stirring to dissolve the sugar. Add the quince pieces, lemon and orange zests, and cheesecloth bundle and reduce the heat to very low.

❦ Cut a round of parchment (baking) paper the diameter of the pan, place over the quinces, and top with a heatproof plate. Cover the pan and cook very slowly for 6–7 hours, using a heat diffuser if cooking on a gas burner. The quinces will be tender and a lovely red. Alternatively, place the covered pan in a 200°F (95°C) oven for 8–9 hours.

❦ Remove the pan from the stove top or the oven, carefully remove the plate and parchment, and discard the cheesecloth bundle. Let the quinces cool in their cooking liquid. Transfer to a large serving bowl. Serve in bowls with a few tablespoons of the juice spooned over the top. The quinces can be stored in the refrigerator for up to 10 days.

serves 6

Alpes-Maritimes

Fougassette

sweet christmas bread

A richer, sweet version of the regional fougasse *bread,* fougassette *is popular around Nice and along the Côte d'Azur. There, it is served as an alternative to* pompe à l'huile, *an olive oil–based sweet bread, during the Christmas season. The use of orange flower water gives the bread a distinctive aroma.*

SPONGE

1 cup (5 oz / 155 g) bread (hard-wheat) flour

¾ cup (6 fl oz / 180 ml) lukewarm water

1 cake (1 oz / 30 g) fresh yeast, or 2½ teaspoons (1 envelope) active dry yeast

DOUGH

1¾ cups (9 oz / 260 g) bread (hard-wheat) flour

pinch of salt

3 eggs, lightly beaten

6 tablespoons (3 oz / 90 g) granulated sugar

2 tablespoons orange flower water

⅓ cup (3 fl oz / 80 ml) olive oil

confectioners' (icing) sugar, for dusting

♛ To make the sponge, place the flour in a small bowl. Place the lukewarm water in a cup, crumble in the yeast, and stir to dissolve. Pour the dissolved yeast into the flour and stir until blended. Cover the bowl with oil-coated plastic wrap and let rise in a warm place until doubled in bulk, 30–45 minutes.

♛ To make the dough, in a food processor fitted with the plastic blade, combine the flour and salt in the processor and add the sponge, eggs, granulated sugar, and orange flower water. Process, pulsing occasionally and adding the oil in a steady stream, until the mixture comes together.

♛ Turn the dough out onto a lightly floured work surface and form into a ball. Place in a lightly oiled bowl, turn to coat with oil, cover the bowl with a damp kitchen towel, and let the dough rise until doubled in bulk, about 1 hour.

♛ Transfer the dough to a floured work surface and knead briefly. Using a rolling pin, roll into a large rectangle about 11 by 15 inches (28 by 38 cm) and transfer to an ungreased baking sheet. Using a sharp knife, make 8 to 10 diagonal slits outward from the center of the dough, like the veins on a leaf, spacing them 2½ inches (6 cm) apart and stopping about 1 inch (2.5 cm) from the edge. Using your fingers, pull the slits open wide, so they do not close during baking. Cover the dough with a damp kitchen towel and let rest for 20 minutes.

♛ Preheat an oven to 400°F (200°C). Have ready a fine-nozzled mister filled with water.

♛ Remove the towel, place the bread in the oven, and quickly spray 3 gusts of water into the top and bottom of the oven. Bake until the bread is golden, about 25 minutes, misting the oven again 5 minutes before removing the bread from it. (The misting ensures a crisper result.)

♛ Transfer the bread to a rack to cool and then sift the confectioners' sugar evenly over the surface. Serve at room temperature.

makes 1 loaf

Vaucluse

Compôte de Fruits Secs

compote of mixed dried fruits

The Provençaux consider two to three tablespoons placed in a small bowl a sufficient serving of this simple compote, as it is dense and rich. A cinnamon-flavored ice cream is sometimes offered as an accompaniment, but these fruits are usually enjoyed unadorned to savor their sweetness before imbibing strong coffee. Crème fraîche, although nontraditional, complements the fruits as well.

Always buy plump, moist dried fruit, as heavily dried ones tend to disintegrate on cooking.

1½ cups (12 fl oz/375 ml) water

½ cup (4 oz/125 g) sugar

1 lb (500 g) mixed dried fruits such as prunes, pears, peaches, apple rings, nectarines, and figs

½ cup (3 oz/90 g) dark raisins

½ cup (3 oz/90 g) golden raisins (sultanas)

4 pieces cinnamon stick, each about 1½ inches (4 cm) long

4 whole cloves

8 cardamom pods

½ teaspoon freshly grated nutmeg

1 cup (8 fl oz/250 ml) fresh orange juice

¼ cup (2 fl oz/60 ml) Cognac or other brandy

♛ In a nonaluminum saucepan over medium heat, combine the water and sugar and bring to a simmer, stirring to dissolve the sugar.

♛ Add the dried fruits, raisins, cinnamon, cloves, cardamom, nutmeg, and orange juice and heat gently until the fruits plump and swell. This should take about 7 minutes for moist dried fruits and longer for drier fruits. The fruit should remain slightly chewy to the bite.

♛ Remove from the heat, stir in the Cognac or brandy, and allow to cool before refrigerating. Cover and refrigerate for up to 1 week. Serve warmed or at room temperature, spooned into small glass bowls or stemmed glasses.

serves 6–8

Alpes-Maritimes

Croissants aux Pignons

pine nut crescents

Said to have originated in Nice, these cookies have gained a reputation that has taken them farther afield. Many of the pine trees that once grew along the coast have been cleared to make way for houses and for plantings of eucalyptus, which are less vulnerable to fire. This makes the pignolats, as the cookies are also called in Nice, even more special and more desirable.

1 cup (5 oz/155 g) pine nuts

1 whole egg, plus 3 egg whites

2¼ cups (9 oz/280 g) ground almonds

1 cup (7 oz/220 g) plus 3 tablespoons superfine (caster) sugar

♛ Preheat an oven to 375°F (190°C). Butter a baking sheet.

♛ Spread the pine nuts in an even layer on a plate or wooden board. Break the whole egg into a wide, shallow bowl and beat with a fork until blended.

♛ In a bowl, combine the ground almonds, sugar, and egg whites. Using a whisk or handheld electric mixer, beat until a firm dough forms. Using the palms of your hands, form the dough into walnut-sized balls. Roll each ball first in the beaten egg and then in the pine nuts to coat evenly. Press each coated ball against the work surface with your fingers to elongate it into a crescent with a flattened underside, then place on the prepared baking sheet. Bake the crescents until golden, 15–20 minutes. Let cool completely on the baking sheet. Using a metal spatula, slide them onto a plate and serve.

makes 16–20 cookies

Picturesque Old Nice offers a maze of narrow streets and enticing shops.

Le Gros Souper

In Provence, food is used to express certain Christian rituals, with various ingredients and recipes carrying specific symbolism. One of the foremost examples of this is the elaborate Christmas Eve supper, *le gros souper*. It is one of the great holiday traditions of Provence, even more symbolic than the meal on December 25.

To honor the Holy Trinity, the table is laid with three cloths, each overlapping a larger one beneath, and set with three candles. Seven items, among them bulbs of garlic, branches of sage, and sheaves of wheat, dress the table to represent Stations of the Cross. More traditionally, instead of wheat sheaves, the table carried wheat sprouted weeks earlier by children, on December 4. Often a whole raw fish is plated as decoration, to recall the miracles of Christ. For the end of the meal, but set out on a sideboard or a nearby table at the start, are the thirteen desserts *(les treize desserts)*, the number representing Christ and his apostles at the Last Supper.

Although nowadays the time-consuming ritual of the traditional meal is less closely followed, the thirteen desserts remain sacred to most Provençaux. The first four are raisins, figs, almonds, and hazelnuts (filberts), to symbolize the four mendicant orders of friars (and also the ingredients in a popular seasonal tart, *tarte aux mendiants*). Among other offerings are grapes, melons, dates, other nuts, and the soft, white nougat of Montélimar and Sault and its cousin, a stunning black nougat containing nuts embedded in caramelized sugar. Local candies such as *calissons d'Aix* and *les Nostradamus de Salon*, or the fruit-flavored spun-sugar *berlingots*, sit alongside gleaming *fruits confits*.

Made especially for this night and for the festive season to come is the olive oil–based round sweet bread known as *la pompe à l'huile*, which is traditionally broken apart with the hands rather than cut with a knife. In Nice, the briochelike orange-scented *fougassette*, the local sweet version of *fougasse*, replaces *la pompe*.

This "nativity supper" is usually centered around steamed or boiled salt cod, for the meal must be simple and light enough to leave appetite for the next day's feast of goose or turkey. It must also be served so that the family is able to arrive at the local church in time for midnight mass.

Vaucluse

Fruits Confits aux Épices

spiced candied fruits

The candied fruits can be eaten plain with coffee. They can also be used to top ice cream or to decorate cakes, or can be dipped in chocolate.

2 oranges

1 each pink or yellow grapefruit and lemon

5 oz (155 g) kumquats

2½ cups (1 lb/500 g) superfine (caster) sugar, plus sugar for coating (2 cups/14 oz/440 g)

2 star anise, each broken in 2 or 3 pieces

1 cinnamon stick, broken into 3 equal pieces

1 vanilla bean, split lengthwise

☙ The night before cooking, cut the oranges, grapefruit, and lemon into slices ⅛ inch (3 mm) thick. Leave the kumquats whole if small or halve if large. Lay the pieces on a cake rack, brush with hot water, and allow to dry slightly overnight.

☙ The next day, in a wide saucepan over medium heat, combine 2 cups (16 fl oz/500 ml) water and the 2½ cups (1 lb/500 g) sugar and bring to a boil, stirring to dissolve the sugar. Add the spices and place the fruits in the pan. Reduce the heat to low, cover the fruits with a piece of parchment (baking) paper cut to fit the diameter of the pan, and simmer gently until the skins are soft and translucent, about 20 minutes. Remove from the heat, cover, and let the fruits cool in the syrup at room temperature.

☙ The following day, using a wide slotted spatula, carefully lift the fruits onto a cake rack, disturbing the flesh as little as possible. Let drain fully, at least 2 hours.

☙ Preheat an oven to 250°F (120°C). Line a baking sheet with parchment paper.

☙ Transfer the fruits to the prepared baking sheet and place in the oven for about 30 minutes. The fruits should be dry and shiny; do not allow them to color. Remove from the oven and let stand until tepid.

☙ Spread the sugar for coating on a plate and roll the fruit pieces in the sugar, coating evenly. Store in an airtight tin at room temperature for up to 2 weeks.

makes about 1¼ lb (625 g) candied citrus fruits

Alpes-Maritimes

Oranges Caramélisées à l'Eau de Fleur d'Oranger

caramelized oranges with orange
flower water

*The orange flower water made in Grasse in the
Cannes hinterlands has become a favorite flavoring
ingredient of the Provençaux. Here it enhances
a simple refreshing dessert using navel oranges.
Substitute blood oranges when in season.*

6 navel oranges or blood oranges

2 teaspoons orange flower water, or to taste

½ cup (4 oz / 125 g) plus 1 tablespoon sugar

¾ cup (6 fl oz / 180 ml) water

❧ Using a citrus zester, remove the zest from 1
orange in long threads. Using a sharp knife, cut a thin
slice off the top and bottom of each orange to expose
the flesh. Stand the orange upright and thickly slice
off the remaining peel in strips, carefully following
the contour of the orange and removing all the
white pith and membrane. Cut each orange crosswise into slices ⅛ inch (3 mm) thick. Spread the
orange slices on a serving plate, arranging them
attractively in 2 or 3 layers. Scatter the zest over the
top and drizzle with the orange flower water.

❧ No more than 45 minutes before serving the
oranges, combine the sugar and water in a small
saucepan and place over medium heat, stirring constantly to dissolve the sugar. When the mixture
reaches a boil, continue to boil without stirring until
it turns a light beige. Lift and swirl the pan to distribute the color and return to medium heat. Using
a pastry brush dampened with water, brush down the
pan sides to release the sugar crystals. Continue to
boil until the sugar turns a dark caramel color. The
whole process should take about 15 minutes.

❧ Immediately pour the caramel over the oranges,
working from the center outward, but not quite to
the edges, and distributing the caramel evenly. It will
set quickly. Using a spoon and fork, "crack open" the
caramel in front of the diners, then serve the orange
slices on individual plates.

serves 6

Vaucluse

Merveilles

little marvels

These little biscuits, also known as oreillettes, bugnes, or galans, depending on the region, are common everywhere in Provence, up the Rhône to Lyons, and even along the Riviera into Italy, where they are called crostoli. The shapes of deep-fried pastry dough dredged with confectioners' sugar are a favorite sweet for serving with Champagne, after-dinner coffee, or afternoon tea, or to accompany fresh berry desserts. They may be stored for a couple of days in an airtight tin, but they are best when freshly made.

DOUGH

1½ cups (7½ oz/235 g) plus 2 tablespoons all-purpose (plain) flour

3 tablespoons unsalted butter, melted and cooled

2 eggs, lightly beaten

2 tablespoons milk or water

2 teaspoons orange flower water

2 tablespoons granulated sugar

grated zest of 1 orange

grapeseed, peanut, or vegetable oil for deep-frying

1 cup (4 oz/125 g) confectioners' (icing) sugar

❧ To make the dough, place the flour in a large bowl. Make a well in the center and add the cooled butter, eggs, milk or water, and orange flower water. Using a wooden spoon, stir to mix the ingredients in the well, then slowly incorporate into the well the granulated sugar and finally the grated zest. Continuing to stir, incorporate the flour from the sides of the well until a homogenous dough forms. Using floured hands, shape the dough into a ball, cover with plastic wrap, and let rest in a cool place about 2 hours. If the weather is hot, refrigerate the dough.

❧ On a lightly floured work surface, roll out the dough ⅛ inch (3 mm) thick. Using a fluted pastry wheel or a sharp knife, cut half of the pastry sheet into long strips about 2 inches (5 cm) wide. Cut across the strips at 1⅛-inch (3-cm) intervals to form rectangles. Using a fork, make small impressions around the edge of each rectangle.

❧ To make the finished plate of cookies more interesting, vary how you cut the remaining pastry: leave some strips longer, some wider, and cut some into elongated triangles. Make 2 parallel lengthwise slits

in some of the longer strips and 2 parallel vertical slits in some of the shorter strips. In the center of some of the triangles, cut a horizontal slit; bend the top point of the triangle and pull it partly through the slit. Some of the long strips can be knotted; other pieces can be pleated into rough bowlike shapes.

❧ Pour the oil to a depth of 3–4 inches (7.5–10 cm) into a large saucepan and heat to 325°F (165°C) on a deep-frying thermometer.

❧ Working in batches, add the cookies, a few at a time, to the hot oil and fry, turning the cookies in the oil once or twice, until golden and slightly puffed, 1–1½ minutes. Using a slotted spoon or wire skimmer, transfer to paper towels to drain.

❧ Spread the confectioners' sugar on a large plate and coat the warm cookies with the sugar. Serve the cookies at room temperature.

serves 8–10

LE GLOSSAIRE

The following entries cover key Provençal ingredients and basic techniques called for throughout the book. Look for Provençal and other French ingredients in specialty-food stores and well-stocked supermarkets. For information on items not found below, please refer to the index.

ANCHOVIES

Arranged on top of *pissaladière*, puréed with olives to make *tapenade*, or simmered in a sauce with tomatoes and garlic for haricots verts, anchovies—*anchois*—are a popular element of Provençal cooking. Fresh anchovies are excellent grilled, panfried, or lightly marinated and served raw. Whole anchovies layered with salt have the best flavor of the preserved products. Buy them in bulk or in 1- to 2-pound (500-g to 1-kg) tins. While anchovy fillets in olive oil are commonly available in tins, look for the higher-quality imported anchovies packed in glass jars. Avoid anchovies packed in other types of oil.

TO PREPARE WHOLE SALTED ANCHOVIES, rinse gently under running cold water. If a less assertive flavor is desired, soak for 10 minutes before proceeding. Scrape the skin away with the tip of a knife and cut away the dorsal fin. Press each anchovy open, flattening it carefully from head to tail end. Lift away the backbone, then separate the fillets. Rinse gently again, then dry on paper towels. The fillets can be used immediately or placed in a glass or other nonaluminum container, covered with olive oil, and refrigerated for up to 2 weeks.

ARTICHOKES

This Mediterranean native, called *artichaut* in French, is cultivated for its thistlelike flower, which is harvested before it blooms. Two sizes are commonly used in Provençal recipes: small, purple-leaved, chokeless specimens, which are typically eaten raw or lightly blanched; and medium or large, green-leaved globes with a prickly choke and thorn-tipped leaves.

TO PREPARE ARTICHOKES, add the juice of 1 lemon to a bowl of cold water. Trim the stem from each artichoke, leaving 1 inch (2.5 cm) intact for small artichokes, 2 inches (5 cm) for large globes. Peel off the outer leaves until you reach the tender yellow inner leaves. Lay the artichoke on its side and cut off the tough green tops of the leaves until only the tender, edible portion remains. Cut the artichoke lengthwise into halves or quarters, or as directed in individual recipes. (Very small, chokeless artichokes are often left whole.) If there are fibrous hairs surrounding the heart (this is the choke), run the tip of a small paring knife between the heart and the hairs, then scoop out the hairs with a spoon. Drop the halves or quarters into the lemon water, then drain well before using.

BACON

Sautéed with aromatics and vegetables or used in meat dishes such as daubes, bacon is an essential ingredient in many Provençal recipes. French cooks prefer to purchase bacon unsliced and with the rind intact. To approximate this thick, flavorful *lard fumé,* look for smoked slab bacon at fine markets and butcher shops. Stack 2 or 3 thick slices and then cut crosswise into squares or thin strips to make the *lardons* used in fillings, soups, sauces, and stews.

BELL PEPPERS

Vegetables, rather than meat, are at the heart of Provençal cuisine, and firm, shiny green, red, and yellow bell peppers—*les poivrons*—are among the most appreciated of the bountiful garden harvest. Also known as capsicums, peppers are an important ingredient in the region's trademark ratatouille; are used in salads, sautés, and braises; and are also stuffed. Some recipes call for roasting and peeling peppers to heighten their natural sweetness and to make them more tender.

TO ROAST BELL PEPPERS, preheat a broiler (griller). Cut each pepper in half lengthwise and remove the stem, seeds, and veins. Place the pepper halves, skin side up, on a baking sheet, slip under the broiler about 4 inches (10 cm) from the heat source, and broil (grill) until the skin is blackened and blistered, 5–8 minutes. Remove from the broiler, place in a bowl, cover, let steam for a few minutes, and then peel away the blackened skin. Use the peppers as directed in individual recipes.

BOUQUET GARNI

One of the most common ways of adding flavor to a dish in Provence, as in all of France, is to use a bundle of herbs called a bouquet garni. The classic bouquet garni includes only three herbs: fresh flat-leaf (Italian) parsley sprigs, fresh thyme sprigs, and bay leaves. When a recipe calls for a bouquet garni, use 3 large parsley sprigs, 2 large thyme sprigs, and 1 bay leaf. For a large bouquet garni, use 4 large parsley sprigs, 3 medium-sized thyme sprigs, and 1 large bay leaf. Lay the thyme and bay on the parsley sprigs, "pleat" the parsley sprigs to hold the other herbs firmly in the center, tightly wind kitchen string around the whole packet, and then tie securely, leaving a tail of string to permit easy removal of the herb bundle from the dish. If a recipe calls for one or more additions to the bouquet, such as a small celery or fennel stalk or an oregano sprig, bind them into the bundle with the other ingredients. The herb sprigs must be perfectly fresh, as any sign of mustiness will diminish the flavor of the dish.

CAPERS

The unopened flower bud of a Mediterranean trailing shrub, the caper—*câpre* in French, *tapeno* in Provençal dialect—is an indispensable ingredient in *tapenade* and adds piquant flavor to sauces for everything from rabbit and beef to salt cod and pasta. Provence is known for its small, deep green capers, which are labeled "non-pareil," an acknowledgment of their excellence. Capers packed in sea salt retain their intense floral flavor and firm texture, but brined and vinegared capers are commonly available in the south. Rinse all three types before using. For a more subtle flavor, soak them in water to cover for 10–15 minutes and then drain. When buying salted capers, make sure that the salt is white and dry; they can be kept in the refrigerator for up to 1 year.

CHICKPEA FLOUR
A fine, pale yellow flour ground from dried chickpeas (also known as garbanzo beans), chickpea flour lends a rich and nutty flavor to savory crepes and fritters. In Nice, *la farine de pois chiches* is the essential ingredient in classic treats such as *socca* and French-fried *panisses*. The flour can be found in specialty shops and health-food stores and in Italian, Indian, Greek, and Spanish markets. If the flour is unavailable, grind dried chickpeas, a small amount at a time, in a clean coffee grinder.

CROUTONS
A crouton is a piece of crisped bread used as a crunchy, appetizing addition to soups or as a base for holding roasted red peppers (capsicums), baked fresh goat cheese, a bit of pâté, or a smear of *tapenade* or other dip. Depending on their use and the whim of the cook, croutons can vary in size from small squares for dropping into soup to baguette-sized or larger rounds that match the size of the ingredients that will sit on them, whether a slice of goat cheese for a salad or some *sauce rouille* for a fish soup. Sometimes a cook will rub the bread pieces with garlic, and sometimes not, and then will toast them in the oven, panfry them in oil, or grill them on a stove-top ridged grill pan or over a fire.

TO TOAST CROUTONS, preheat the oven to 300°F (150°C). Rub the bread pieces with garlic, if desired, brush well with olive oil, arrange on a baking sheet, and toast in the oven until pale gold and dry to the touch, 15–18 minutes. TO PANFRY CROUTONS, again rub the bread pieces with garlic or not, then heat 1 inch (2.5 cm) of olive oil in a frying pan over high heat. Add the bread pieces to the hot oil in a single layer and fry until golden on the first side, about 1 minute. Turn and fry, adding more oil as needed, until golden on the second side, about 1 minute longer. Transfer to paper towels to drain. TO GRILL CROUTONS, again rub with garlic or not and brush well with olive oil. Preheat a stove-top ridged grill pan over medium-high heat, or prepare a fire in a grill. Grill the bread pieces on the first side until lightly browned, about 1 minute. Rotate the pieces 45 degrees and continue to grill on the same side for about 1 minute longer, to create attractive grill marks. Turn and brown without rotating on the second side, about 1 minute longer.

CUTTLEFISH
Abundant in the waters of the Mediterranean, the cuttlefish—*seiche* in French—is flatter, thicker, and meatier than its close relative, the squid, and is generally preferred over the latter for its succulence. The solid white cuttlebone in the center helps to differentiate the two; the squid has a transparent quill. Provençal cooks most often stuff and bake these hardy cephalopods, or they braise them with peas, tomatoes, or other vegetables. If a cuttlefish is particularly large, it requires pounding to tenderize the meat before cooking. Large squid can be used in place of cuttlefish in most recipes. To clean cuttlefish, follow the directions for squid (page 250).

FAVA BEANS
Slipped from their large pods, pale green fava beans, also known as broad beans, have a slightly bitter flavor and a dense texture. In spring, the first tiny *fèves*, or *fèvettes*, of the season are eaten raw directly from their pods. Most mature ones are sautéed simply with garlic or combined with other vegetables such as haricots verts or artichokes. Fresh and dried fava beans are markedly different in flavor and should not be substituted for each other in recipes. With the exception of the new season's beans, favas require peeling, as the thin skin covering the beans can be tough and bitter.

TO PREPARE FRESH FAVA BEANS, split the pods with your fingers and remove the beans. To peel them easily, blanch the shelled beans in boiling water for about 30 seconds. Drain, cool slightly under cold water, and then simply pinch each bean to slip it from its skin.

FIGS
Sweet, succulent *figues* first arrived on the southern coast of France from Asia Minor more than three thousand years ago. Fragile and highly perishable, fresh figs are a luxury. Popular varieties include the golden Smyrna and the deep purple Mission. Although delicate in flavor, figs are versatile in the kitchen. The fresh fruit is excellent macerated, poached, baked, glazed on tarts, or transformed into jam. Once dried, figs become even sweeter and gain a firm, chewy texture that is perfect for braises, stuffings, and cakes. Figs do not ripen off the tree, so choose fresh fruits that are soft but smooth, with a plump shape and a firm stem. Eat the fresh fruits as soon as possible after purchasing, keeping them at room temperature in a single layer to prevent bruises. When buying dried figs, look for ones that are still moist and flexible. Store dried figs in an airtight container away from light and heat.

HAM
Jambon cru, also known as *jambon sec,* is the raw, unsmoked ham of France. Prized raw hams such as *jambon de montagne* are dry-cured and air-aged in cool, mountain breezes to create their finely textured and delicately flavored meat. *Jambon de Bayonne* from the Basque country is widely considered the finest of the French cured hams, but products from the Ardennes, the

Savoy, the Massif Central, and the Alpes de Provence are also excellent. Spanish *serrano* (from the mountain) or Italian prosciutto (with the ham from Parma considered the best) are also good choices in recipes calling for *jambon cru*. For cooking, avoid packages of paper-thin slices, and instead ask the butcher to cut the ham into thicker pieces. Cooked ham, *jambon cuit* or *jambon blanc*, is also used throughout France.

HAZELNUTS

French cultivation of plump, sweet *noisettes* is small and limited to the southwest, Corsica, and southern Languedoc-Roussillon. In Provence, hazelnuts, also known as filberts, are one of the thirteen treats served on Christmas Eve symbolizing Christ and the Apostles at the Last Supper. Rich and slightly sweet, hazelnuts are generally used in desserts, but they also appear as a garnish on salads, vegetables, and other savory dishes. Pressed into a fragrant oil, the nut adds depth of flavor to a variety of sauces and dressings. Avoid buying hazelnuts already chopped, for whole nuts have the best flavor and texture.

TO TOAST AND PEEL HAZELNUTS, spread the nuts in a single layer on a baking sheet or shallow pan. Toast them at 325°F (165°C) for 15–20 minutes, or until they are fragrant, shaking the pan twice during this time to ensure even coloration. Remove from the oven and, while still warm, rub the hazelnuts briskly in a clean kitchen towel to remove their brown skins. As with all nuts, toasting hazelnuts deepens their flavor and improves their texture.

HERBES DE PROVENCE

Provençal home cooks and herb purveyors alike carefully guard their recipes for this fragrant blend of dried herbs. The number and proportions vary from producer to producer, but thyme, marjoram, savory, oregano, basil, rosemary, fennel seed, and lavender flowers are typically part of the mix. Rubbed with *herbes de Provence* and olive oil, roasted meats and poultry are infused with a distinctively rustic flavor. Look in the spice section of quality markets for the little clay crocks in which the herb blend is traditionally packed.

LAVENDER

In the south of France, especially in Haute Provence, the heady scent of lavender drifts from large fields that stretch across the hillsides. While true lavender grows wild above 2,400 feet (800 m) and is still collected by hand to make lavender essence, the cultivated hybrid, lavandin, accounts for most of the modern supply. The flowers add their fragrance to the famous perfumes made in the city of Grasse, not far from Nice. Lavender is also appreciated by the region's cooks, lending its distinctive sweetness to vinegars, sauces, honey, ice cream, and drinks, as well as savory stews and roasts. Be sure to use only chemical-free lavender from an organic garden or flowers packaged specifically for cooking, as those sold for floral arrangements have been treated with chemicals. Look for small, dried flowers in the bulk herb section of health-food stores or the baking aisle of fine grocers. They should retain a vivid violet hue and flowery fragrance.

MUSHROOMS

Twice a year, after the spring rains and during the cooling days of autumn, these earthy treasures appear in forests throughout Provence. Passionate about foraging, entire families will gather for a mushroom expedition, looking beneath familiar trees and around old stumps for their favorite varieties. Although some of these mushrooms are now cultivated, those found in the wild still have the fullest flavor.

CÈPE With its firm texture, rich flavor, and plump profile, the cèpe is sought after throughout Europe. A wild mushroom that cannot be cultivated, it has a light brown cap topping its thick stem and an unusually sweet fragrance. The cèpe is most commonly available dried in the United States. To reconstitute, soak in water for 1 hour or more for the best flavor and texture. Drain before using.

CHANTERELLE This bright yellow, delicately fluted mushroom is named for its elegant shape (from the Greek *kantharos,* a tall drinking vessel). Chanterelles grow only in the wild in wooded areas and have a flavor with hints of fresh apricots. A rarer black variety has a finer texture and a deeper flavor, in spite of its rather intimidating French name, *trompette de la mort,* or "trumpet of death." Take care not to overcook chanterelles, for they toughen easily.

MOREL The morel possesses an intense, musky aroma prized by foragers. Its long, oval cap sports a network of deep crevices. Expensive, fragile, and delicate in flavor, the morel is classically enjoyed in simple yet elegant dishes. Before cooking fresh morels, rinse them briefly in plenty of water to remove the grit trapped in their honeycombed caps.

SANGUIN Beneath pine trees grows one of the most loved mushrooms in Provence. Named for the deep red stains that appear when it is cut, the *sanguin* has a buff to creamy, slightly concave cap lightly streaked with green. Although plentiful in the autumn throughout Provence, it is difficult to find elsewhere in France. Also known as the pine mushroom, the *sanguin* is occasionally sold at farmers' markets and specialty grocers. If needed, substitute fresh shiitake mushrooms, which have the texture if not the deep flavor of the *sanguin*.

OLIVE OIL

The Greeks planted the first olive trees in Provence during the sixth century B.C., and the Romans arrived five hundred years later to perfect the art of pressing olive oil. Gnarled olive trees with their green-gray leaves and dark fruit cover the countryside of the Midi. The finest olive groves of the region stretch west from the peak of Mount Ventoux along the littoral and around the ancient village of Les Baux. There are over one hundred olive oil mills in Provence today, each producing an oil with distinctive color and flavor. The region boasts a handful of areas that have been granted an *appellation d'origine contrôlée* (traditional production area status), and local labels carry this important recognition. Among them, olive oil from Nyons (the northern Vaucluse and southern Drôme), pressed almost wholly from *tanches* ripened to the point of wrinkling, has a particularly fruity flavor. Baux Valley, in the Bouches-du-Rhône, is home to an olive oil that relies on a blend of varieties, *grossane, salonenque, picholine,* and *aglandau*. Even the tiny *cailletiers*

olives of Nice are pressed into oil. The finest olive oils are made by virtually the same method as they have been for centuries. In late autumn and winter, ripe olives are harvested and washed in cold water. After being crushed to a paste, with great care to prevent breaking their pits, the olives are packed onto fibrous mats and pressed to extract their fruity, green oil. Only oil obtained from the first cold pressing of olives and with less than 1 percent acidity can carry the term *extra virgin* on the label. Save the fruitiest, most expensive extra-virgin olive oils for dressing salads and drizzling over finished dishes, where the flavor can be best appreciated. Filtered and refined oil, labeled "pure" or simply "olive oil," has a higher smoke point and a lighter flavor. Use this clearer, less fruity oil in cooking and baking, for it will not burn as readily and will meld better with other ingredients. Olive oil's high level of monounsaturated fatty acid (almost 75 percent) makes it an integral component of what has been identified as the healthful Mediterranean diet.

PUFF PASTRY

Dishes made with puff pastry look very grand, but making the pastry appears far more difficult than it actually is. The pastry can also be purchased. For the best quality, buy from a good cake shop that uses butter, not margarine. If only a portion of the pastry is used, the remainder may be frozen as described below.

3¼ cups (1 lb/500 g) all-purpose (plain) flour

pinch of salt

2½ tablespoons unsalted butter, at room temperature, plus 2 cups (1 lb/500 g) unsalted butter, chilled

1 cup (8 fl oz/250 ml) water

❦ In the bowl of a stand mixer fitted with the paddle attachment, combine the flour, salt, and room-temperature butter. Beating slowly at first and then increasing the speed to medium, beat the ingredients, slowing adding the water in a thin stream at the same time, until the ingredients are mixed together into a firm dough and form a ball. (Alternatively, place the flour on a work surface, make a well in the center, and add the salt, room-temperature butter, and water. Using your fingers, combine the ingredients and form the dough into a ball.) Transfer the dough to a work surface, reshape into a ball with the heels of your hands, cover with plastic wrap, and refrigerate for 30 minutes.

❦ Using a rolling pin, beat the chilled butter between sheets of parchment (baking) paper into a rectangle about ¾ inch (2 cm) thick. Remove the dough from the refrigerator. On a floured work surface, roll out the chilled dough into a round about 11 inches (28 cm) in diameter. Remove the paper from the rectangle of butter, place the butter in the center of the dough round, and fold the edges of the dough over the butter to enclose completely. Tap the dough with the rolling pin to ensure that it adheres to the butter.

❦ Using the rolling pin and flouring the work surface and pin often but lightly, roll out the dough into a rectangle about 20 inches (50 cm) long by 7 inches (18 cm) wide. Take care to apply pressure evenly and not to squeeze the butter from the dough. Keep the ends as square as possible. Fold the pastry into thirds by folding it toward you and then back over itself.

❦ Firmly gripping the folded rectangle, rotate it 90 degrees so that the seam is on your left. Roll out the dough into a rectangle of the same size and again fold it into thirds. You have now completed 2 "turns." Dust the dough with flour and cover with plastic wrap or with parchment (baking) paper and a kitchen towel, tucking the ends in well so that they do not dehydrate. Let rest in the refrigerator for 1 hour.

❦ Remove the dough from the refrigerator and repeat the rolling and folding to complete 2 more turns. Again, wrap the dough and return to the refrigerator to rest for 1 hour. Repeat the process one more time, again completing 2 turns.

❦ Once you have completed 6 turns, the pastry dough is ready to use. It may be used immediately or stored in the refrigerator, well wrapped, for up to 3 days. The pastry may be frozen; ideally, for best results, it should be frozen after 4 turns, and the final 2 turns completed after thawing. To freeze the pastry, wrap airtight in plastic wrap and freeze for up to 2 weeks. Transfer to the refrigerator for 1 day to thaw, then remove and bring to room temperature before rolling.

makes 2½ lb (1.25 kg) pastry

PASTIS

Sipped with leisure during a hot afternoon, pastis is a way of life in the south of France. A glass of pastis—one part liqueur mixed with about three parts cold water—is a common aperitif before a meal or in the village square after a game of *pétanque*. Well-loved brands include Ricard, Duval, Jeannot, Pernod, and Pastis 51. The strong, clear, licorice-flavored liqueur also finds its way into the kitchen, where its flavor especially complements seafood.

PORK RIND

French butchers sell bacon with the rind, or *la couenne,* still intact. Before slicing the bacon, cooks trim off the rind and use large pieces of it to line the bottom of a pan, thereby preventing large cuts of meat from sticking, or place it over meats to protect any portion not covered by sauce, keeping it from drying out during cooking. Small pieces of rind are stewed in meat dishes to provide texture. Look for pork rind that is free of nitrate and nitrites. Freeze leftovers for use in other recipes.

RABBIT

Filled with wild herbs and roasted, simmered in a *civet* with red wine and mushrooms, or baked with *tapenade,* rabbit is much appreciated in Provence. Domesticated rabbits have a more delicate flavor and texture than the *lapins de garenne* that live among the brush-covered hills of the Midi. Large rabbits are best cooked by braising to keep their meat moist and tender. Whole rabbits are available at specialty markets and fine butchers. To purchase just the saddle, order from companies that specialize in game.

SEA SALT

In the *salins,* or salt marshes, along the southern coast of France, skilled workers known as *paludiers* have raked and harvested large flakes of sea salt by hand since antiquity. Created by the controlled evaporation of water from the lowlands of the Mediterranean, sea salt from Provence is either fine, ideal for dissolving quickly during cooking, or coarse, for adding a pleasant crunch just before serving. A subtle scent of violets infuses the finest salt, known as *fleur de sel,* or "salt flower," for its bloom on the surface of salt deposits. Free of additives, sea salt is appreciated for its rich mineral notes. Look for both fine and coarse sea salt in the spice section of specialty markets and better supermarkets. If needed, kosher salt can be substituted for fine sea salt. Other salts, however, cannot replace the unique flavor and finishing texture of *fleur de sel.*

SNAILS

While the large, fleshy *escargots bourguignons* help define French cuisine around the world, Provençal cooks are more likely to use the little gray common snails, *petits gris,* native to the Mediterranean shores. Many believe that snails gathered from vineyards, also known as milk snails, have the best flavor, but they are also the most difficult to find. Look in gourmet markets for shelled snails canned in salt brine. Their cleaned and dried shells can be purchased separately for serving or garnishing. Fresh and frozen snails are increasingly available from specialty farms by mail order.

SQUID

The mild, sweet flesh of squid, known as *calmar* in French or *tautenne* in Provençal dialect, complements the flavors of a wide range of dishes. It is a popular food all along the Mediterranean, where its size varies from small to quite large. Squid can toughen when overheated, so it should be cooked briefly or simmered gently.

TO CLEAN SQUID, pull the head and tentacles from the body pouch, then discard the clinging innards. Just below the eyes, cut off the tentacles and reserve them, discarding the eye portion. Squeeze the cut end of the tentacles to expel the hard, round beak, discarding it. Pull out and discard the long, transparent quill from inside the body pouch. Rinse the pouch and tentacles thoroughly under running cold water. Some recipes call for peeling the gray membrane from the pouch. Other recipes leave the membrane intact, as it dissolves readily when cooked, to color a sauce. Cut the body or leave whole as directed in individual recipes.

TRUFFLES

The humble appearance of truffles belies their intense aroma and flavor, so valued by chefs in France and beyond that they are known as black diamonds. Although the Périgord region is famous for its truffle market, black truffles grow more abundantly in Provence, which supplies 60 percent of the French market. The growth of these underground fungi among the roots of elm and oak trees, the exact weather conditions required for the fungi to grow, the intuition and experience needed to find them, and their inimitably earthy, much desired flavor all contribute to the costliness of truffles. Traditionally, truffle hunters employed trained pigs to sniff out the buried delicacies, but nowadays dogs are more popular for indicating the immediate area where truffles can be found. Shaved into paper-thin slices with a special tool, truffles garnish egg and potato dishes and savory sauces. Truffles also appear classically in pâtés, with foie gras, and, for the ultimate decadence, baked whole in brioche or puff pastry. Appearing first in November and then peaking in January and February, fresh black truffles are a rare and expensive luxury. Order them from fine grocers or mail-order truffle companies. Also available are less expensive (and less fragrant) summer truffles, sliced into a jar with winter truffle juice. Truffle juice boosts the flavor of sauces, while the slices add their musky flavor to dishes both simple and special. Puréed winter truffles and truffle oil are two convenient, albeit less flavorful, forms. Purchase the finest-quality truffles that you can afford and avoid any that list "flavoring" as an ingredient, revealing chemical additives that will leave a harsh aftertaste in dishes.

STOCKS

If you are making particularly rich sauces and need a beef stock with a more gelatinous quality, add 1 pig's foot or chicken back with the other ingredients. If a recipe calls for light chicken stock, increase the amount of water by 2 cups (16 fl oz/500 ml). Freshly made stocks will keep in the refrigerator for up to 6 days. To prevent deterioration, after the third day, bring them to a boil and boil for 2 minutes. Stocks may be frozen for up to 3 months.

BEEF STOCK

⅓ cup (3 oz/90 g) olive oil

10 lb (5 kg) beef shank, cut crosswise into 3-inch (7.5-cm) lengths

2 large yellow onions, chopped

2 large carrots, sliced

2 celery stalks, each cut crosswise into thirds

1 leek, including tender green tops, halved lengthwise

½ turnip, studded with 2 whole cloves

mushroom trimmings (optional)

4 large fresh flat-leaf (Italian) parsley sprigs

½ bay leaf

8 peppercorns

4 qt (4 l) water

⚜ In a large stockpot over high heat, warm the olive oil. Add the beef shank and brown, turning two or three times, until richly colored. Add the onions and carrots, and continue to cook, turning as necessary, until the onions are nicely caramelized and the edges of the carrot slices are browned. Add the remaining ingredients. Bring to a boil over high heat, reduce the heat to low, and simmer very slowly, uncovered, for at least 6 hours. Do not let the stock boil. Skim from time to time, particularly in the first 30 minutes when most of the impurities rise to the top. Add warm water as needed to keep the ingredients covered.

⚜ Strain the stock through a colander placed over a large bowl. Discard the solids. Let cool, then cover and refrigerate overnight. The next day, scoop off and discard the fat from the surface, strain the stock through a fine-mesh sieve, and use the stock immediately or store until needed.

makes about 3 qt (3 l)

CHICKEN STOCK

4–5 lb (2–2.5 kg) chicken backs, wing tips, and necks, skinned

2 yellow onions, chopped

2 carrots, sliced

1 celery stalk, sliced

¼ small turnip, studded with 2 whole cloves

1 leek, including tender green tops, halved lengthwise

3 fresh flat-leaf (Italian) parsley sprigs

8 peppercorns

3 qt (3 l) water

⚜ In a stockpot, combine all the ingredients. Bring to a boil over high heat, reduce the heat to low, and simmer very slowly, uncovered, for at least 3 hours. Do not let the stock boil,. Skim from time to time, particularly in the first 30 minutes when most of the impurities rise to the top. Add warm water as needed to keep the ingredients covered.

⚜ Strain the stock through a colander placed over a large bowl. Discard the solids. Let cool, then cover and refrigerate overnight. The next day, scoop off and discard the fat from the surface, strain the stock through a fine-mesh sieve, and use the stock immediately or store until needed.

makes about 2½ qt (2.5 l)

FISH STOCK

about 2 lb (1 kg) frames and heads of 3 or 4 small fish, such as whiting or flathead, or 2 larger fish, such as snapper or porgy

1 yellow onion, very finely chopped

1 small carrot, very finely sliced

½ celery stalk, finely sliced

½ leek, including tender green tops, finely chopped

mushroom trimmings (optional)

3 fresh flat-leaf (Italian) parsley sprigs

4 peppercorns

about 6 cups (48 fl oz/1.5 kg) water

⚜ Remove the gills from the fish heads and rinse away any signs of blood. Place all the fish in a stockpot. Add the remaining ingredients and the water as needed to cover the solids by 1 inch (2.5 cm). Place over medium heat and bring just to a boil. Reduce the heat to low and simmer slowly, uncovered, for no more than 20 minutes. Skim off any foam or scum that forms on the surface.

⚜ Remove the stock from the heat and strain through a colander placed over a large bowl. Discard the solids. Rinse the pot and return the strained stock to it. Place over medium-high heat, bring to a boil, and cook, uncovered, until reduced by one-third. If a recipe calls for jellied fish stock, reduce the stock by one-half.

⚜ Remove from the heat and strain through a fine-mesh sieve placed over a bowl. Strain again through a sieve lined with cheesecloth (muslin). Use the stock immediately or store until needed.

makes 4 cups (32 fl oz/1 l) stock or 3 cups (24 fl oz/750 ml) jellied stock

INDEX

ACKNOWLEDGMENTS

Diane Holuigue expresses her indebtedness to the huge team that contributed to the look, the design, and the heart of the book. Thanks also go to my husband, whose patience has been tried for the tenth time in this domain, to Wendely Harvey for bringing me to Weldon Owen, to my long-term collaborator Huguette Quennoy, to my right-hand pâtissière Loretta Sartori, and to the chefs and friends that have made me so welcome in Provence over many, many years, particularly Provençal chef extraordinaire Roger Vergé, Jean-Marc Larrue, Kathie Alex, and the wonderful André Perez, for their willingness to troop yet again through the fish and truffle markets, introduce me to their favorite suppliers, and give of their profound knowledge of techniques, recipes, and secrets so this book may be much more authentic than it ever could have been from my experience alone.

Noel Barnhurst wishes to thank his assistant, Noriko Akiyama.

George Dolese wishes to thank Leslie Busch, food stylist, and Elisabet der Nederlanden, food styling assistant, for their stellar work in preparing the food for photography. Thanks also go to Royal Hawaiian Seafood and to The Butler and the Chef and Champ de Mars for their generous use of props.

Jason Lowe thanks Gaye, Miranda, and Angela.

Weldon Owen thanks Desne Ahlers for writing the captions and for contributing her proofreading skills and Thy Tran for contributing her culinary expertise to the writing of the glossary text. We also thank Linda Bouchard for her expert computer layout and production, Ken DellaPenta for indexing the book, Annette Herskovits for her translation services, and Kathy Schermerhorn for color work.

OXMOOR HOUSE INC.

Oxmoor House books are distributed by Sunset Books
80 Willow Road, Menlo Park, CA 94025
Telephone: 650-321-3600 Fax: 650-324-1532

Vice President/General Manager: Rich Smeby
New Accounts Manager/Special Sales: Brad Moses

Oxmoor House and Sunset Books are divisions of
Southern Progress Corporation

WILLIAMS-SONOMA INC.
Founder and Vice-Chairman: Chuck Williams

WELDON OWEN INC.
Chief Executive Officer: John Owen
President: Terry Newell
Vice President International Sales: Stuart Laurence
Creative Director: Gaye Allen
Publisher: Hannah Rahill
Design Concept: Kari Ontko, India Ink
Art Director: Jamie Leighton
Managing Editor: Judith Dunham
Copyeditor: Sharon Silva
Consulting Editor: Norman Kolpas
Production Director: Chris Hemesath
Production & Reprint Coordinator: Todd Rechner
Editorial Assistant: Dana Goldberg
Prop and Style Director: George Dolese
Calligraphy: Jane Dill

THE SAVORING SERIES
conceived and produced by Weldon Owen Inc.
814 Montgomery Street, San Francisco, CA 94133
Telephone: 415-291-0100, Fax: 415-291-8841

In collaboration with Williams-Sonoma Inc.
3250 Van Ness Avenue, San Francisco, CA 94109

Separations by Colourscan Overseas Co. Pte. Ltd.
Printed in Singapore by Tien Wah Press (Pte.) Ltd.

pp **4–5**: In early spring, the fertile valley spreading below Bonnieux and the mountains of the Lubéron is radiant with cherry blossoms. pp **6–7**: Morning in Arles brings early risers to the Place du Forum and its many cafés. Presiding over the square is a statue of Frédéric Mistral (1830–1914), Nobel Prize–winning poet and leader of the Provençal literary renaissance. pp **8–9**: Spirited bulls of the Camargue, marshland of the Rhône delta, are bred for the *course camarguaise*, a bloodless form of bullfighting and game of skill in which contestants pluck ribbons from the bulls' horns. pp **12–13**: A solumn stone *mas* anchors this farmstead near Bonnieux in the Lubéron.

Savoring is a registered trademark of Weldon Owen Inc.